NOBLE™

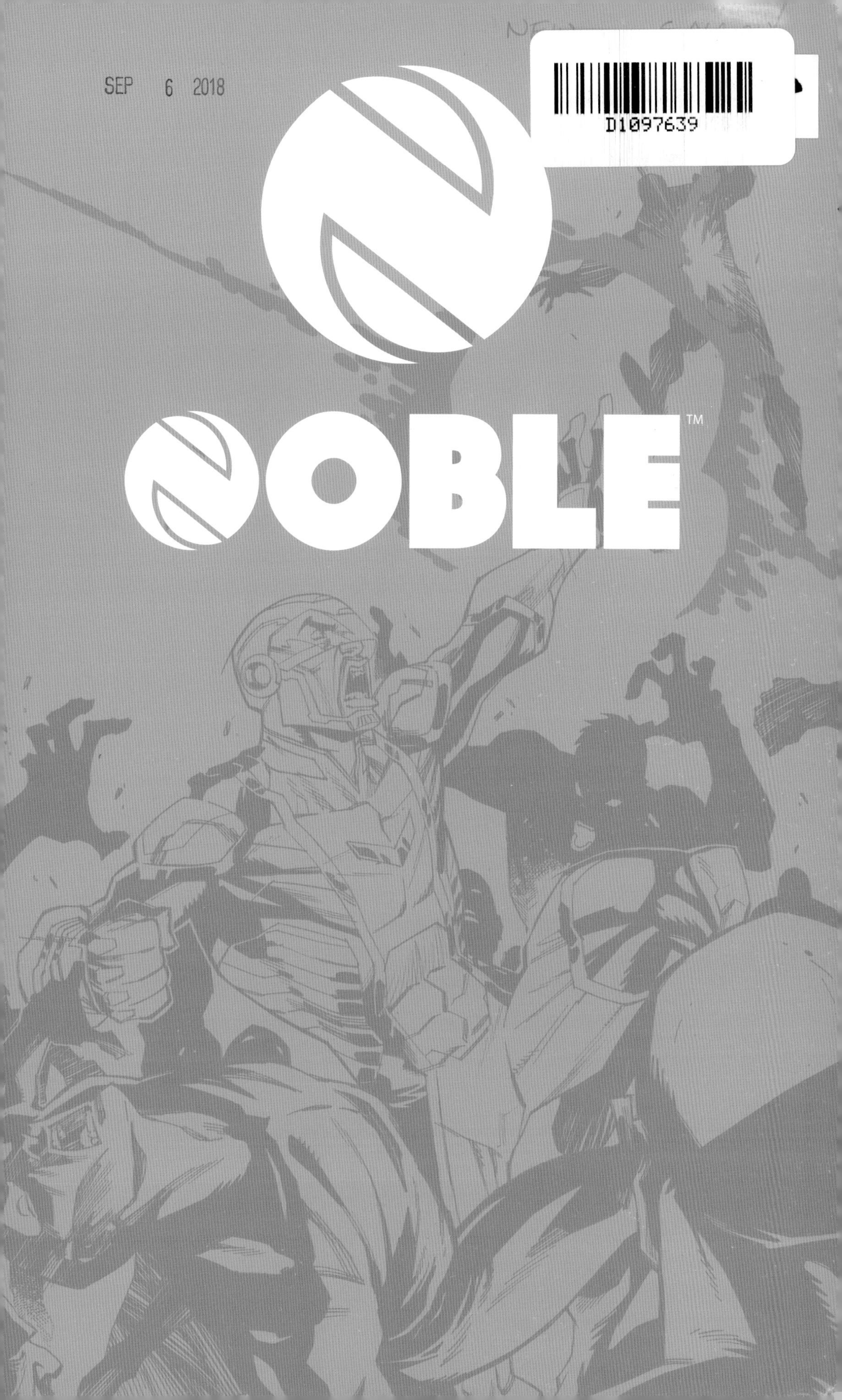

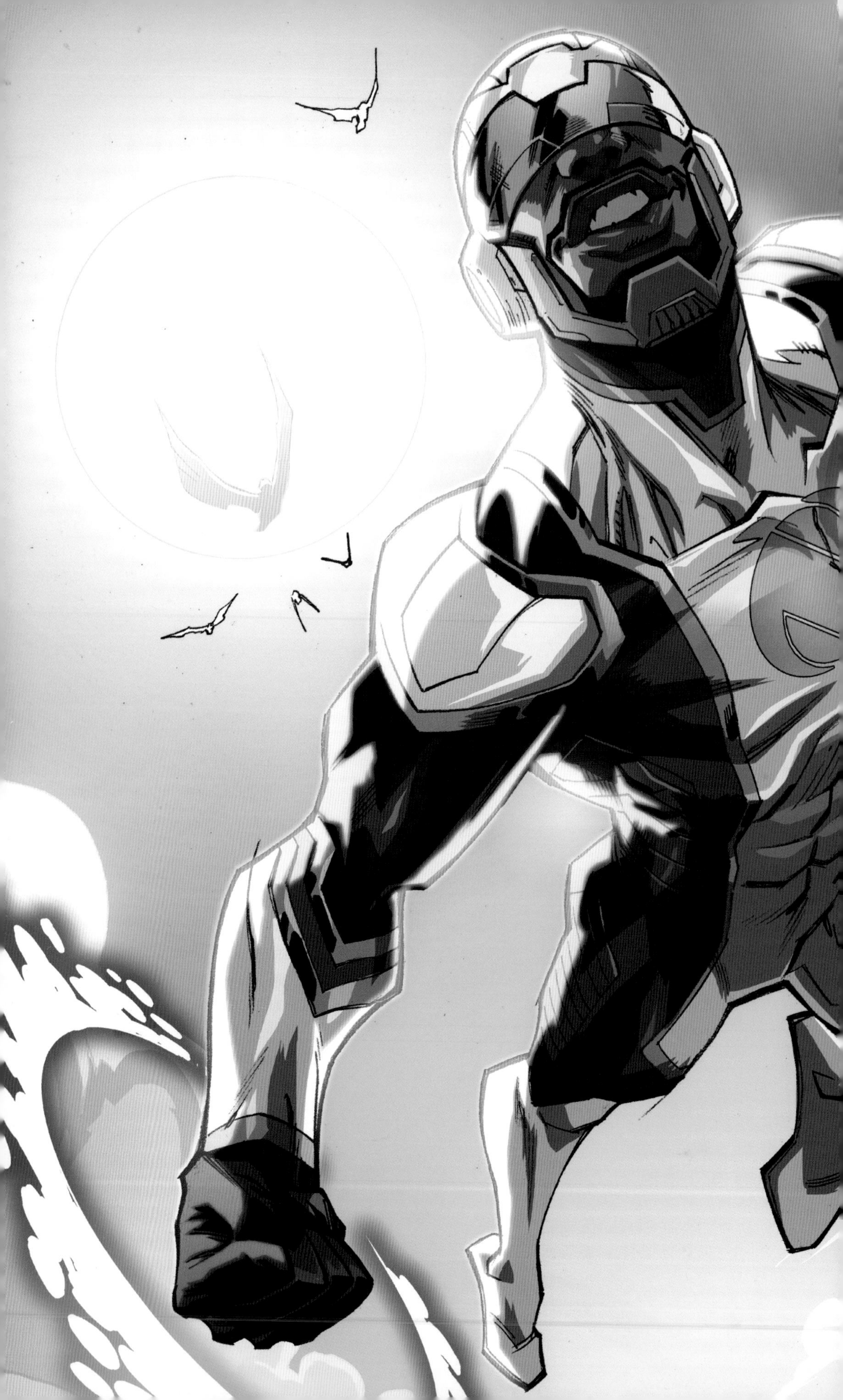

CATALYST PRIME

NOBLE™

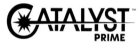

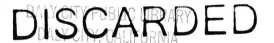

NEVER EVENTS

Written by **BRANDON THOMAS**
Illustrated by **ROGER ROBINSON, WILL ROSADO, JAMAL IGLE,** and **ROBIN RIGGS**
Lettered by **SAIDA TEMOFONTE**
Colored by **CHRISTOPHER SOTOMAYOR, PAUL MOUNTS, SNAKEBITE CORTEZ,** and **JUAN FERNANDEZ**

JOSEPH ILLIDGE • Senior Editor
DESIREE RODRIGUEZ • Editorial Assistant

Cover by **KHARY RANDOLPH** and **EMILIO LOPEZ**

LION FORGE

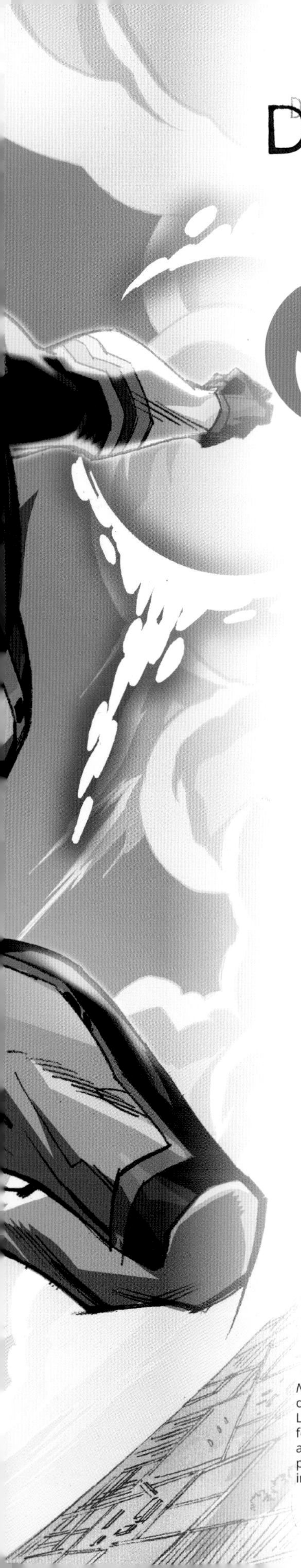

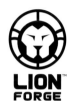

ISBN: 978-1-941302-74-3
Library of Congress Control Number: 2018930957

10 9 8 7 6 5 4 3 2 1

CHAPTER ONE

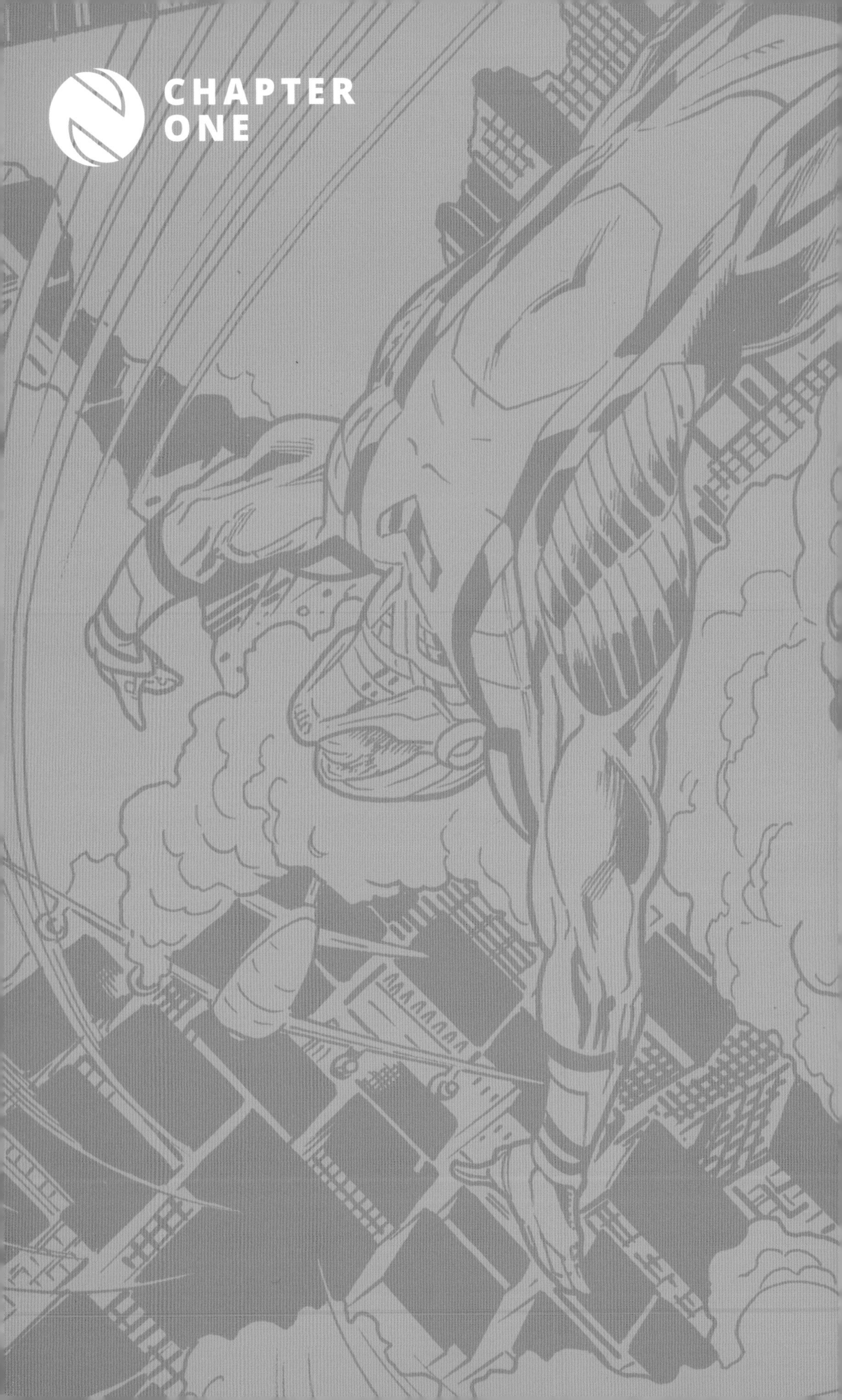

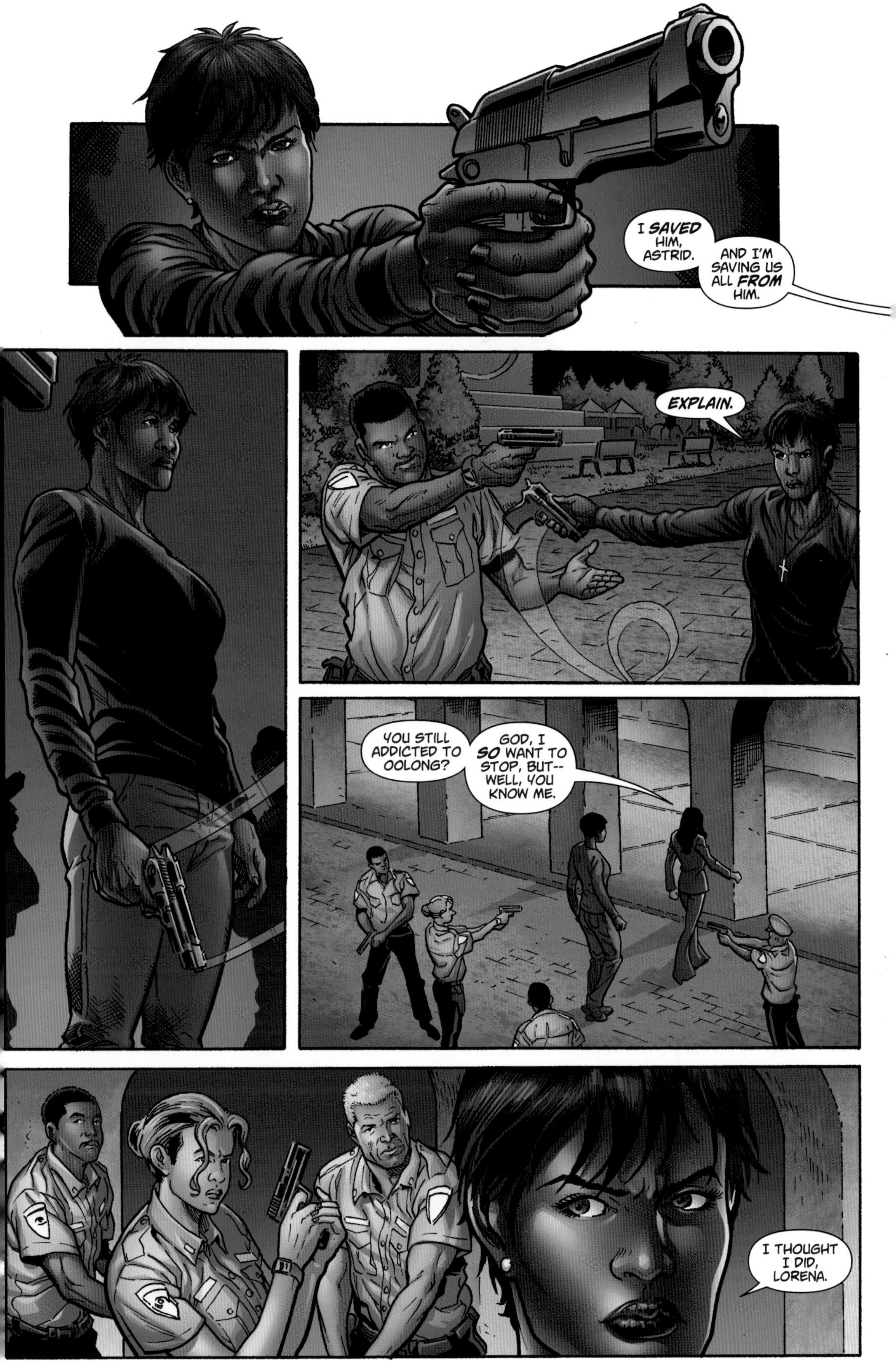
I SAVED HIM, ASTRID.
AND I'M SAVING US ALL FROM HIM.
EXPLAIN.
YOU STILL ADDICTED TO OOLONG?
GOD, I SO WANT TO STOP, BUT-- WELL, YOU KNOW ME.
I THOUGHT I DID, LORENA.

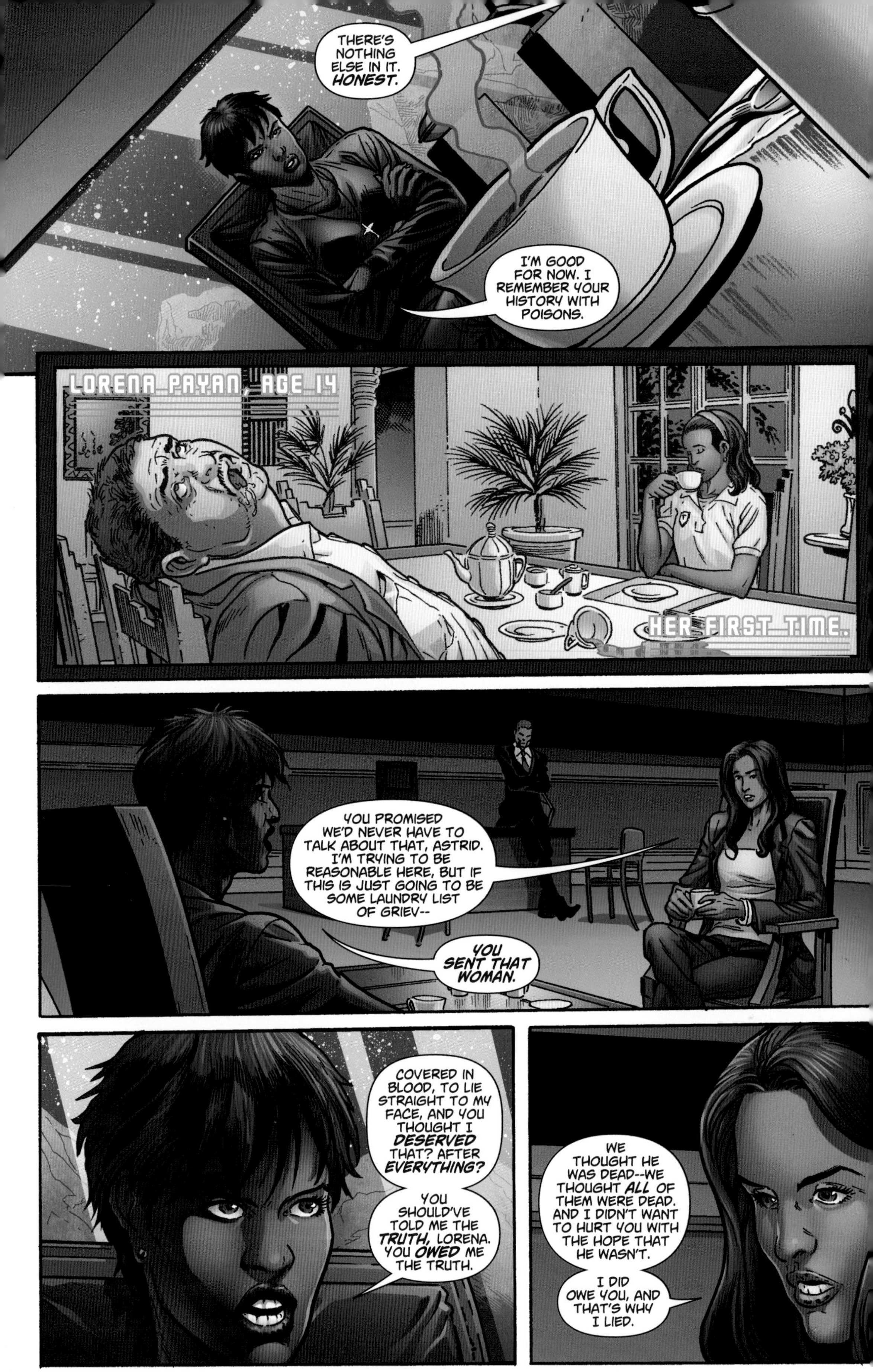
THERE'S NOTHING ELSE IN IT. HONEST.
I'M GOOD FOR NOW. I REMEMBER YOUR HISTORY WITH POISONS.
LORENA PAYAN, AGE 14
HER FIRST TIME.
YOU PROMISED WE'D NEVER HAVE TO TALK ABOUT THAT, ASTRID. I'M TRYING TO BE REASONABLE HERE, BUT IF THIS IS JUST GOING TO BE SOME LAUNDRY LIST OF GRIEV--
YOU SENT THAT WOMAN.
COVERED IN BLOOD, TO LIE STRAIGHT TO MY FACE, AND YOU THOUGHT I DESERVED THAT? AFTER EVERYTHING?
YOU SHOULD'VE TOLD ME THE TRUTH, LORENA. YOU OWED ME THE TRUTH.
WE THOUGHT HE WAS DEAD--WE THOUGHT ALL OF THEM WERE DEAD. AND I DIDN'T WANT TO HURT YOU WITH THE HOPE THAT HE WASN'T.
I DID OWE YOU, AND THAT'S WHY I LIED.

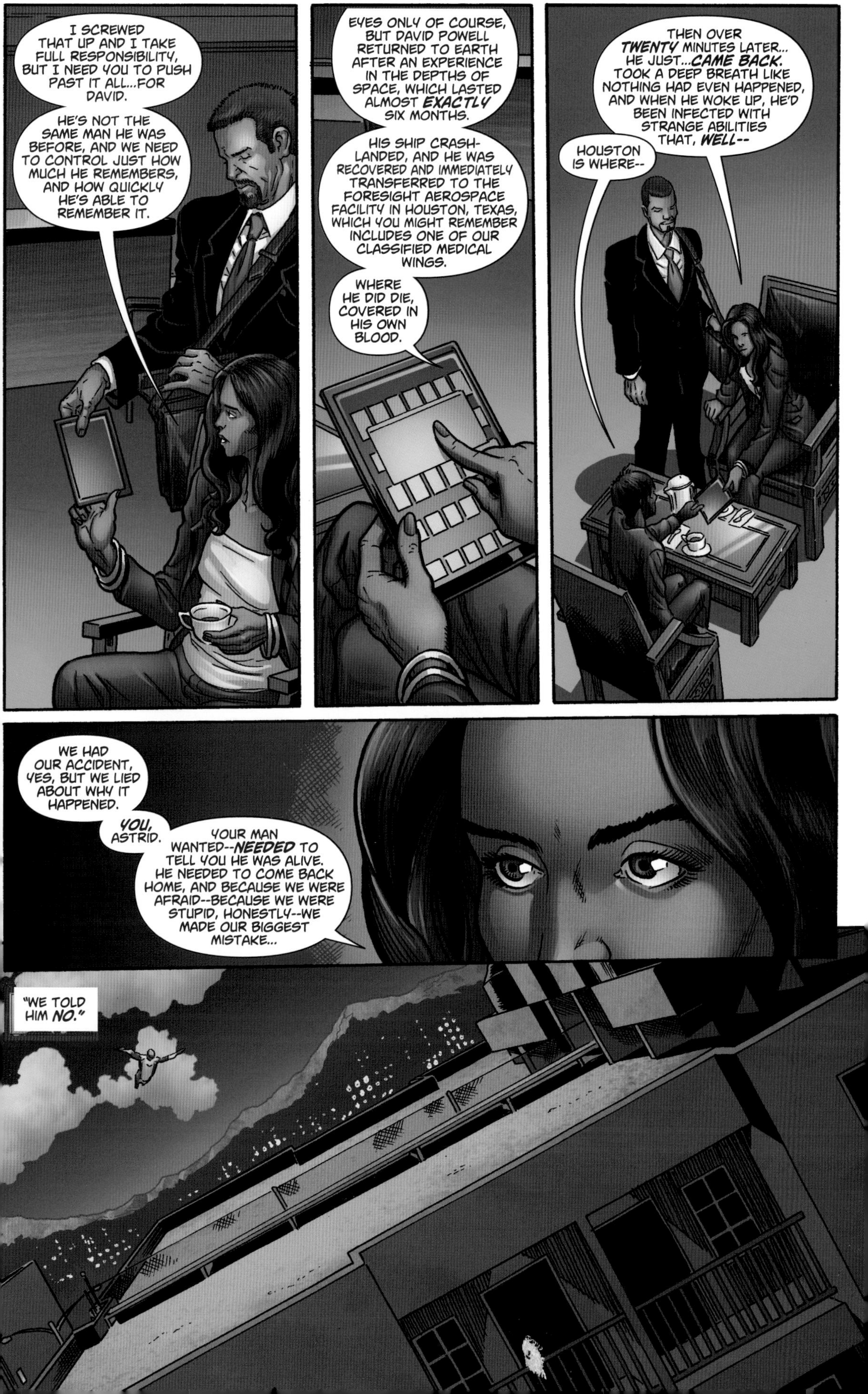

I SCREWED THAT UP AND I TAKE FULL RESPONSIBILITY, BUT I NEED YOU TO PUSH PAST IT ALL...FOR DAVID.
HE'S NOT THE SAME MAN HE WAS BEFORE, AND WE NEED TO CONTROL JUST HOW MUCH HE REMEMBERS, AND HOW QUICKLY HE'S ABLE TO REMEMBER IT.
EYES ONLY OF COURSE, BUT DAVID POWELL RETURNED TO EARTH AFTER AN EXPERIENCE IN THE DEPTHS OF SPACE, WHICH LASTED ALMOST EXACTLY SIX MONTHS.
HIS SHIP CRASH-LANDED, AND HE WAS RECOVERED AND IMMEDIATELY TRANSFERRED TO THE FORESIGHT AEROSPACE FACILITY IN HOUSTON, TEXAS, WHICH YOU MIGHT REMEMBER INCLUDES ONE OF OUR CLASSIFIED MEDICAL WINGS.
WHERE HE DID DIE, COVERED IN HIS OWN BLOOD.
THEN OVER TWENTY MINUTES LATER... HE JUST...CAME BACK. TOOK A DEEP BREATH LIKE NOTHING HAD EVEN HAPPENED, AND WHEN HE WOKE UP, HE'D BEEN INFECTED WITH STRANGE ABILITIES THAT, WELL--
HOUSTON IS WHERE--
WE HAD OUR ACCIDENT, YES, BUT WE LIED ABOUT WHY IT HAPPENED.
YOU, ASTRID.
YOUR MAN WANTED--NEEDED TO TELL YOU HE WAS ALIVE. HE NEEDED TO COME BACK HOME, AND BECAUSE WE WERE AFRAID--BECAUSE WE WERE STUPID, HONESTLY--WE MADE OUR BIGGEST MISTAKE...
"WE TOLD HIM NO."

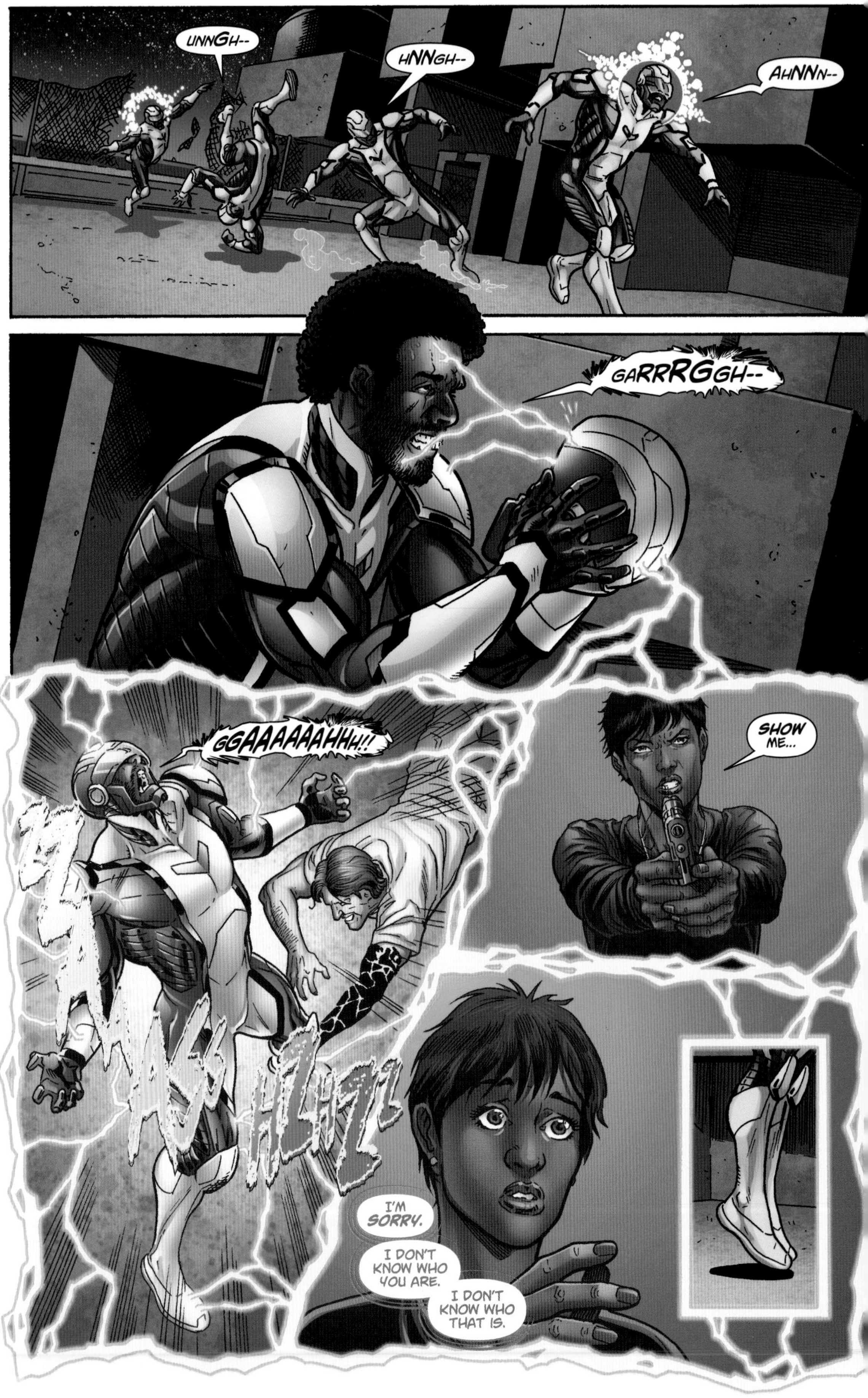
UNNGH--
HNNGH--
AHNNN--
GARRRGGH--
GGAAAAAAHHH!!
SHOW ME...
I'M SORRY.
I DON'T KNOW WHO YOU ARE.
I DON'T KNOW WHO THAT IS.

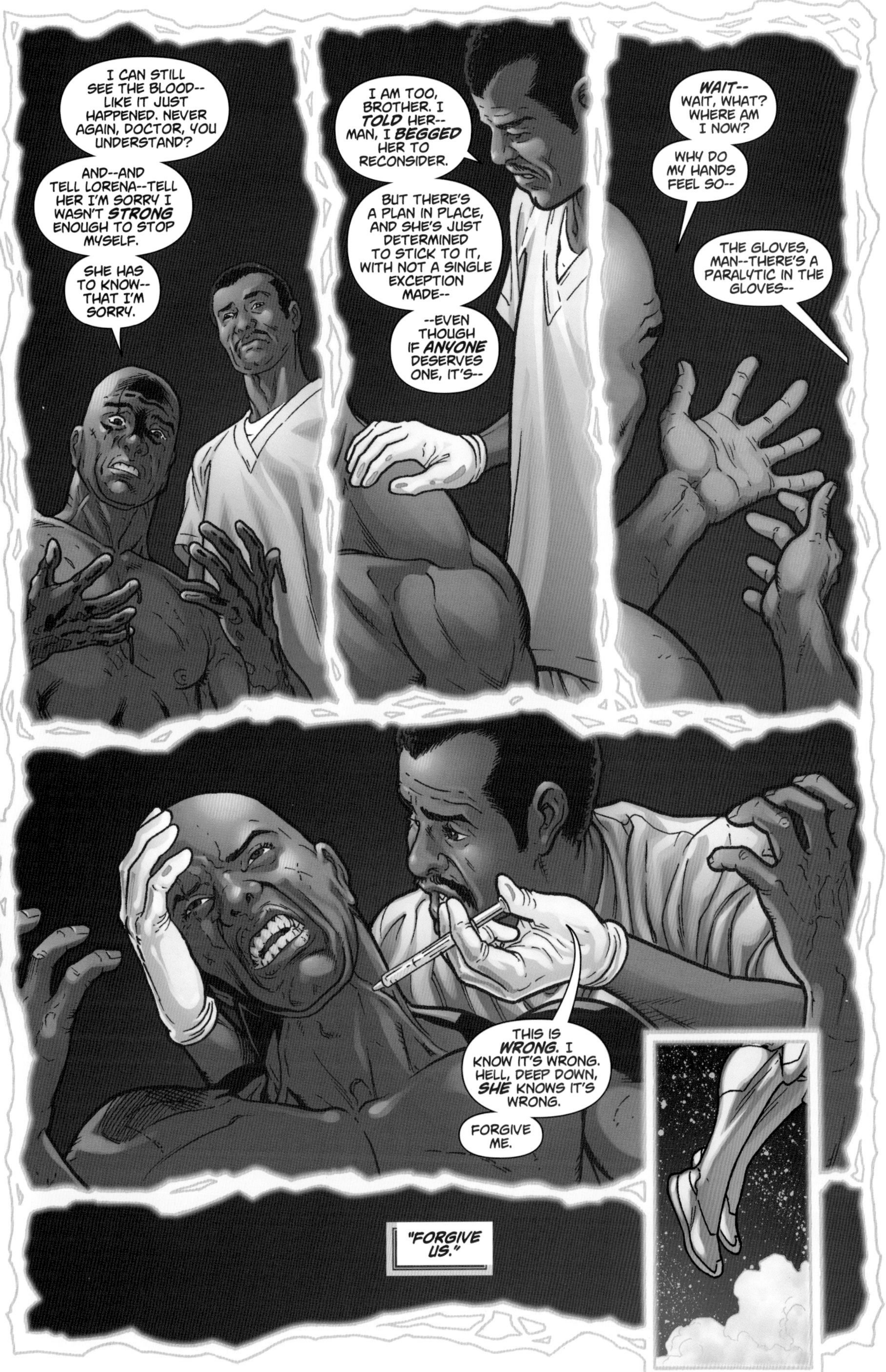
I CAN STILL SEE THE BLOOD-- LIKE IT JUST HAPPENED. NEVER AGAIN, DOCTOR, YOU UNDERSTAND?
AND--AND TELL LORENA--TELL HER I'M SORRY I WASN'T STRONG ENOUGH TO STOP MYSELF.
SHE HAS TO KNOW-- THAT I'M SORRY.
I AM TOO, BROTHER. I TOLD HER-- MAN, I BEGGED HER TO RECONSIDER.
BUT THERE'S A PLAN IN PLACE, AND SHE'S JUST DETERMINED TO STICK TO IT, WITH NOT A SINGLE EXCEPTION MADE--
--EVEN THOUGH IF ANYONE DESERVES ONE, IT'S--
WAIT-- WAIT, WHAT? WHERE AM I NOW?
WHY DO MY HANDS FEEL SO--
THE GLOVES, MAN--THERE'S A PARALYTIC IN THE GLOVES--
THIS IS WRONG. I KNOW IT'S WRONG. HELL, DEEP DOWN, SHE KNOWS IT'S WRONG.
FORGIVE ME.
"FORGIVE US."

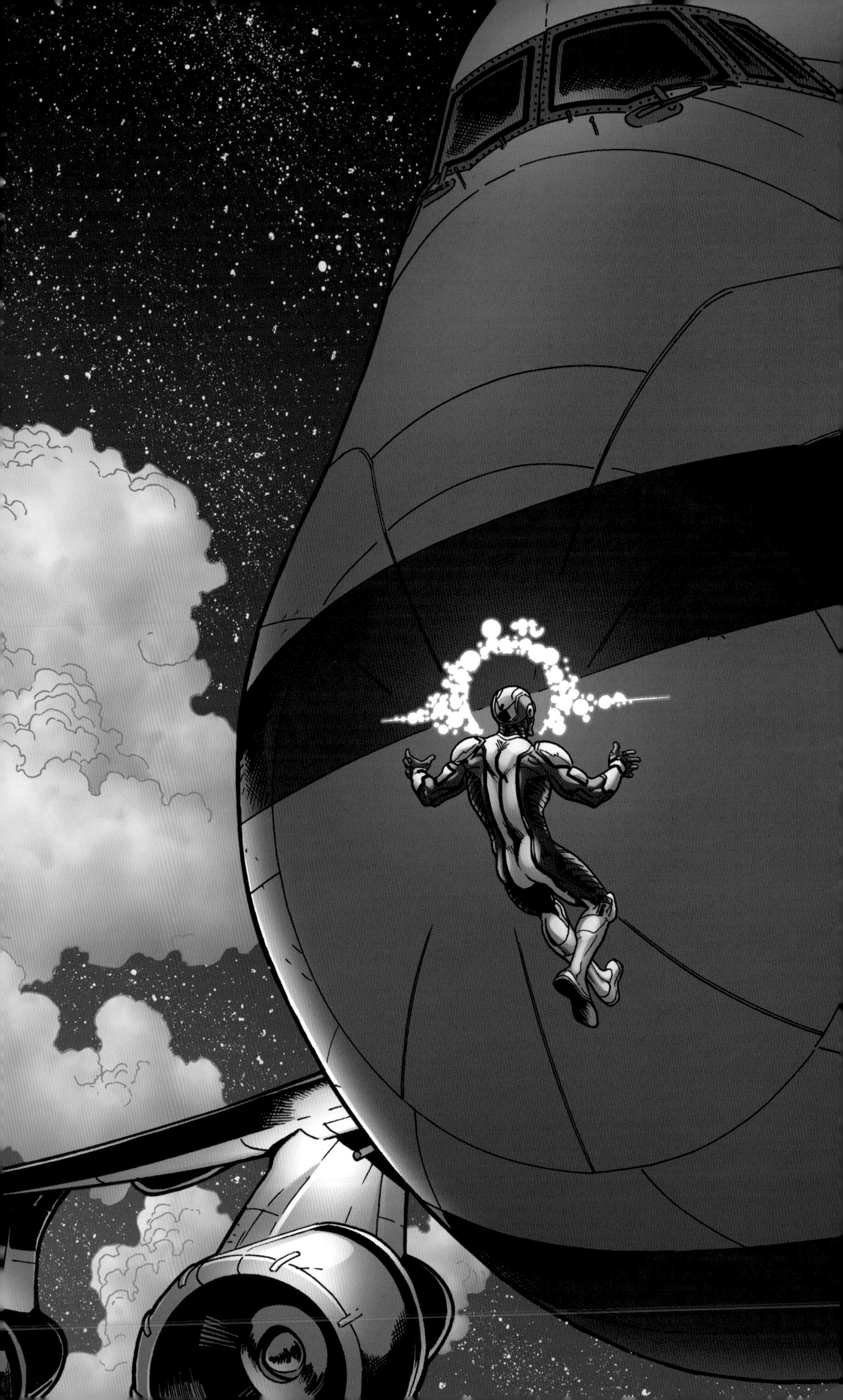

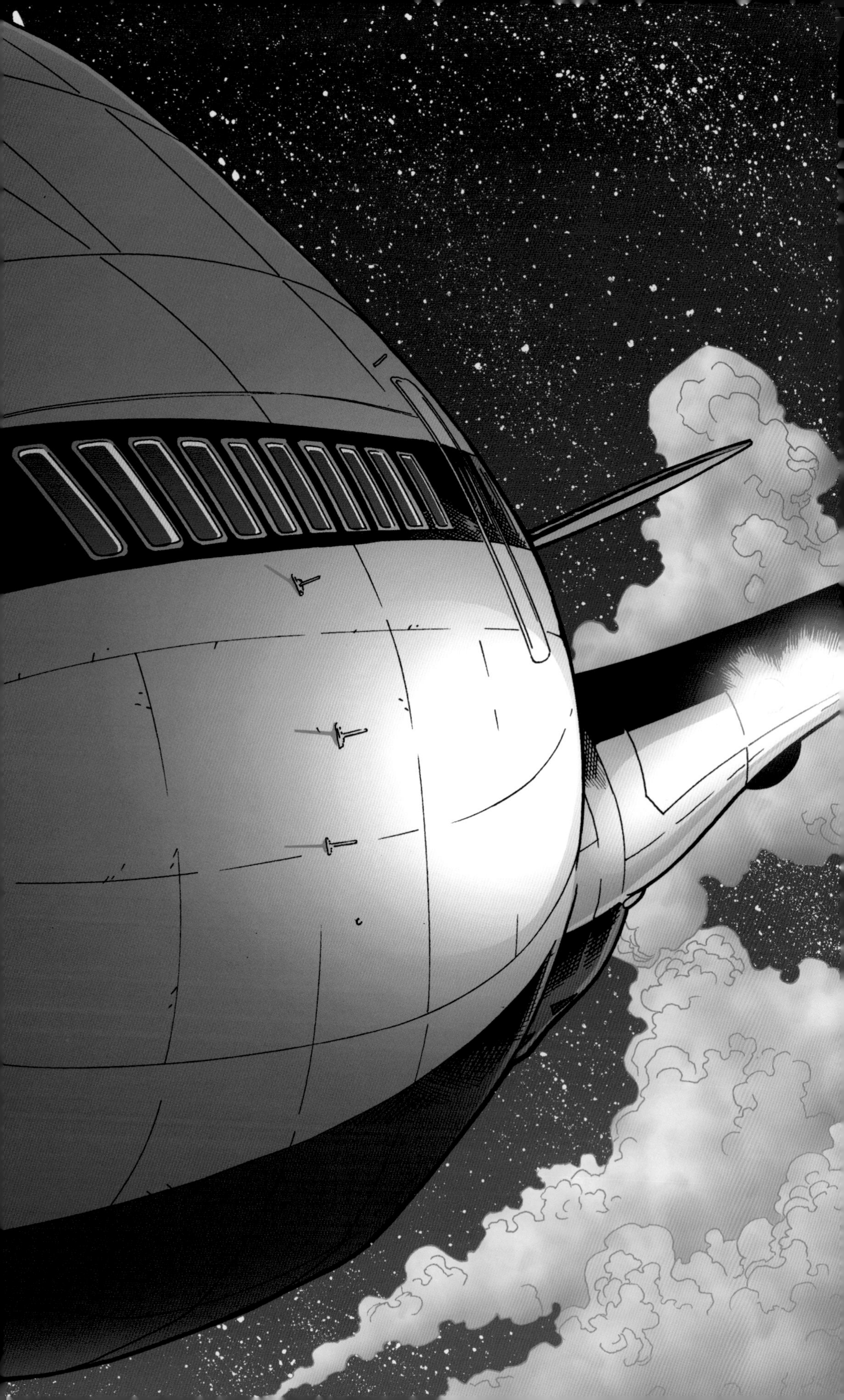

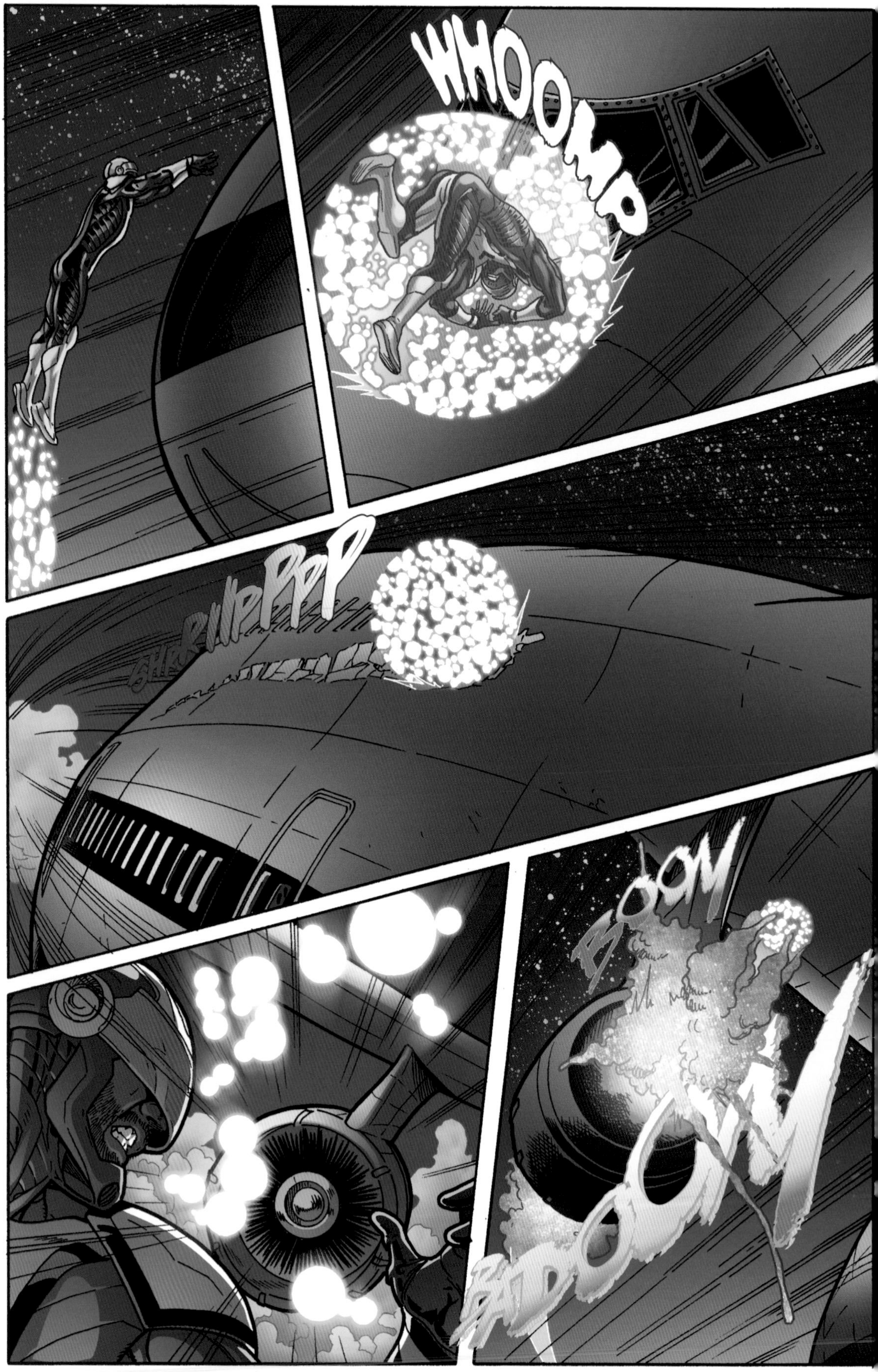
WHOOMP
SHRRIIPPPP
BOOM
BADOOM

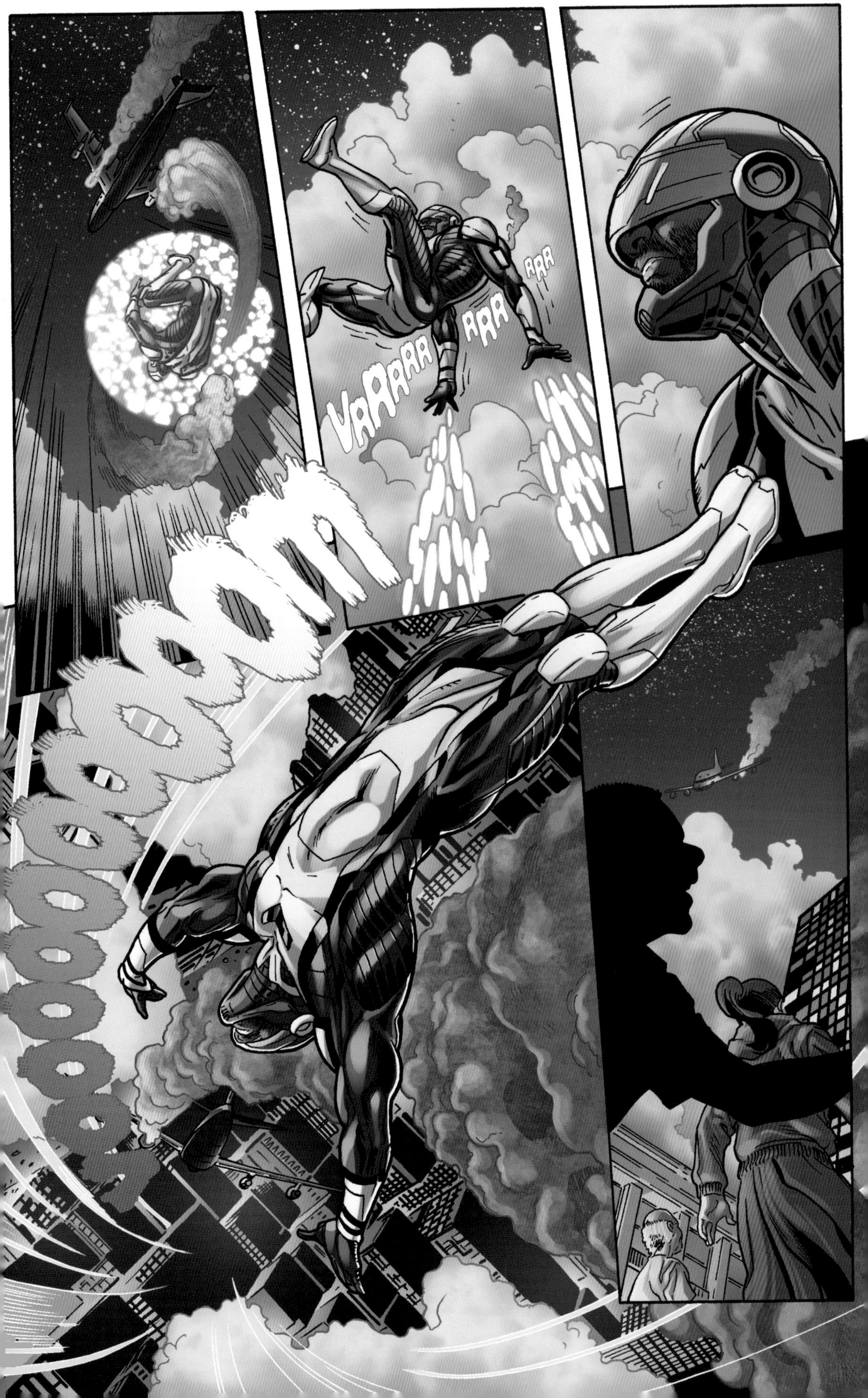

VAAAAAA
AAA
AAA
VOOOOOOOOOOM

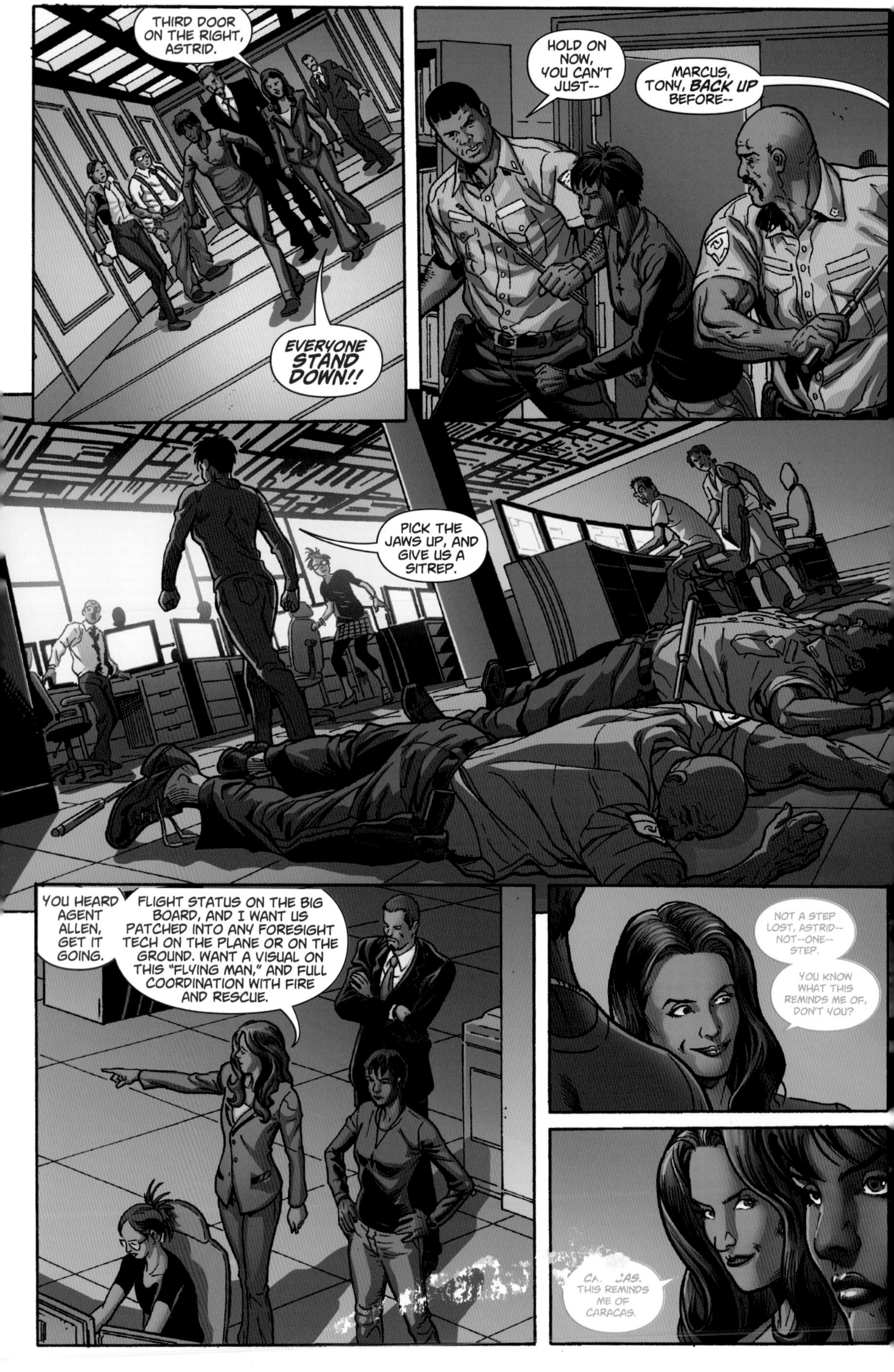

THIRD DOOR ON THE RIGHT, ASTRID.
EVERYONE STAND DOWN!!
HOLD ON NOW, YOU CAN'T JUST--
MARCUS, TONY, BACK UP BEFORE--
PICK THE JAWS UP, AND GIVE US A SITREP.
YOU HEARD AGENT ALLEN, GET IT GOING.
FLIGHT STATUS ON THE BIG BOARD, AND I WANT US PATCHED INTO ANY FORESIGHT TECH ON THE PLANE OR ON THE GROUND. WANT A VISUAL ON THIS "FLYING MAN," AND FULL COORDINATION WITH FIRE AND RESCUE.
NOT A STEP LOST, ASTRID-- NOT--ONE-- STEP.
YOU KNOW WHAT THIS REMINDS ME OF, DON'T YOU?
THIS REMINDS ME OF CARACAS.

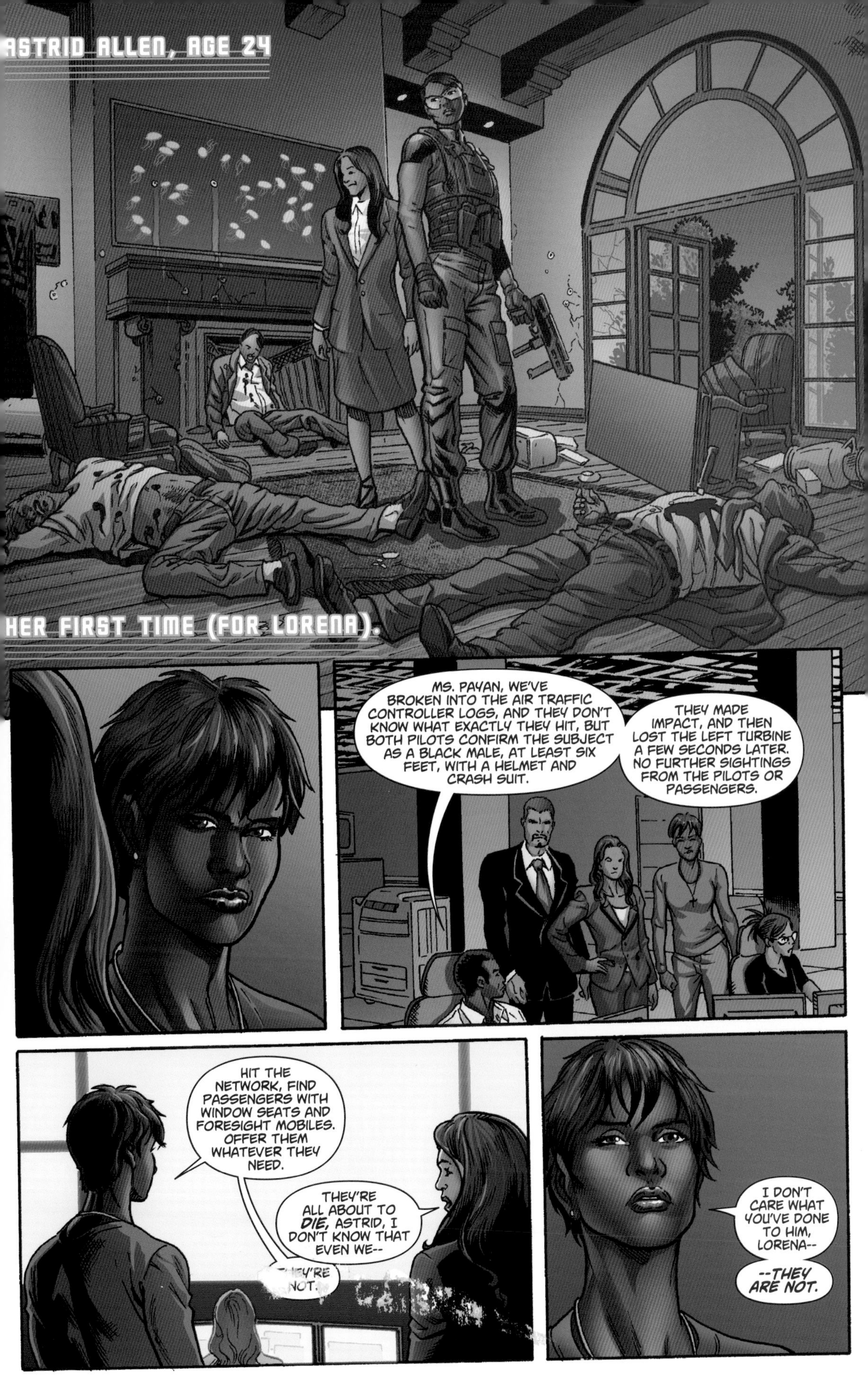
ASTRID ALLEN, AGE 24
HER FIRST TIME (FOR LORENA).
MS. PAYAN, WE'VE BROKEN INTO THE AIR TRAFFIC CONTROLLER LOGS, AND THEY DON'T KNOW WHAT EXACTLY THEY HIT, BUT BOTH PILOTS CONFIRM THE SUBJECT AS A BLACK MALE, AT LEAST SIX FEET, WITH A HELMET AND CRASH SUIT.
THEY MADE IMPACT, AND THEN LOST THE LEFT TURBINE A FEW SECONDS LATER. NO FURTHER SIGHTINGS FROM THE PILOTS OR PASSENGERS.
HIT THE NETWORK, FIND PASSENGERS WITH WINDOW SEATS AND FORESIGHT MOBILES. OFFER THEM WHATEVER THEY NEED.
THEY'RE ALL ABOUT TO *DIE*, ASTRID, I DON'T KNOW THAT EVEN WE--
NOT.
I DON'T CARE WHAT YOU'VE DONE TO HIM, LORENA--
--THEY ARE NOT.

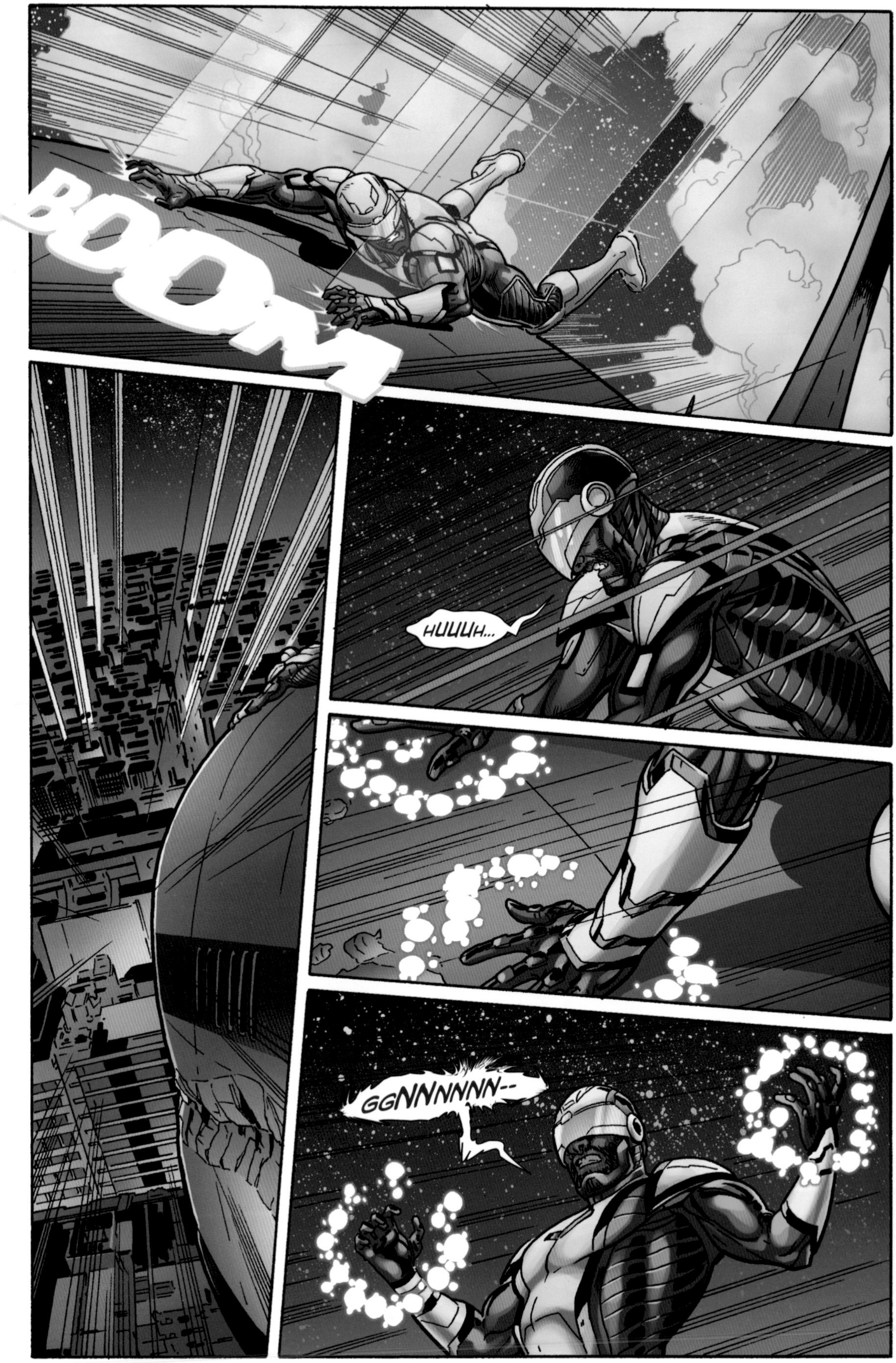
BOOM
HUUUH...
GGNNNNNN--

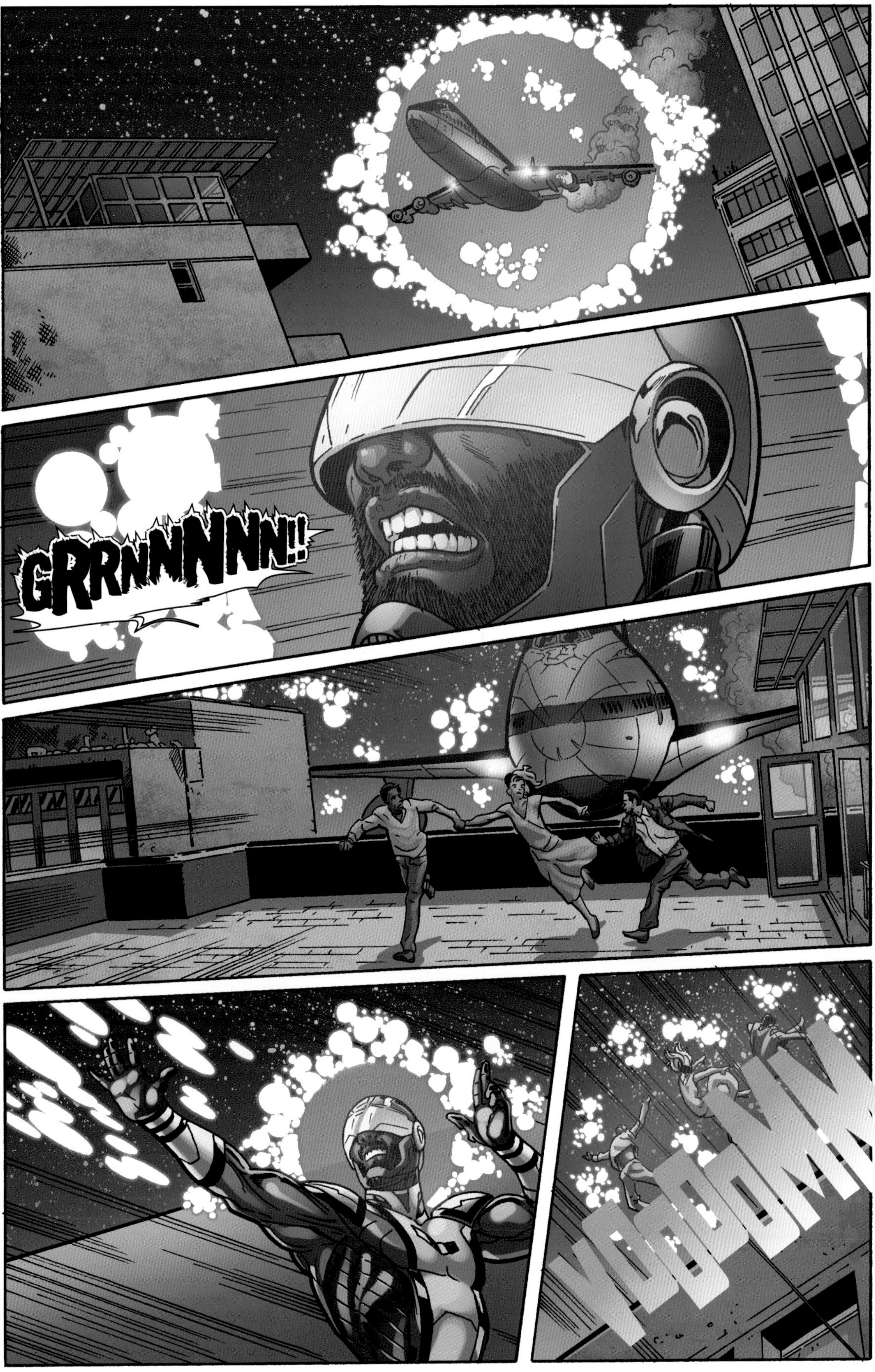
GRRNNNNNN!!
VOOOMM

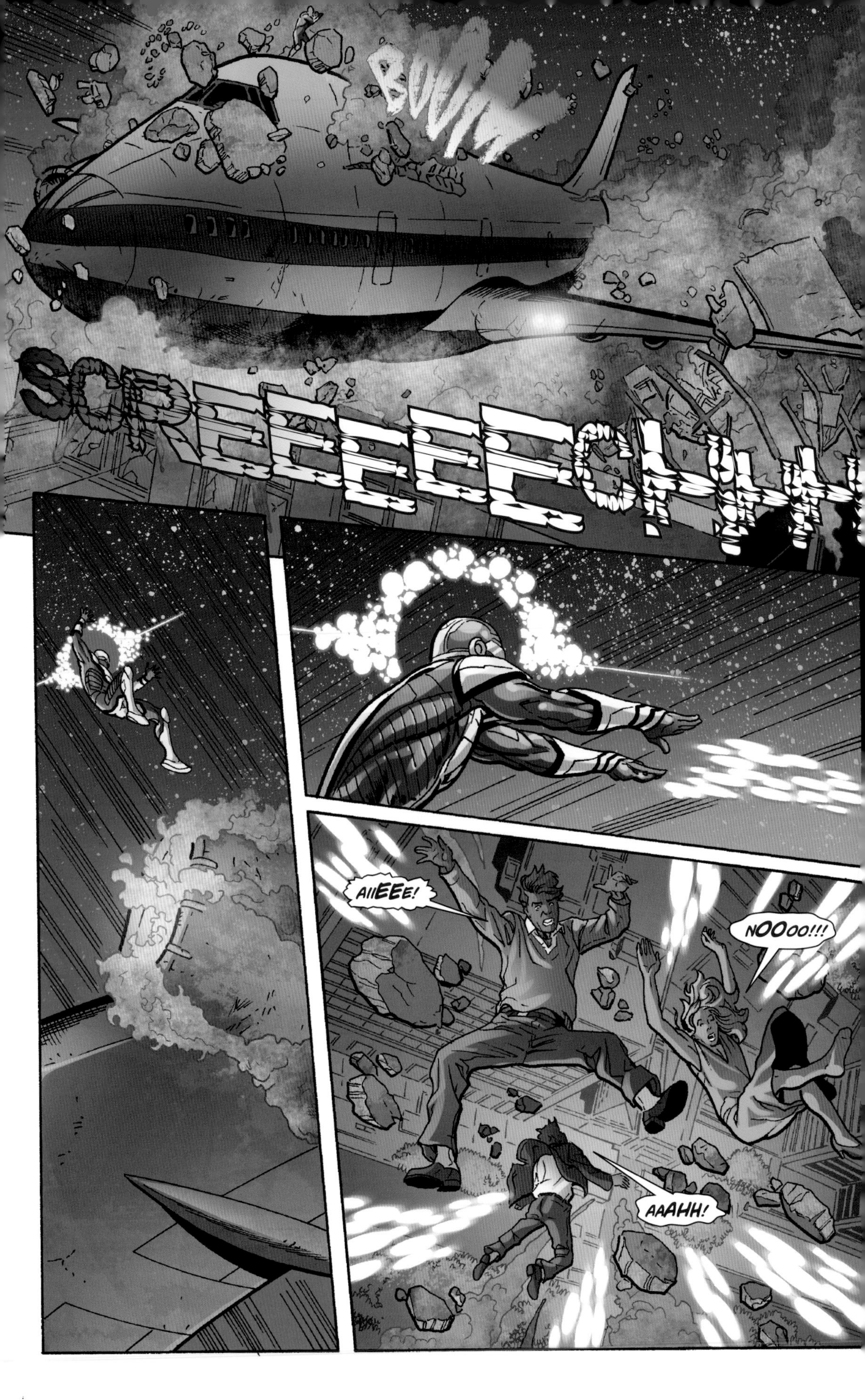
BOOM
SQREEEECHHH
AIIEEE!
NOOoo!!!
AAAHH!

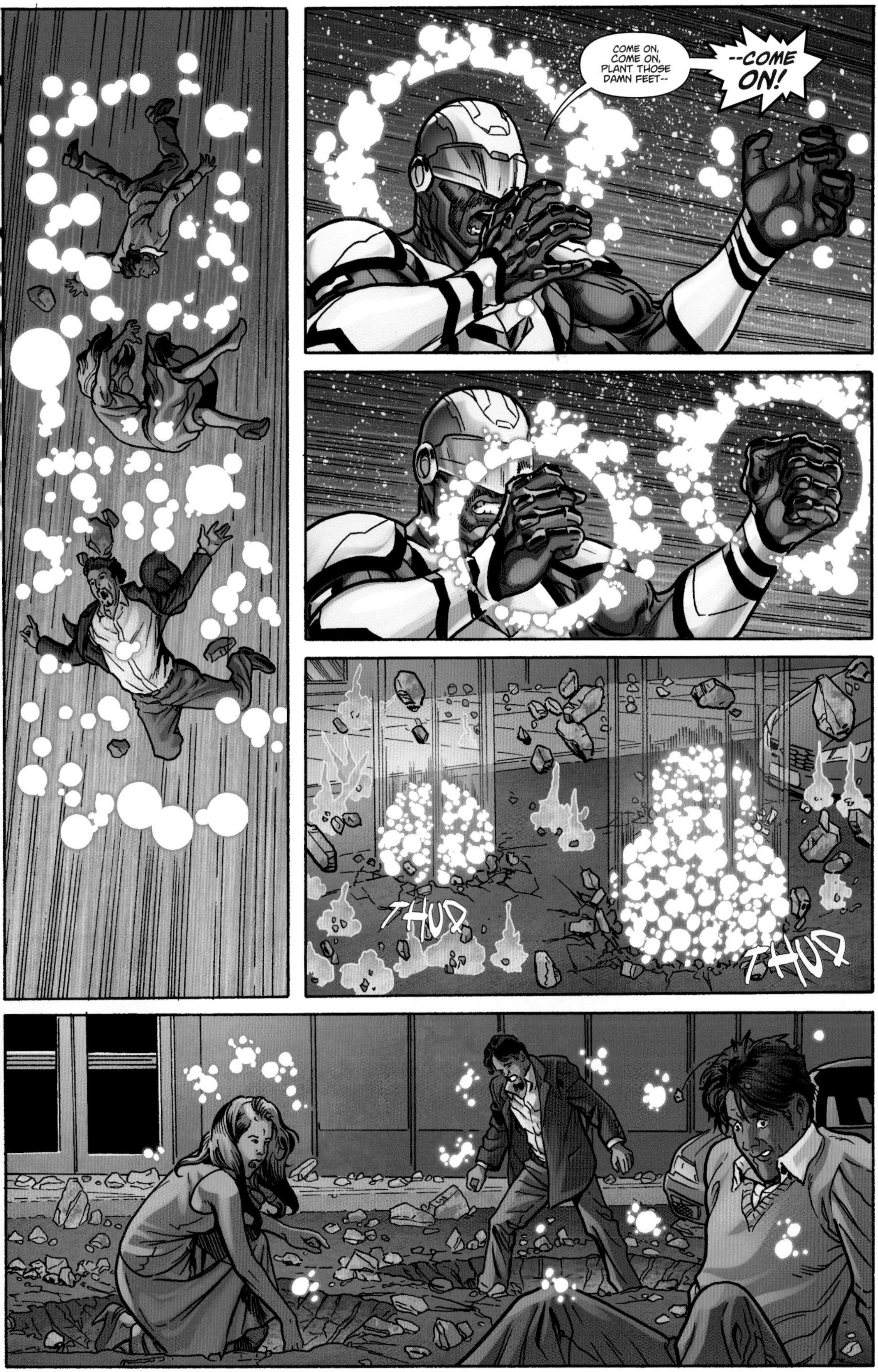
COME ON, COME ON, PLANT THOSE DAMN FEET--
--COME ON!
THUD
THUD

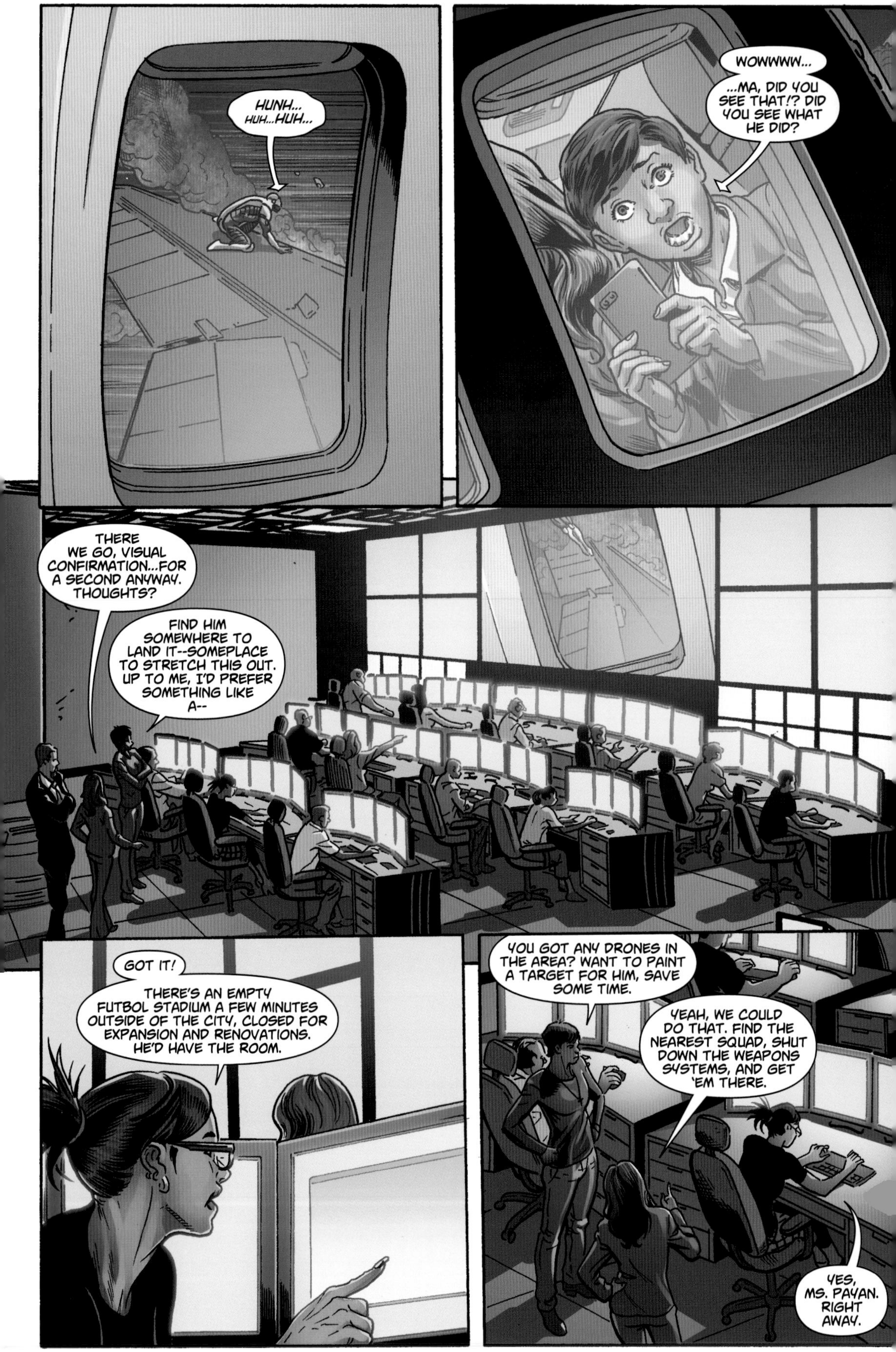
HUNH... HUH...HUH...
WOWWWW...
...MA, DID YOU SEE THAT!? DID YOU SEE WHAT HE DID?
THERE WE GO, VISUAL CONFIRMATION...FOR A SECOND ANYWAY. THOUGHTS?
FIND HIM SOMEWHERE TO LAND IT--SOMEPLACE TO STRETCH THIS OUT. UP TO ME, I'D PREFER SOMETHING LIKE A--
GOT IT!
THERE'S AN EMPTY FUTBOL STADIUM A FEW MINUTES OUTSIDE OF THE CITY, CLOSED FOR EXPANSION AND RENOVATIONS. HE'D HAVE THE ROOM.
YOU GOT ANY DRONES IN THE AREA? WANT TO PAINT A TARGET FOR HIM, SAVE SOME TIME.
YEAH, WE COULD DO THAT. FIND THE NEAREST SQUAD, SHUT DOWN THE WEAPONS SYSTEMS, AND GET 'EM THERE.
YES, MS. PAYAN. RIGHT AWAY.

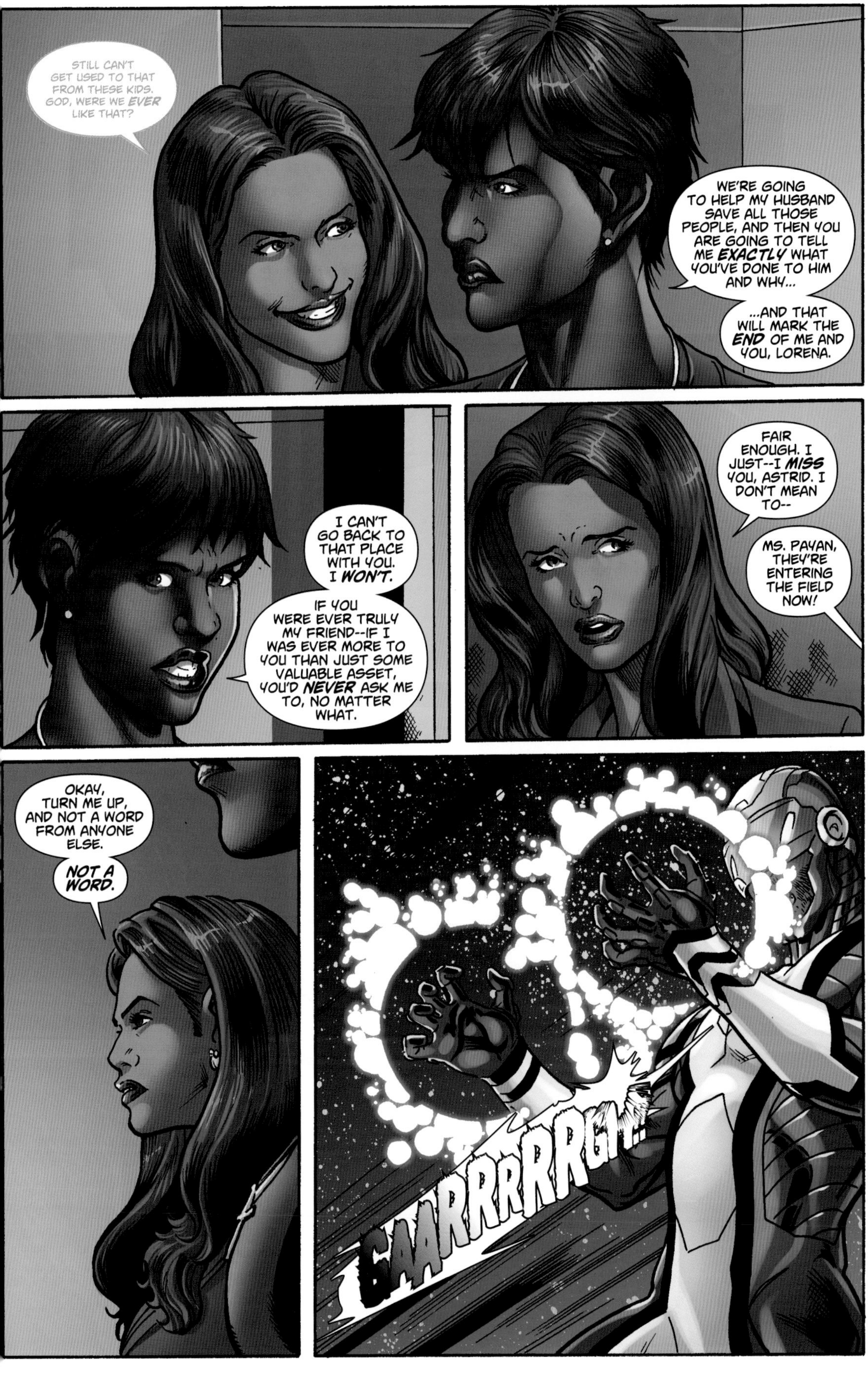
STILL CAN'T GET USED TO THAT FROM THESE KIDS. GOD, WERE WE EVER LIKE THAT?
WE'RE GOING TO HELP MY HUSBAND SAVE ALL THOSE PEOPLE, AND THEN YOU ARE GOING TO TELL ME EXACTLY WHAT YOU'VE DONE TO HIM AND WHY...
...AND THAT WILL MARK THE END OF ME AND YOU, LORENA.
I CAN'T GO BACK TO THAT PLACE WITH YOU. I WON'T.
IF YOU WERE EVER TRULY MY FRIEND--IF I WAS EVER MORE TO YOU THAN JUST SOME VALUABLE ASSET, YOU'D NEVER ASK ME TO, NO MATTER WHAT.
FAIR ENOUGH. I JUST--I MISS YOU, ASTRID. I DON'T MEAN TO--
MS. PAYAN, THEY'RE ENTERING THE FIELD NOW!
OKAY, TURN ME UP, AND NOT A WORD FROM ANYONE ELSE.
NOT A WORD.
GAARRRRRGH!!

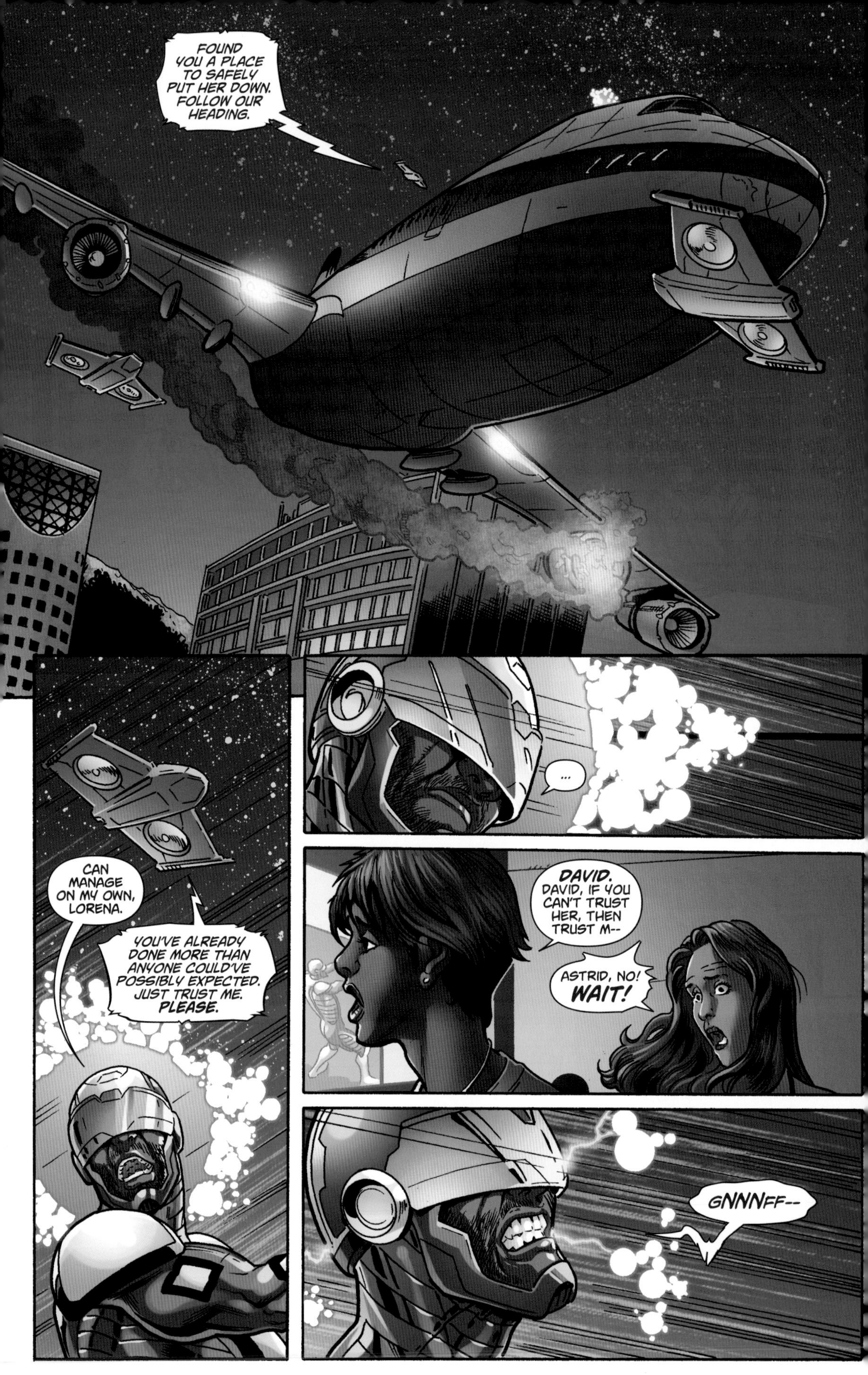
FOUND YOU A PLACE TO SAFELY PUT HER DOWN. FOLLOW OUR HEADING.
CAN MANAGE ON MY OWN, LORENA.
YOU'VE ALREADY DONE MORE THAN ANYONE COULD'VE POSSIBLY EXPECTED. JUST TRUST ME. PLEASE.
...
DAVID. DAVID, IF YOU CAN'T TRUST HER, THEN TRUST M--
ASTRID, NO! WAIT!
GNNNFF--

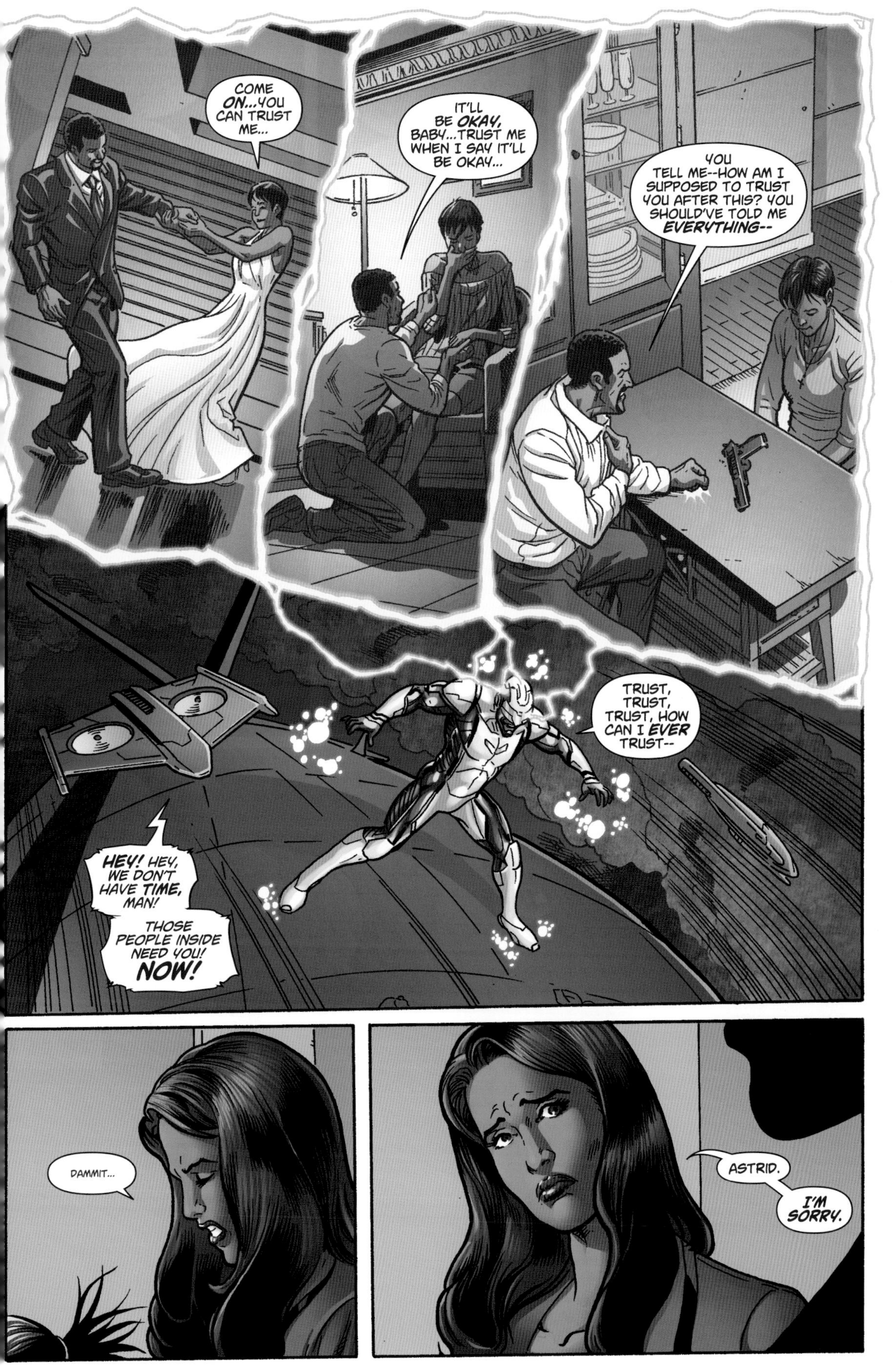
COME ON...YOU CAN TRUST ME...
IT'LL BE OKAY, BABY...TRUST ME WHEN I SAY IT'LL BE OKAY...
YOU TELL ME--HOW AM I SUPPOSED TO TRUST YOU AFTER THIS? YOU SHOULD'VE TOLD ME EVERYTHING--
TRUST, TRUST, TRUST, HOW CAN I EVER TRUST--
HEY! HEY, WE DON'T HAVE TIME, MAN!
THOSE PEOPLE INSIDE NEED YOU! NOW!
DAMMIT...
ASTRID.
I'M SORRY.

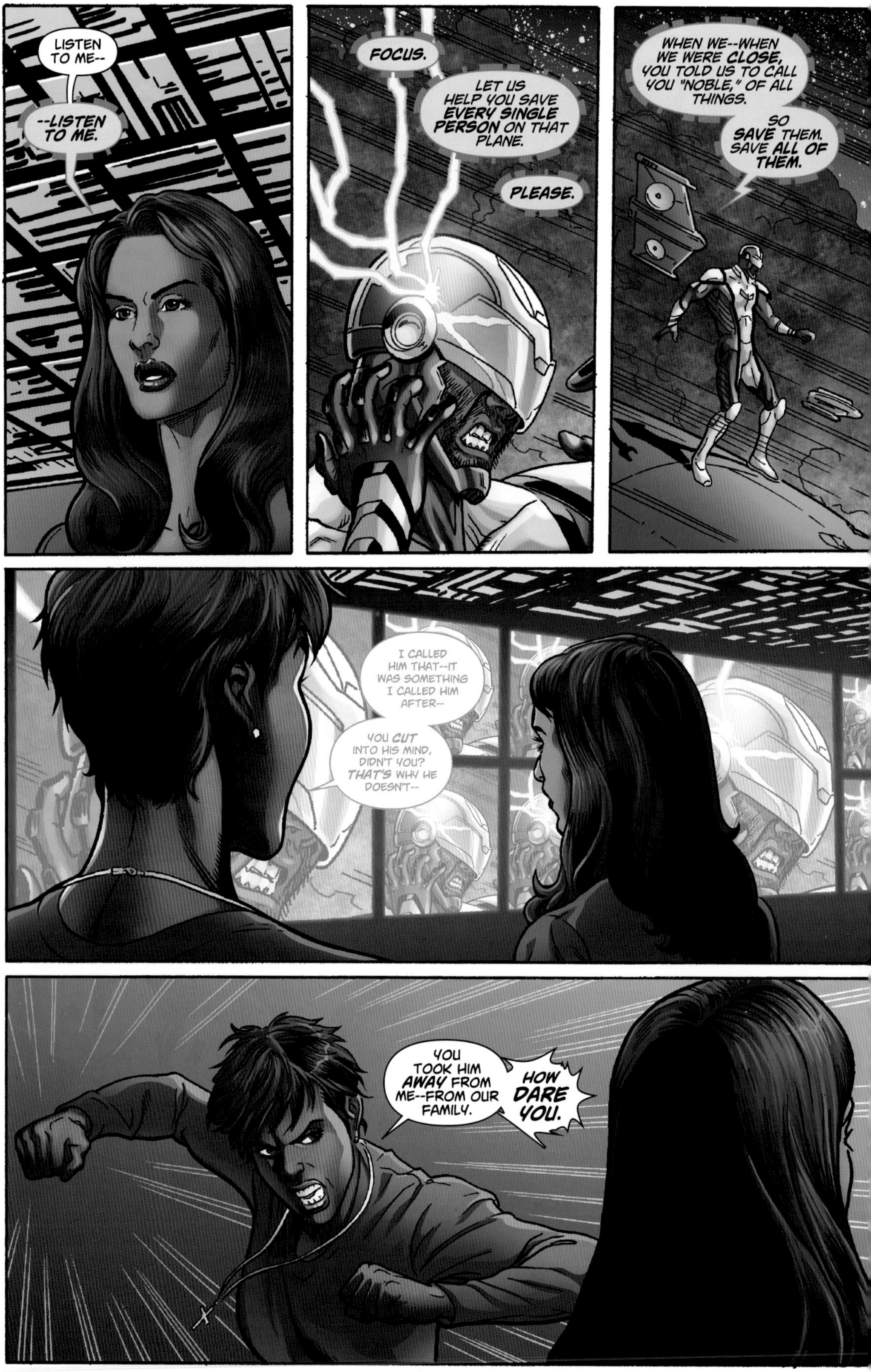
LISTEN TO ME--
--LISTEN TO ME.
FOCUS.
LET US HELP YOU SAVE EVERY SINGLE PERSON ON THAT PLANE.
PLEASE.
WHEN WE--WHEN WE WERE CLOSE, YOU TOLD US TO CALL YOU "NOBLE," OF ALL THINGS.
SO SAVE THEM. SAVE ALL OF THEM.
I CALLED HIM THAT--IT WAS SOMETHING I CALLED HIM AFTER--
YOU CUT INTO HIS MIND, DIDN'T YOU? THAT'S WHY HE DOESN'T--
YOU TOOK HIM AWAY FROM ME--FROM OUR FAMILY.
HOW DARE YOU.

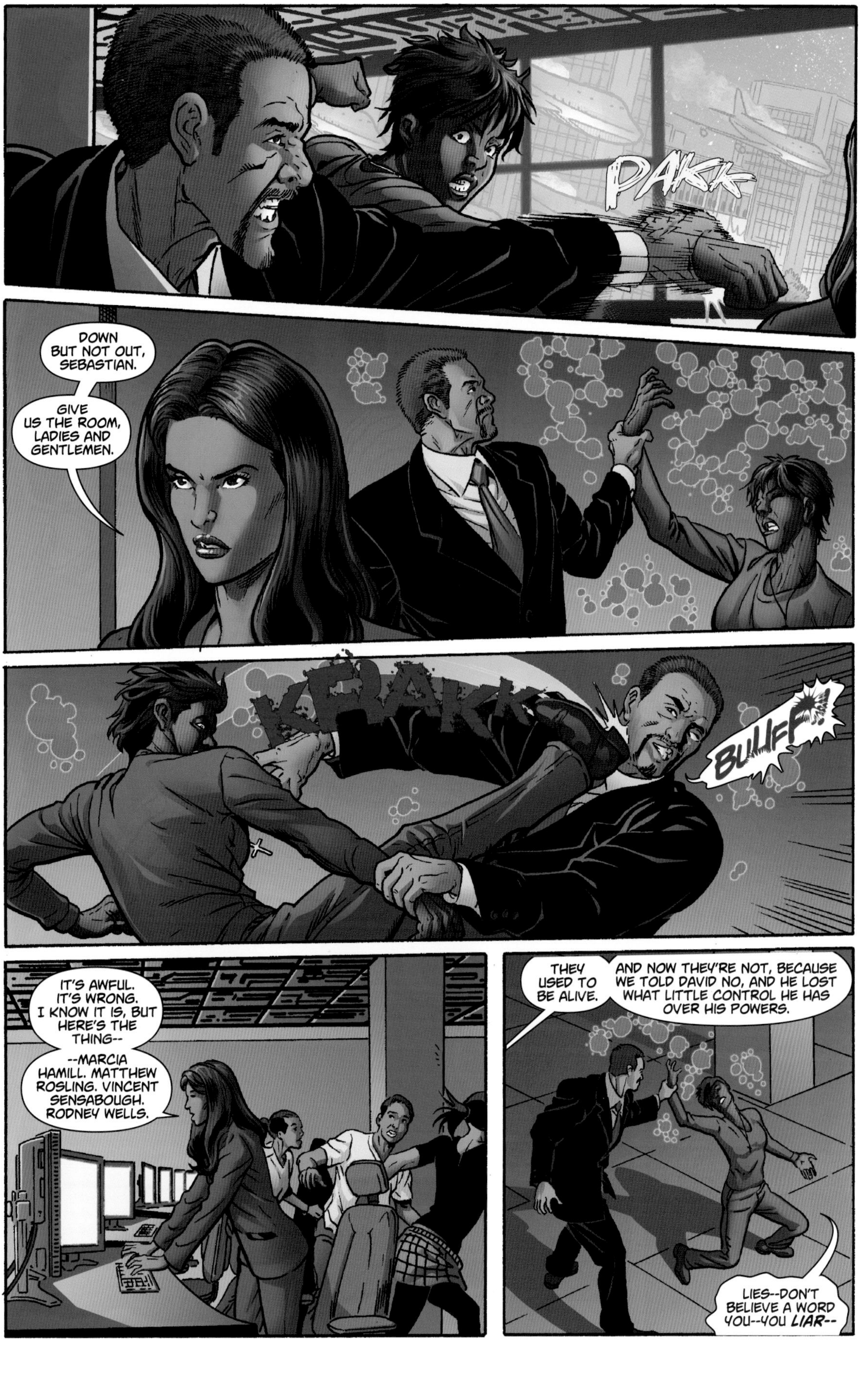
PAKK
DOWN BUT NOT OUT, SEBASTIAN.
GIVE US THE ROOM, LADIES AND GENTLEMEN.
KRAKK
BULLFF
IT'S AWFUL. IT'S WRONG. I KNOW IT IS, BUT HERE'S THE THING--
--MARCIA HAMILL. MATTHEW ROSLING. VINCENT SENSABOUGH. RODNEY WELLS.
THEY USED TO BE ALIVE.
AND NOW THEY'RE NOT, BECAUSE WE TOLD DAVID NO, AND HE LOST WHAT LITTLE CONTROL HE HAS OVER HIS POWERS.
LIES--DON'T BELIEVE A WORD YOU--YOU *LIAR*--

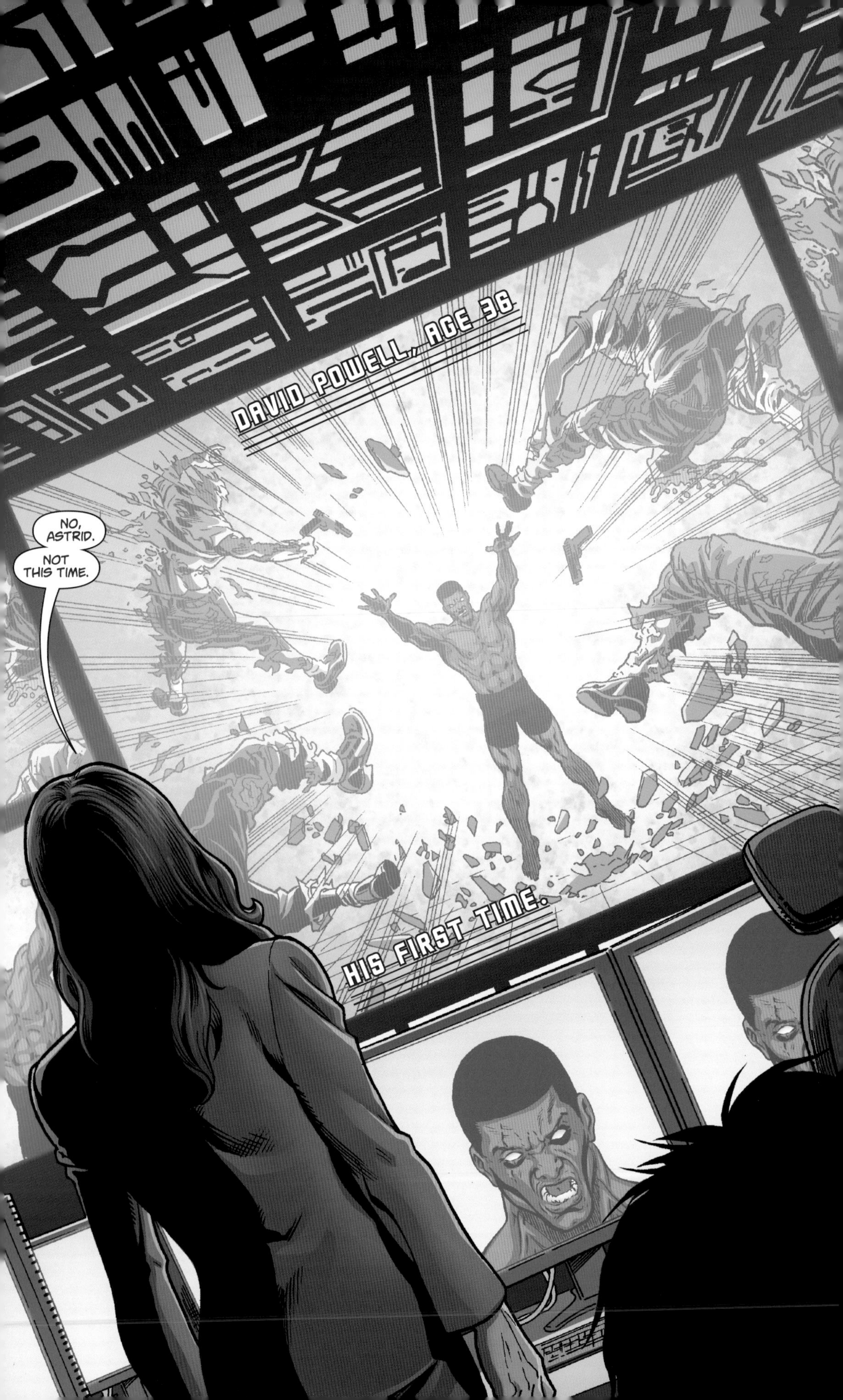
DAVID POWELL, AGE 36
NO, ASTRID.
NOT THIS TIME.
HIS FIRST TIME.

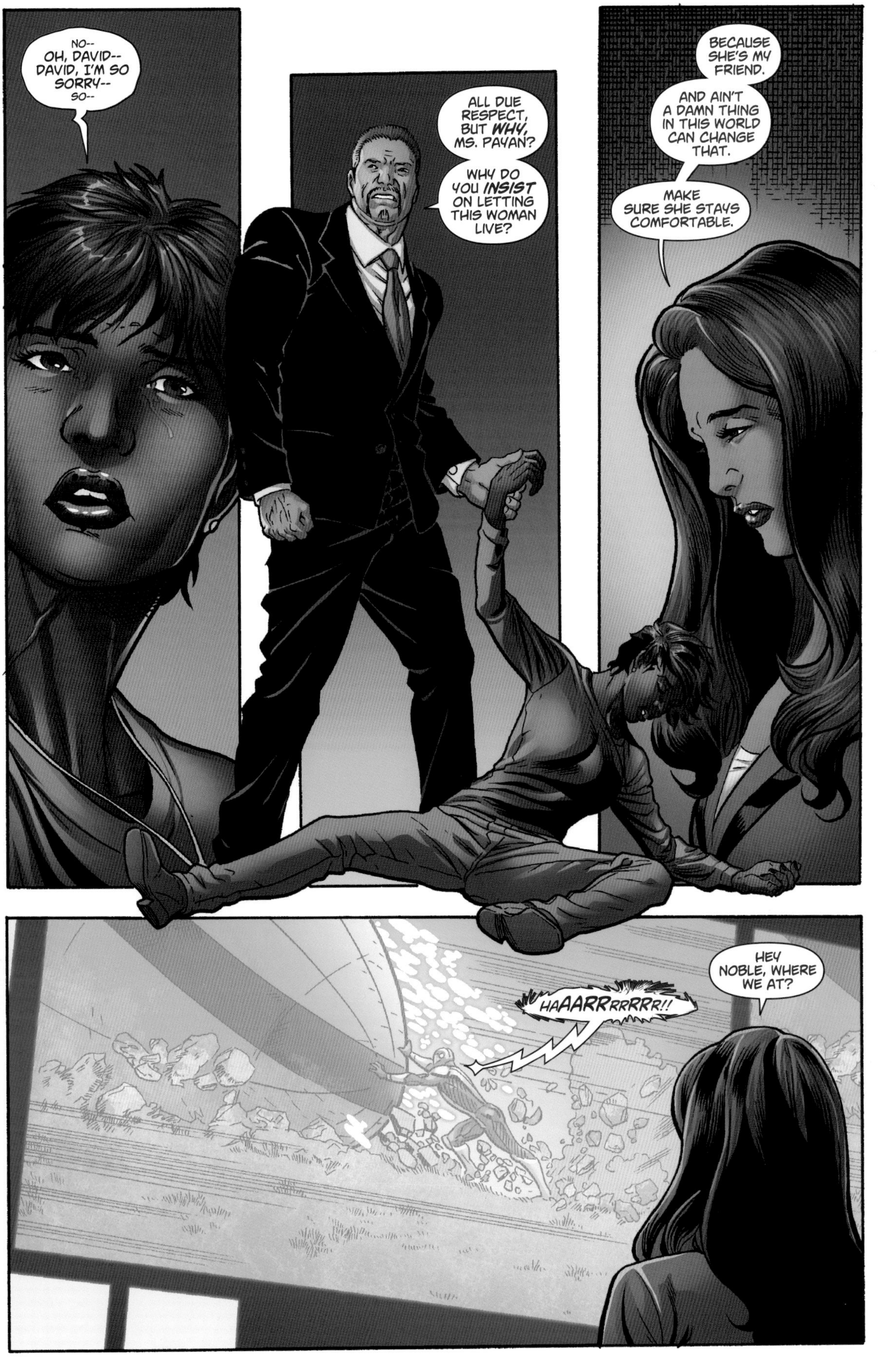
NO-- OH, DAVID-- DAVID, I'M SO SORRY-- SO--
ALL DUE RESPECT, BUT WHY, MS. PAYAN?
WHY DO YOU INSIST ON LETTING THIS WOMAN LIVE?
BECAUSE SHE'S MY FRIEND.
AND AIN'T A DAMN THING IN THIS WORLD CAN CHANGE THAT.
MAKE SURE SHE STAYS COMFORTABLE.
HAAARRRRRRR!!
HEY NOBLE, WHERE WE AT?

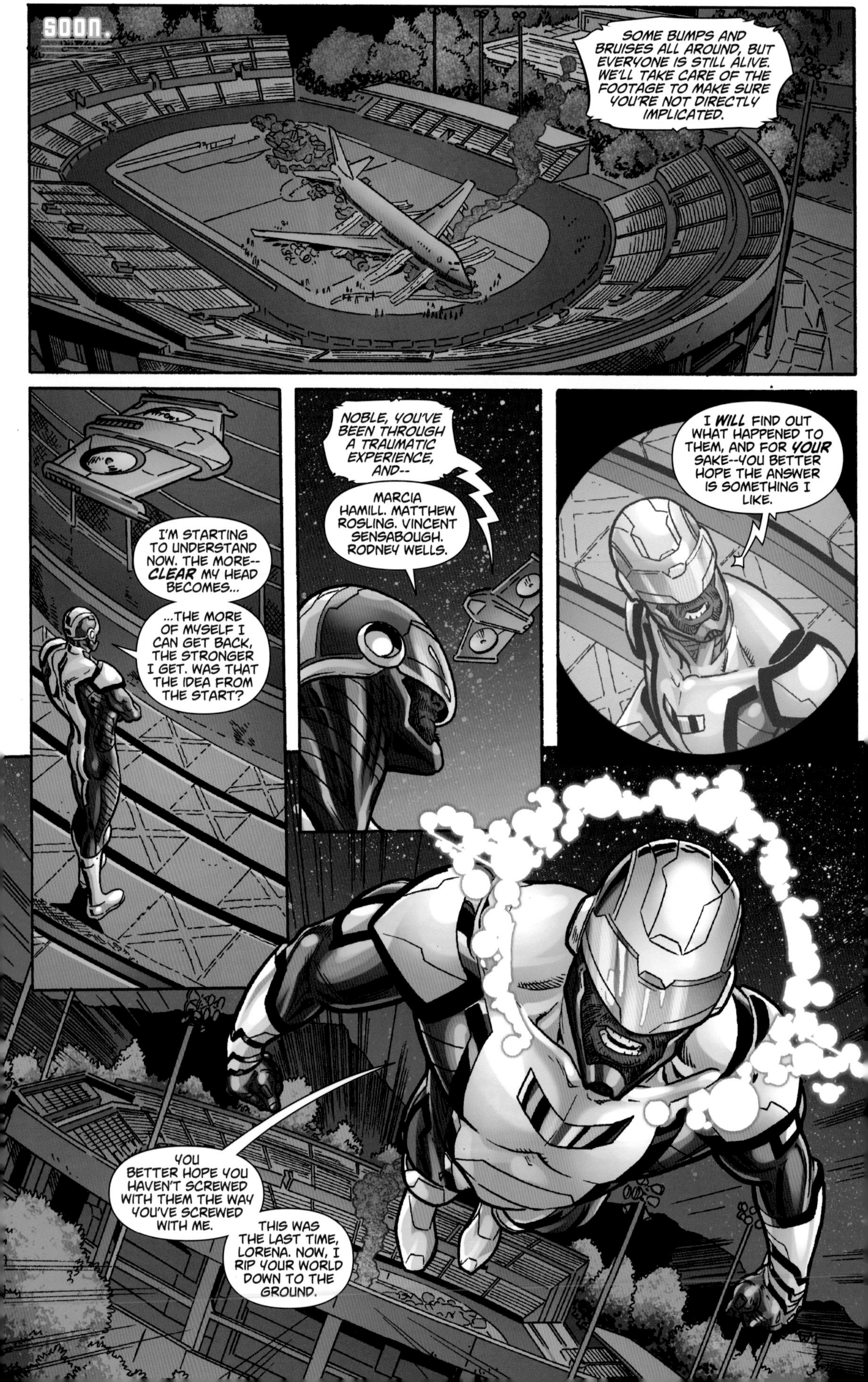
SOON.
SOME BUMPS AND BRUISES ALL AROUND, BUT EVERYONE IS STILL ALIVE. WE'LL TAKE CARE OF THE FOOTAGE TO MAKE SURE YOU'RE NOT DIRECTLY IMPLICATED.
I'M STARTING TO UNDERSTAND NOW. THE MORE--CLEAR MY HEAD BECOMES...
...THE MORE OF MYSELF I CAN GET BACK, THE STRONGER I GET. WAS THAT THE IDEA FROM THE START?
NOBLE, YOU'VE BEEN THROUGH A TRAUMATIC EXPERIENCE, AND--
MARCIA HAMILL. MATTHEW ROSLING. VINCENT SENSABOUGH. RODNEY WELLS.
I WILL FIND OUT WHAT HAPPENED TO THEM, AND FOR YOUR SAKE--YOU BETTER HOPE THE ANSWER IS SOMETHING I LIKE.
YOU BETTER HOPE YOU HAVEN'T SCREWED WITH THEM THE WAY YOU'VE SCREWED WITH ME.
THIS WAS THE LAST TIME, LORENA. NOW, I RIP YOUR WORLD DOWN TO THE GROUND.

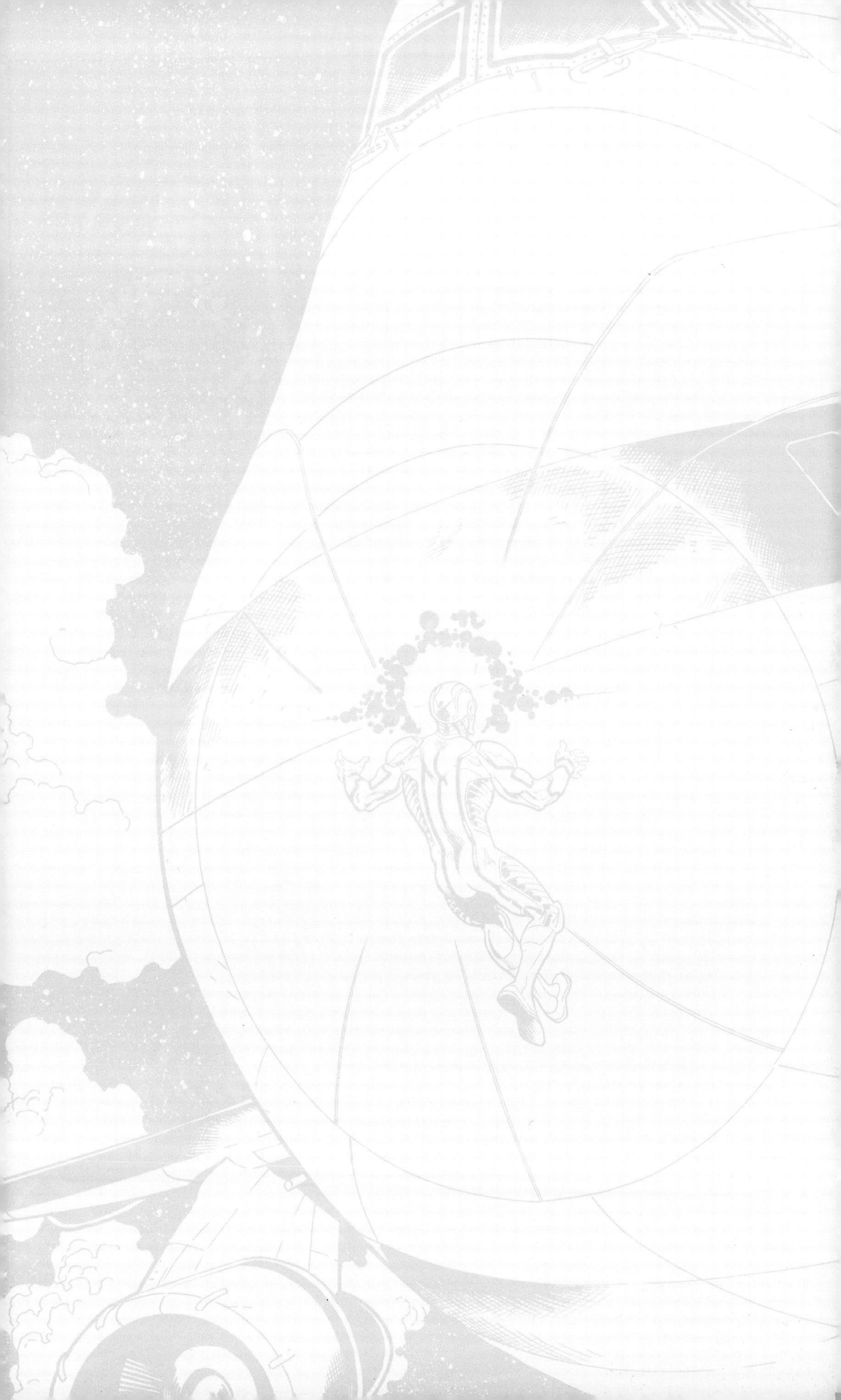

CHAPTER TWO

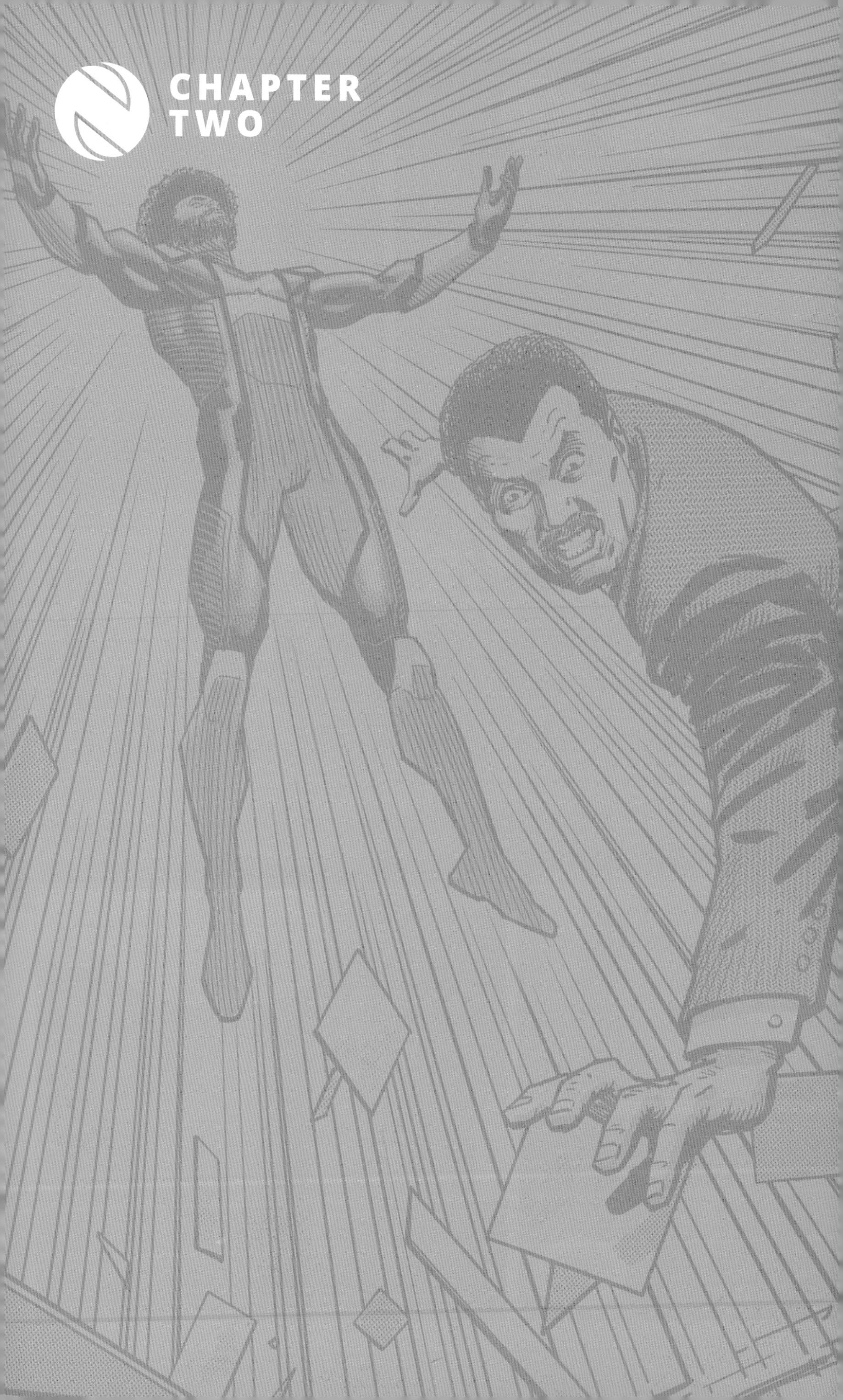

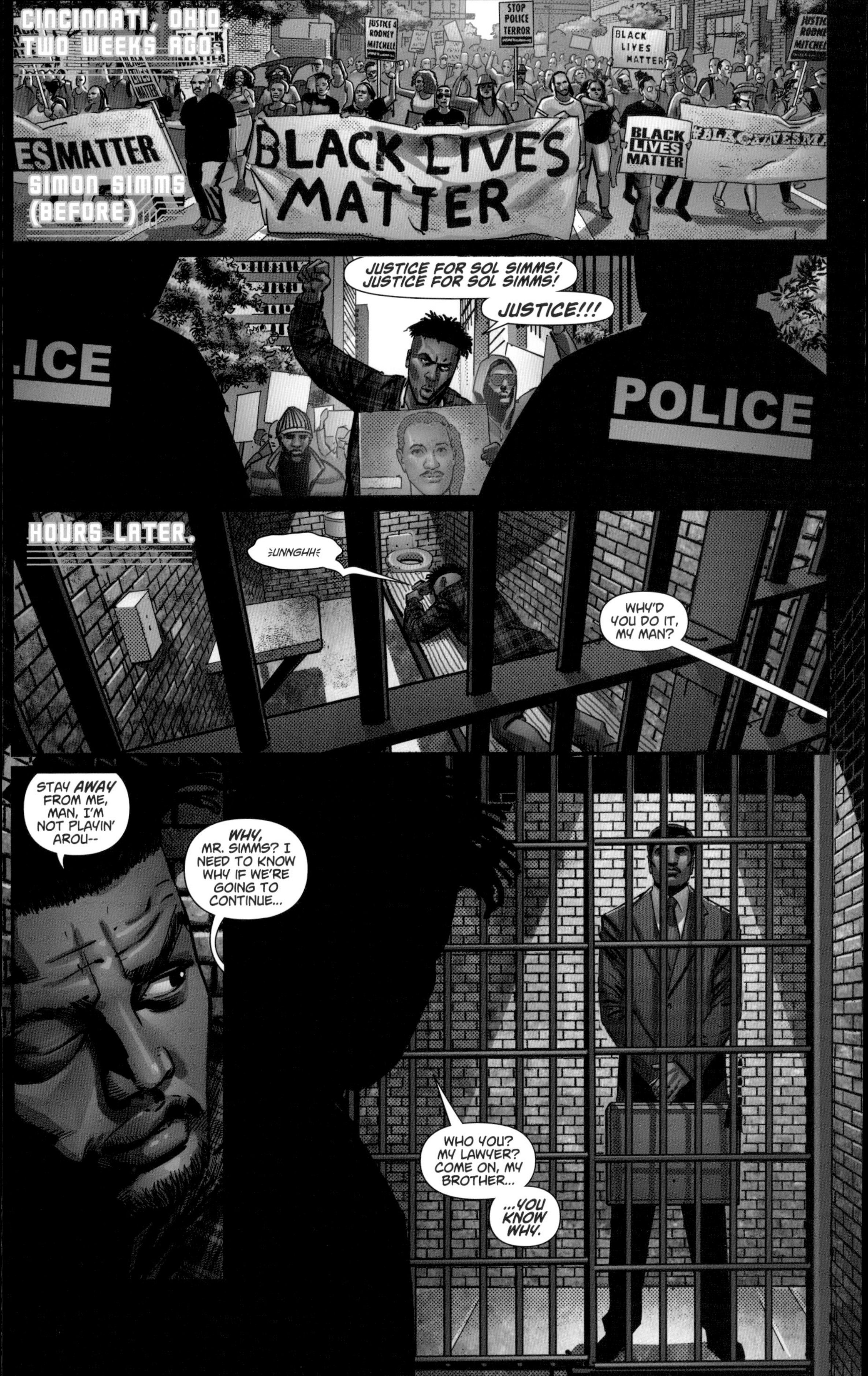
CINCINNATI, OHIO. TWO WEEKS AGO.
JUSTICE 4 RODNEY MITCHELL
STOP POLICE TERROR
BLACK LIVES MATTER
BLACK LIVES MATTER
BLACK LIVES MATTER
SIMON SIMMS (BEFORE)
JUSTICE FOR SOL SIMMS! JUSTICE FOR SOL SIMMS!
JUSTICE!!!
POLICE
HOURS LATER.
UNNGHH
WHY'D YOU DO IT, MY MAN?
STAY AWAY FROM ME, MAN, I'M NOT PLAYIN' AROU--
WHY, MR. SIMMS? I NEED TO KNOW WHY IF WE'RE GOING TO CONTINUE...
WHO YOU? MY LAWYER? COME ON, MY BROTHER...
...YOU KNOW WHY.

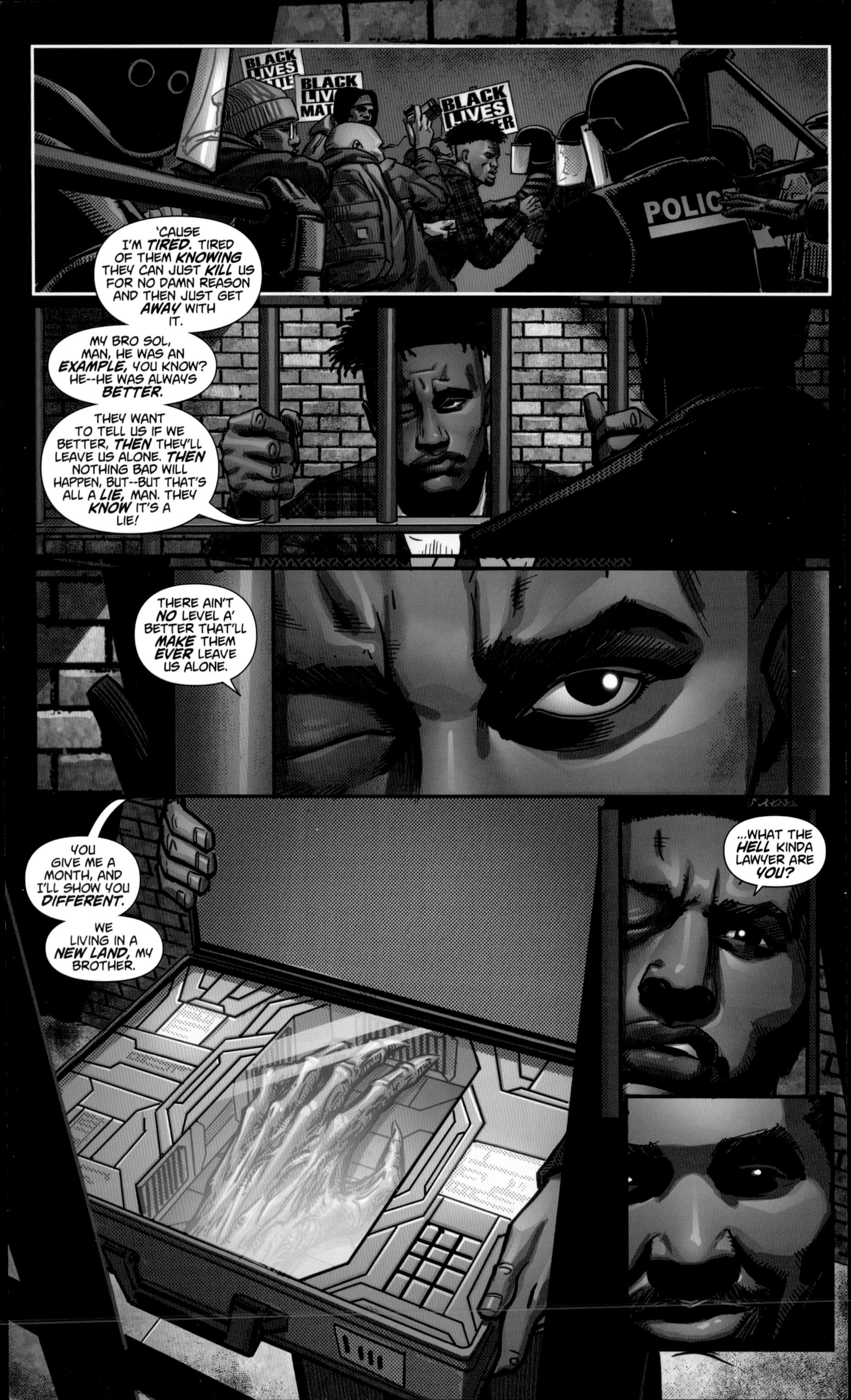
BLACK LIVES MATTER
BLACK LIVES MAT
BLACK LIVES
POLIC
'CAUSE I'M TIRED. TIRED OF THEM KNOWING THEY CAN JUST KILL US FOR NO DAMN REASON AND THEN JUST GET AWAY WITH IT.
MY BRO SOL, MAN, HE WAS AN EXAMPLE, YOU KNOW? HE--HE WAS ALWAYS BETTER.
THEY WANT TO TELL US IF WE BETTER, THEN THEY'LL LEAVE US ALONE. THEN NOTHING BAD WILL HAPPEN, BUT--BUT THAT'S ALL A LIE, MAN. THEY KNOW IT'S A LIE!
THERE AIN'T NO LEVEL A' BETTER THAT'LL MAKE THEM EVER LEAVE US ALONE.
...WHAT THE HELL KINDA LAWYER ARE YOU?
YOU GIVE ME A MONTH, AND I'LL SHOW YOU DIFFERENT.
WE LIVING IN A NEW LAND, MY BROTHER.

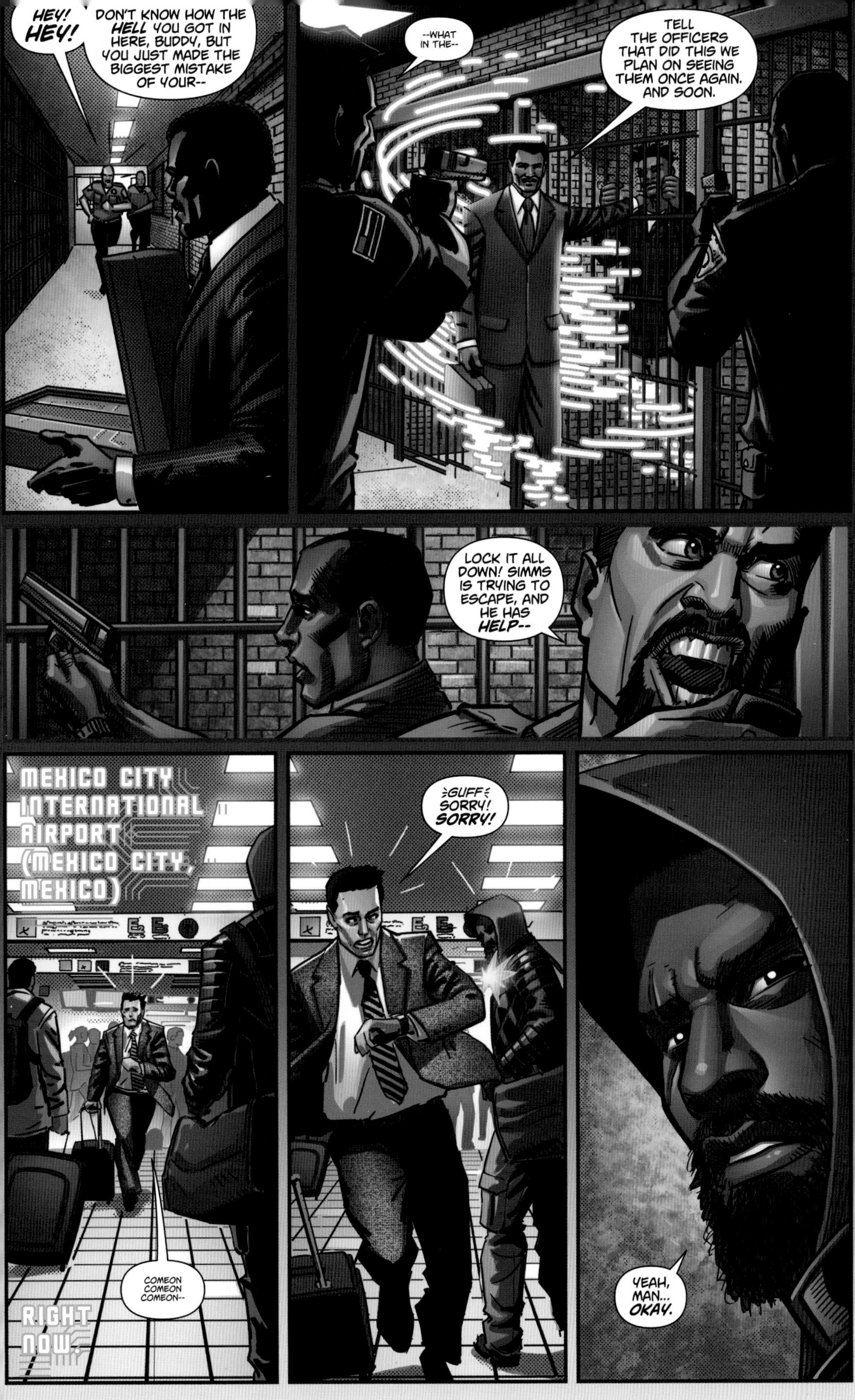
HEY! HEY!
DON'T KNOW HOW THE HELL YOU GOT IN HERE, BUDDY, BUT YOU JUST MADE THE BIGGEST MISTAKE OF YOUR--
--WHAT IN THE--
TELL THE OFFICERS THAT DID THIS WE PLAN ON SEEING THEM ONCE AGAIN. AND SOON.
LOCK IT ALL DOWN! SIMMS IS TRYING TO ESCAPE, AND HE HAS HELP--
MEXICO CITY INTERNATIONAL AIRPORT (MEXICO CITY, MEXICO)
RIGHT NOW.
COMEON COMEON COMEON--
GUFF
SORRY! SORRY!
YEAH, MAN... OKAY.

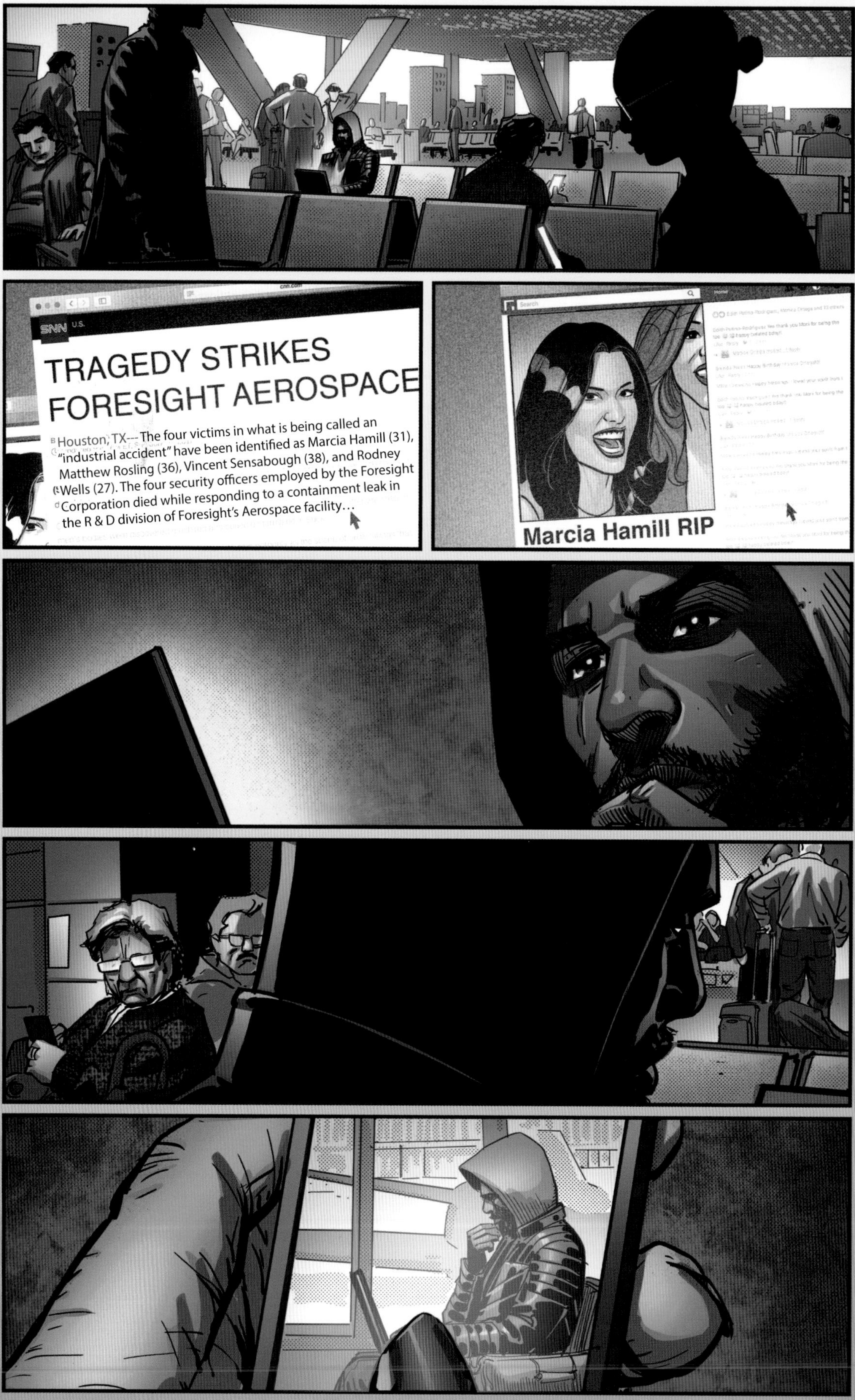

cnn.com
SNN U.S.
TRAGEDY STRIKES FORESIGHT AEROSPACE
Houston, TX-- The four victims in what is being called an "industrial accident" have been identified as Marcia Hamill (31), Matthew Rosling (36), Vincent Sensabough (38), and Rodney Wells (27). The four security officers employed by the Foresight Corporation died while responding to a containment leak in the R & D division of Foresight's Aerospace facility...
Search
Home
Marcia Hamill RIP

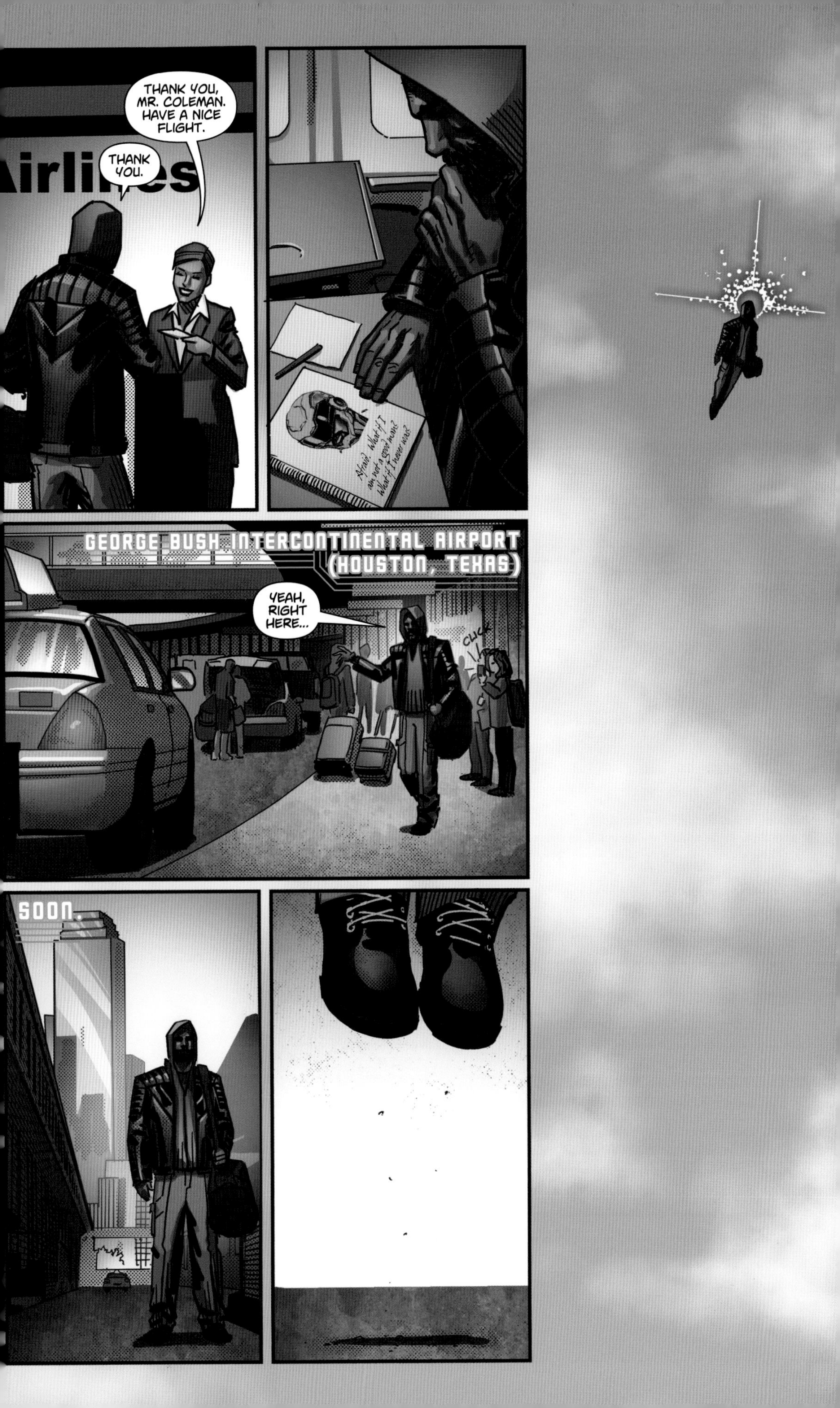

THANK YOU, MR. COLEMAN. HAVE A NICE FLIGHT.
THANK YOU.
Airlines
Afraid. What if I am not a good man? What if I never was?
GEORGE BUSH INTERCONTINENTAL AIRPORT (HOUSTON, TEXAS)
YEAH, RIGHT HERE...
CLICK
SOON.

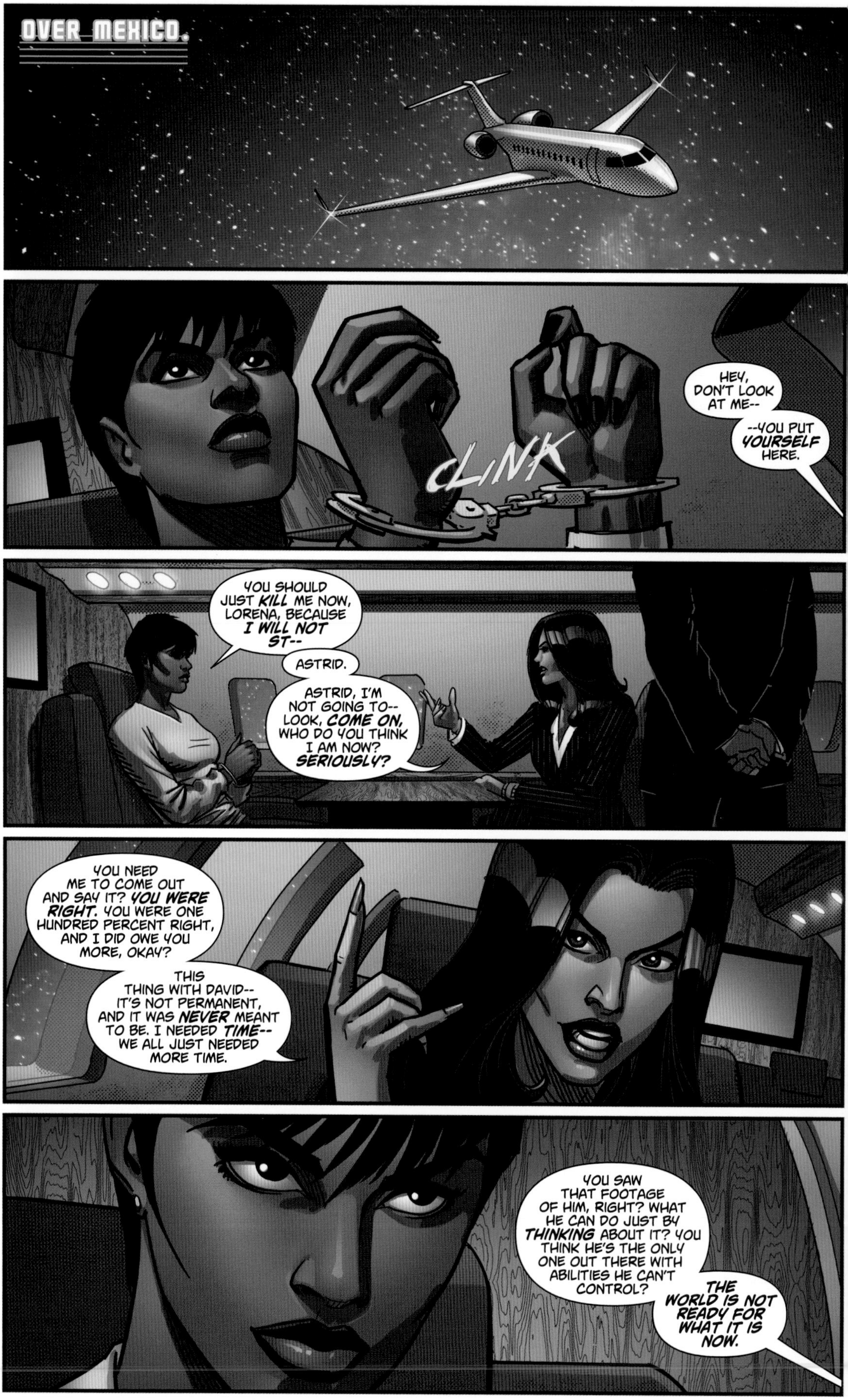
OVER MEXICO.
CLINK
HEY, DON'T LOOK AT ME--
--YOU PUT YOURSELF HERE.
YOU SHOULD JUST KILL ME NOW, LORENA, BECAUSE I WILL NOT ST--
ASTRID.
ASTRID, I'M NOT GOING TO-- LOOK, COME ON, WHO DO YOU THINK I AM NOW? SERIOUSLY?
YOU NEED ME TO COME OUT AND SAY IT? YOU WERE RIGHT. YOU WERE ONE HUNDRED PERCENT RIGHT, AND I DID OWE YOU MORE, OKAY?
THIS THING WITH DAVID-- IT'S NOT PERMANENT, AND IT WAS NEVER MEANT TO BE. I NEEDED TIME-- WE ALL JUST NEEDED MORE TIME.
YOU SAW THAT FOOTAGE OF HIM, RIGHT? WHAT HE CAN DO JUST BY THINKING ABOUT IT? YOU THINK HE'S THE ONLY ONE OUT THERE WITH ABILITIES HE CAN'T CONTROL?
THE WORLD IS NOT READY FOR WHAT IT IS NOW.

IT NEVER IS.

NO, NO--SEE THIS IS THE PROBLEM RIGHT HERE. YOU *THINK* YOU HAVE THE SCOPE OF THE PROBLEM, BUT IT KEEPS CHANGING UP ON US MINUTE BY MINUTE. AND THERE IS *NO GOING BACK NOW.*

MY HUSBAND DOESN'T KNOW WHO HE IS. HE DOESN'T REMEMBER HIS OWN SON'S *NAME,* AND THE "GREATER GOOD" SPEECH IS THE BEST YOU CAN DO?

IF YOU KNOW WHAT'S GOOD FOR YOU-- HAVE YOUR MAN HERE SUCK ME DRY AND BE *DONE* WITH IT.

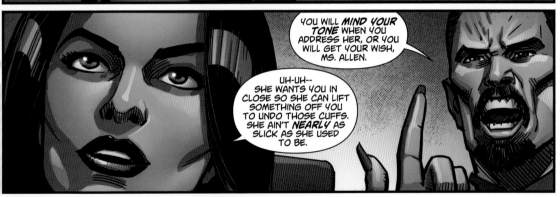

YOU WILL *MIND YOUR TONE* WHEN YOU ADDRESS HER, OR YOU WILL GET YOUR WISH, MS. ALLEN.

UH-UH-- SHE WANTS YOU IN CLOSE SO SHE CAN LIFT SOMETHING OFF YOU TO UNDO THOSE CUFFS. SHE AIN'T *NEARLY* AS SLICK AS SHE USED TO BE.

STILL--I'M GOING TO *HELP* YOU AND DAVID. HELL, I'M HELPING HIM *RIGHT NOW,* CAUSE BOTTOM LINE, *EVENTUALLY,* I NEED YOU BACK ON MY SIDE OF THIS, AND I'M NOT TAKING "NEVER" AS AN ANSWER.

HAVE SOME FOOD BROUGHT BACK, AND *DO NOT* TAKE YOUR EYES OFF THOSE HANDS. I KNOW HOW IT LOOKS NOW, BUT YOU CONSIDER HER ARMED AND EXTREMELY DANGEROUS *AT ALL TIMES.*

WE HAVE A LOCATION?

YES, MA'AM. HE DOES APPEAR HEADED FOR THE HOUSTON FACILITY. USING COMMERCIAL TRAVEL HAS MADE HIM MUCH EASIER TO TRACK.

YEAH, WELL, AFTER HIS LITTLE ACCIDENT A COUPLE DAYS AGO, I'M NOT SURPRISED HE'S BEING MORE CAREFUL. CONTINUE THE CLEAR OUT OF ALL HUMAN ASSETS, AND LEAVE THE DRONES ON PATROL.

JUST ENOUGH TO KEEP HIM FROM GETTING *TOO* SUSPICIOUS, BUT NOT ENOUGH TO PREVENT HIM FROM HAVING THE RUN OF THE PLACE.

MS. PAYAN, WITH ALL DUE RESPECT, WHY ARE--

YEAH, LEMME STOP YOU RIGHT THERE--

--THAT'S THE SECOND TIME THIS WEEK THAT I'VE HAD TO LISTEN TO SOME COLOR COMMENTARY FROM YOU THAT I DIDN'T *SPECIFICALLY* ASK FOR.

NOT GONNA BE A THIRD TIME, UNDERSTAND?

LET'S MAKE IT HAPPEN PEOPLE, AND REMIND THE BOYS IN THE BACK NOT TO FORGET WHAT I SAID ABOUT MS. ALLEN-POWELL'S HANDS. THANK YOU.

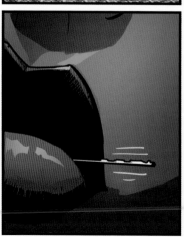

FORESIGHT INDUSTRIES AEROSPACE INITIATIVE
(HOUSTON, TEXAS)

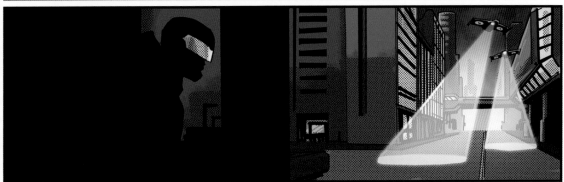

SHOOM

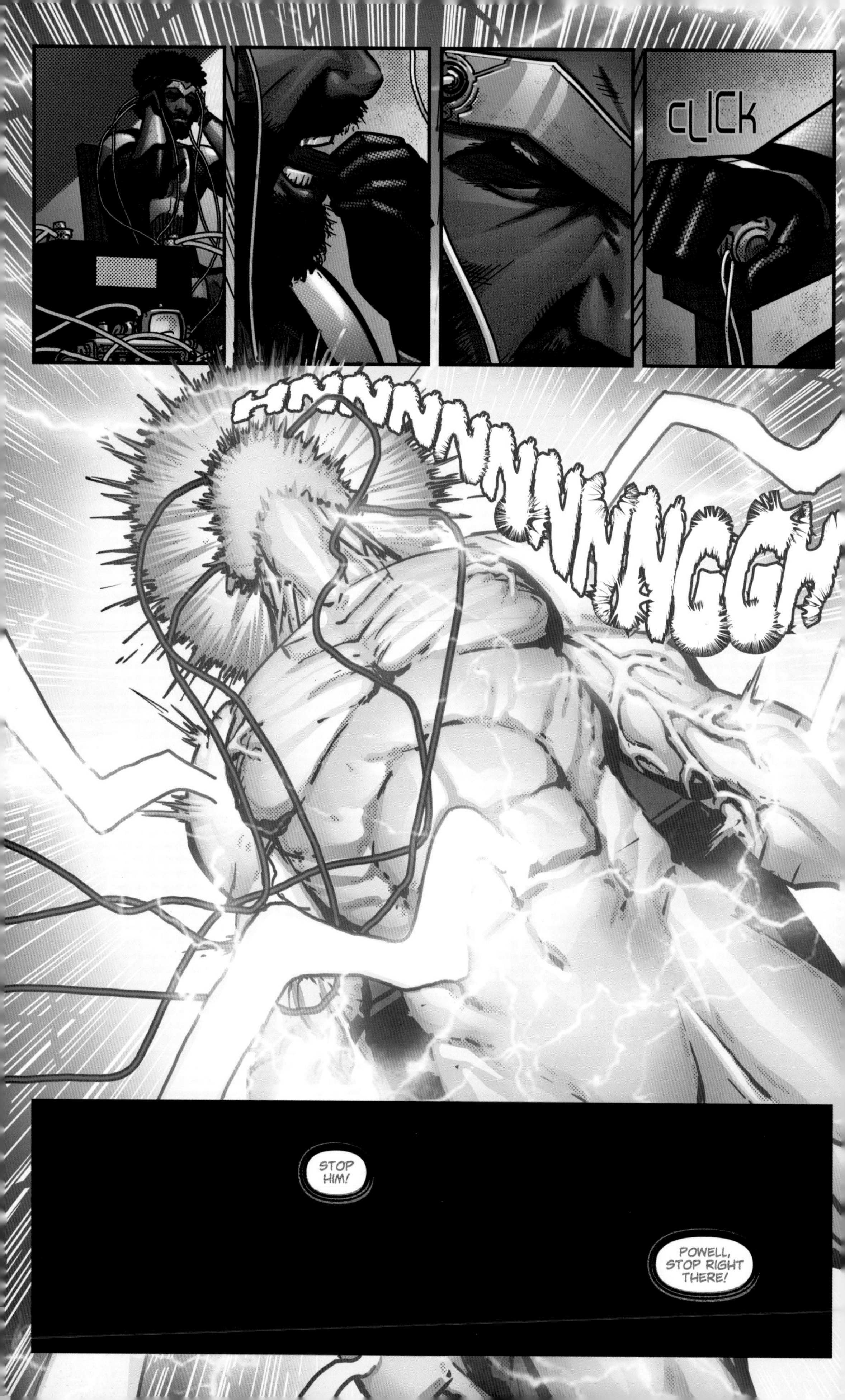
CLICK
HNNNNNNNNNNGGH
STOP HIM!
POWELL, STOP RIGHT THERE!

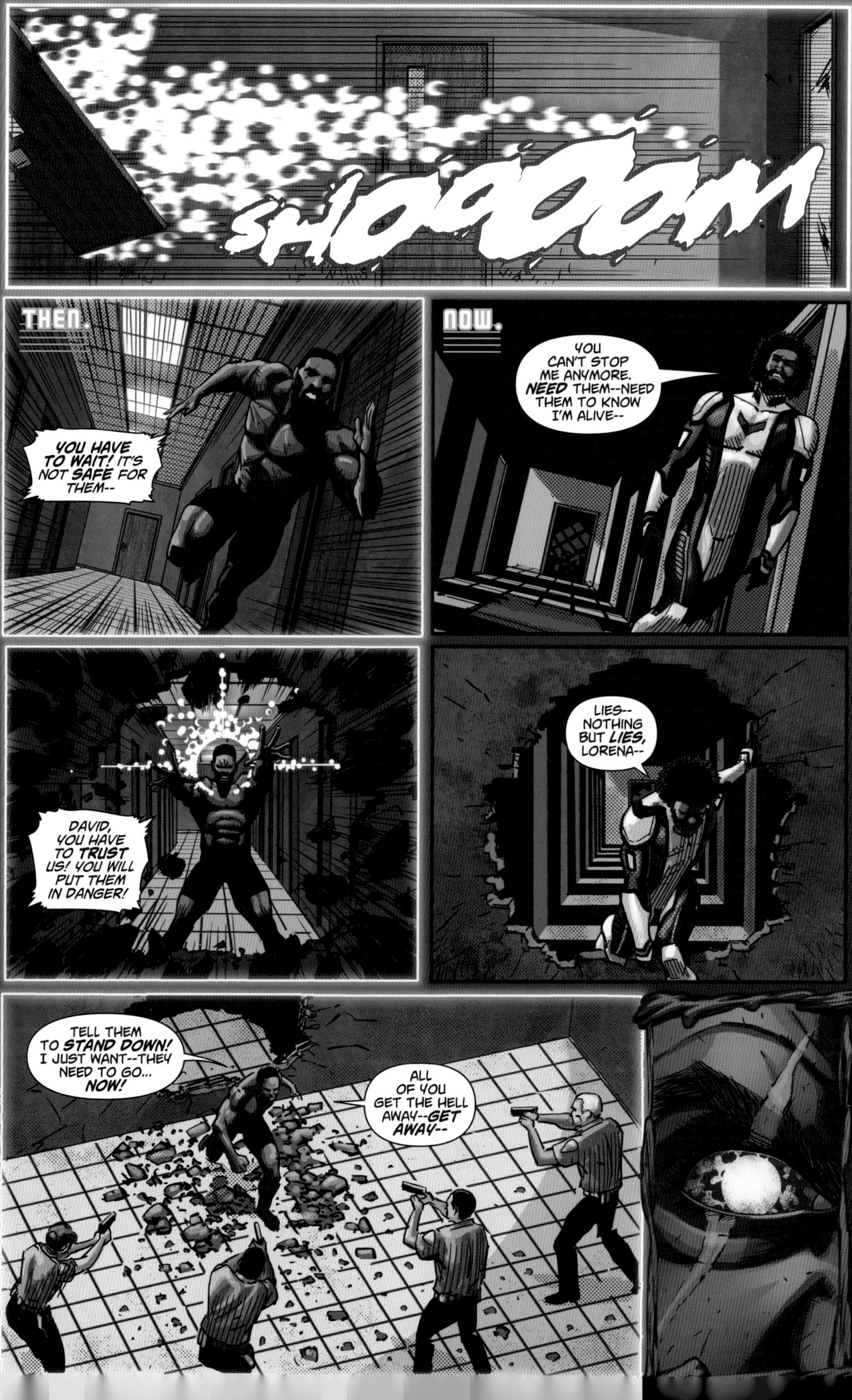
SHOOOOM
THEN.
YOU HAVE TO WAIT! IT'S NOT SAFE FOR THEM--
NOW.
YOU CAN'T STOP ME ANYMORE. NEED THEM--NEED THEM TO KNOW I'M ALIVE--
DAVID, YOU HAVE TO TRUST US! YOU WILL PUT THEM IN DANGER!
LIES-- NOTHING BUT LIES, LORENA--
TELL THEM TO STAND DOWN! I JUST WANT--THEY NEED TO GO... NOW!
ALL OF YOU GET THE HELL AWAY--GET AWAY--

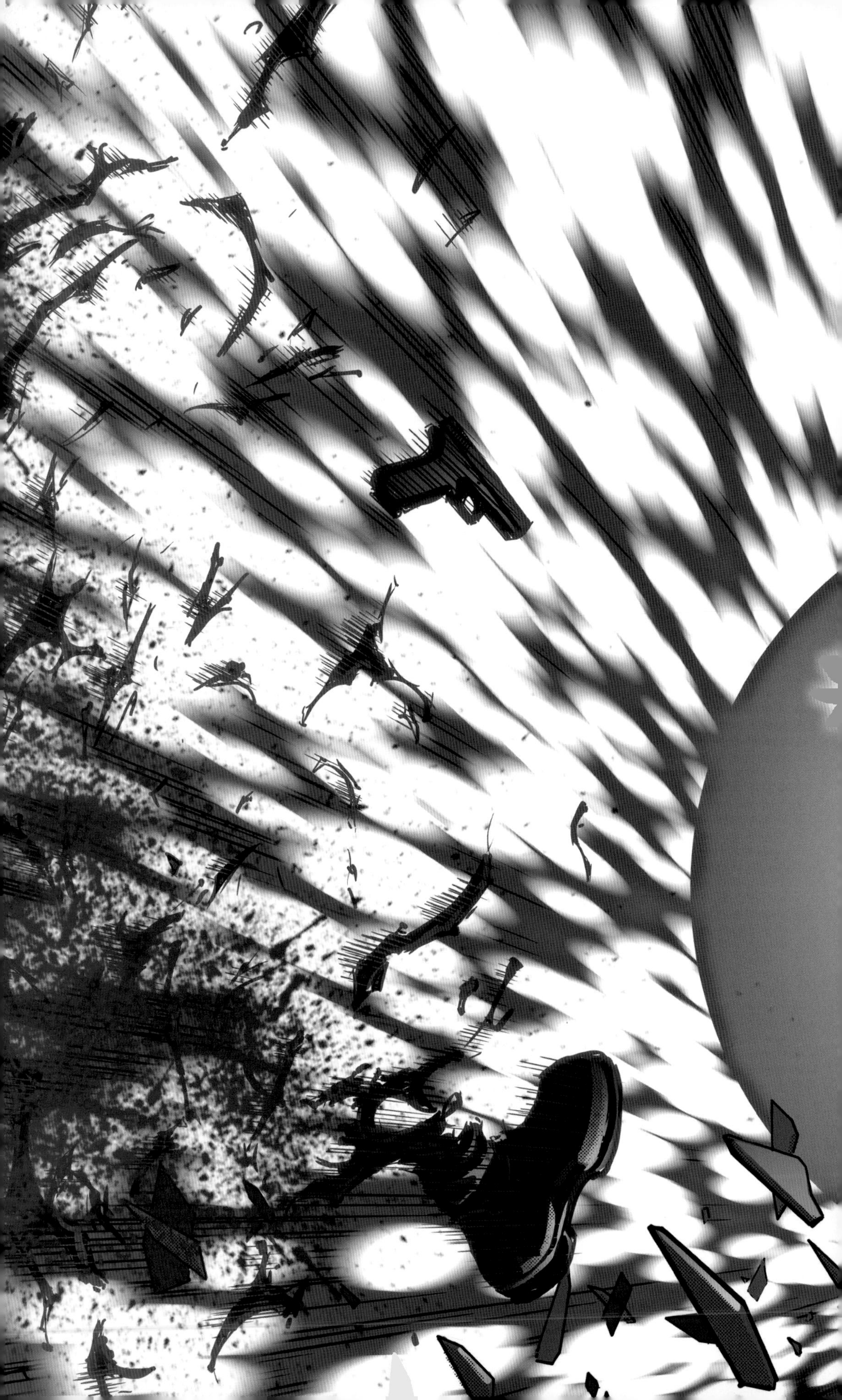

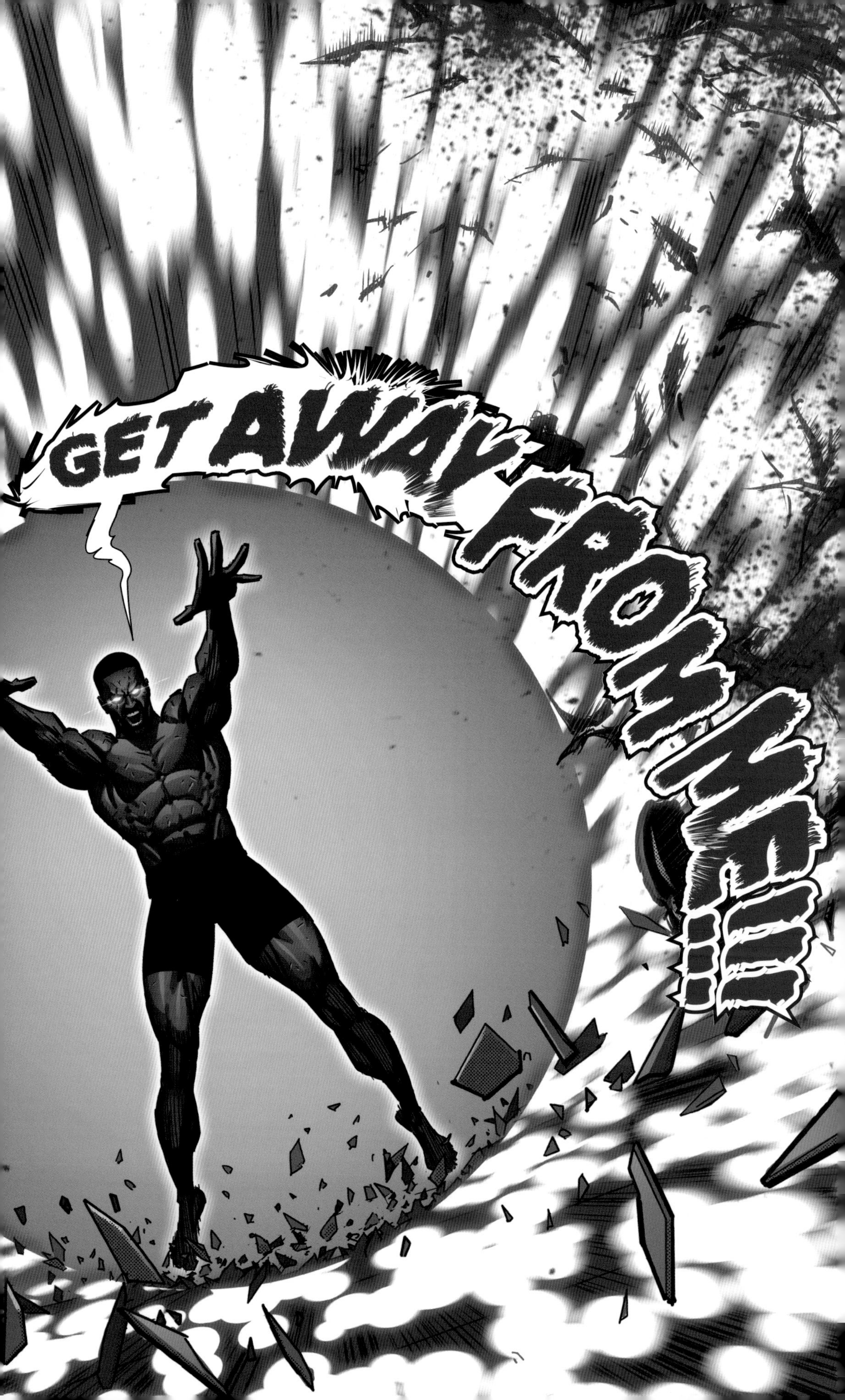
GET AWAY FROM ME!!!

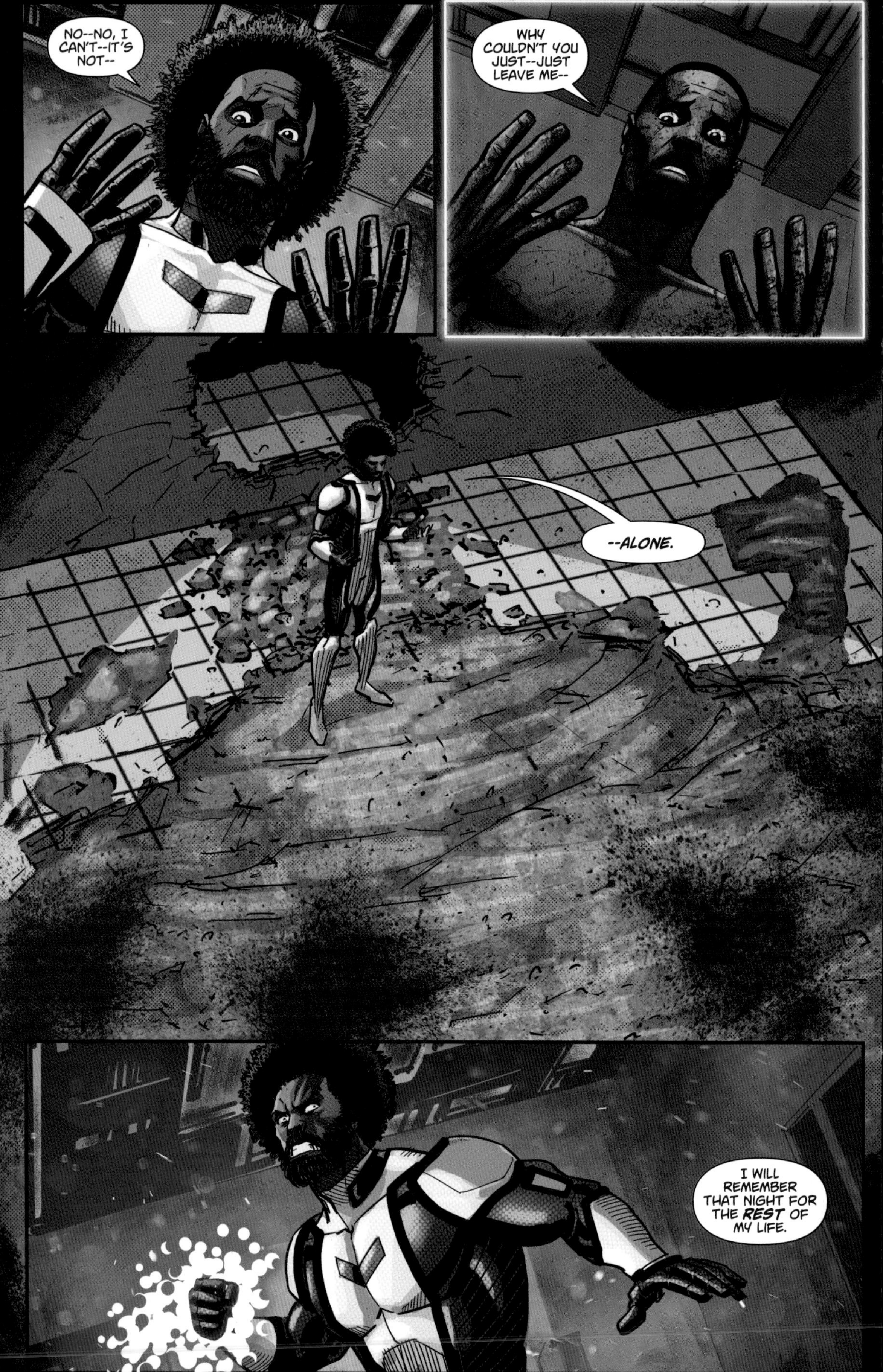
NO--NO, I CAN'T--IT'S NOT--
WHY COULDN'T YOU JUST--JUST LEAVE ME--
--ALONE.
I WILL REMEMBER THAT NIGHT FOR THE REST OF MY LIFE.

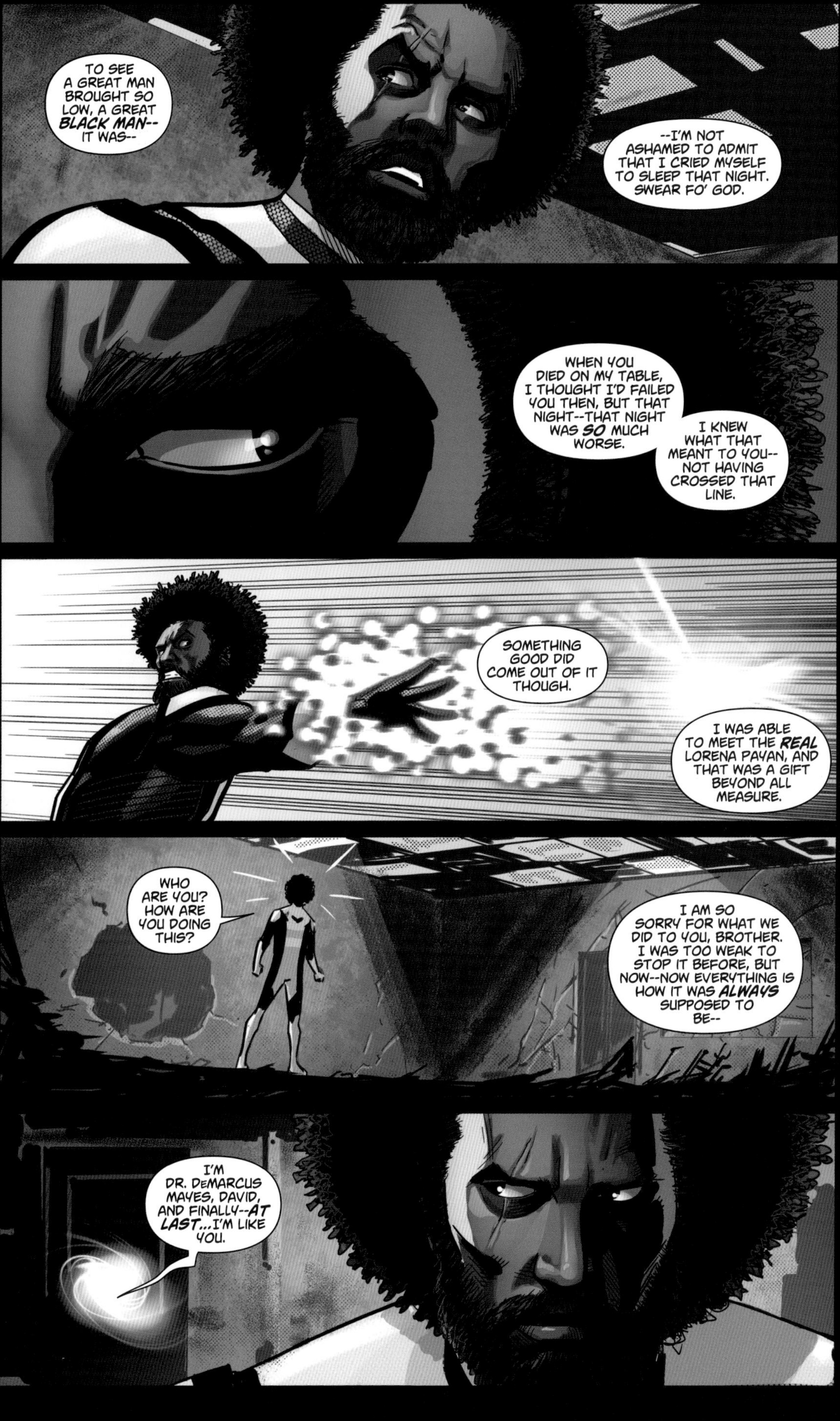
TO SEE A GREAT MAN BROUGHT SO LOW, A GREAT *BLACK MAN*--IT WAS--
--I'M NOT ASHAMED TO ADMIT THAT I CRIED MYSELF TO SLEEP THAT NIGHT. SWEAR FO' GOD.
WHEN YOU DIED ON MY TABLE, I THOUGHT I'D FAILED YOU THEN, BUT THAT NIGHT--THAT NIGHT WAS *SO* MUCH WORSE.
I KNEW WHAT THAT MEANT TO YOU--NOT HAVING CROSSED THAT LINE.
SOMETHING GOOD DID COME OUT OF IT THOUGH.
I WAS ABLE TO MEET THE *REAL* LORENA PAYAN, AND THAT WAS A GIFT BEYOND ALL MEASURE.
WHO ARE YOU? HOW ARE YOU DOING THIS?
I AM SO SORRY FOR WHAT WE DID TO YOU, BROTHER. I WAS TOO WEAK TO STOP IT BEFORE, BUT NOW--NOW EVERYTHING IS HOW IT WAS *ALWAYS* SUPPOSED TO BE--
I'M DR. DeMARCUS MAYES, DAVID, AND FINALLY--*AT LAST*...I'M LIKE YOU.

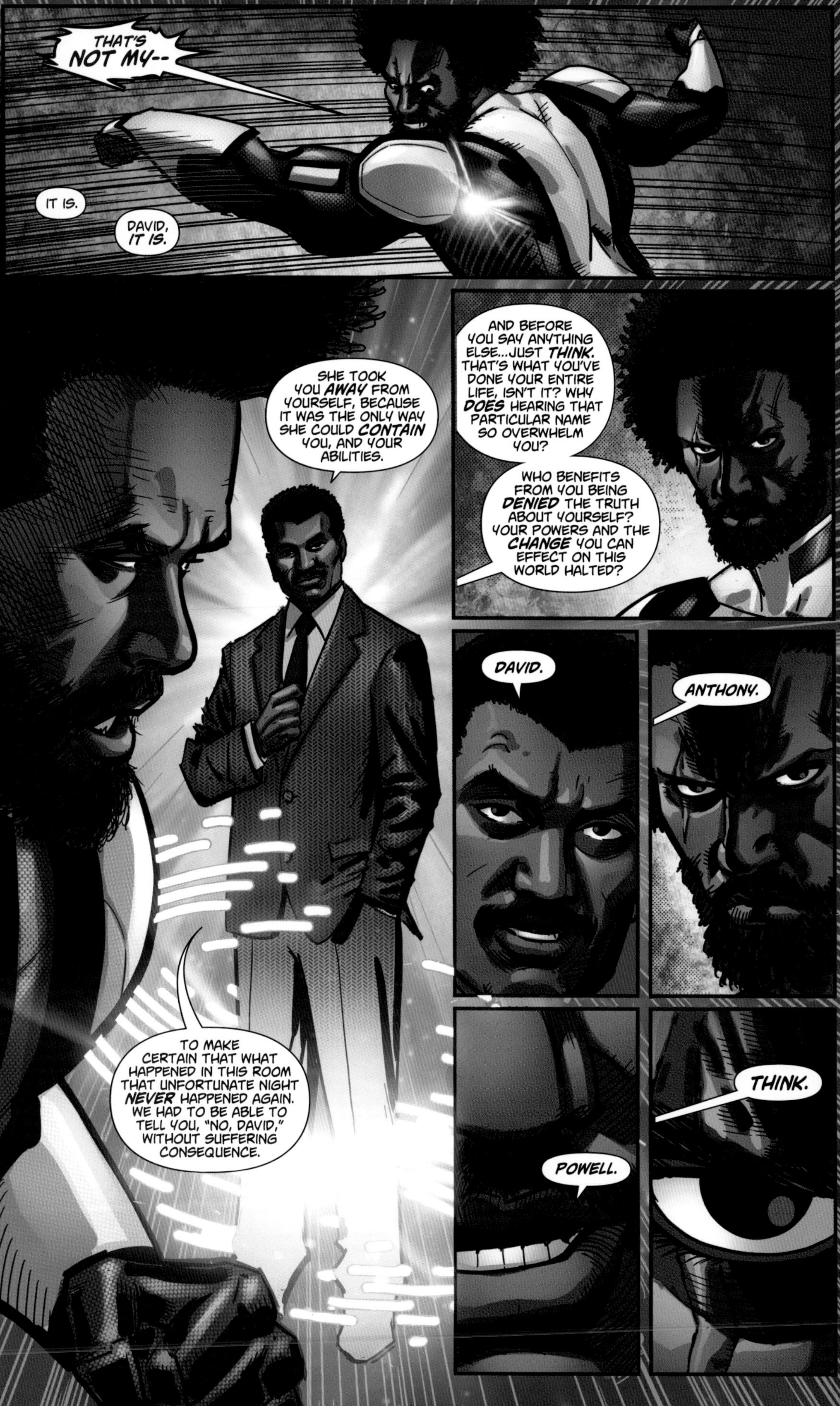
THAT'S NOT MY--
IT IS.
DAVID, IT IS.
SHE TOOK YOU AWAY FROM YOURSELF, BECAUSE IT WAS THE ONLY WAY SHE COULD CONTAIN YOU, AND YOUR ABILITIES.
TO MAKE CERTAIN THAT WHAT HAPPENED IN THIS ROOM THAT UNFORTUNATE NIGHT NEVER HAPPENED AGAIN. WE HAD TO BE ABLE TO TELL YOU, "NO, DAVID," WITHOUT SUFFERING CONSEQUENCE.
AND BEFORE YOU SAY ANYTHING ELSE...JUST THINK. THAT'S WHAT YOU'VE DONE YOUR ENTIRE LIFE, ISN'T IT? WHY DOES HEARING THAT PARTICULAR NAME SO OVERWHELM YOU?
WHO BENEFITS FROM YOU BEING DENIED THE TRUTH ABOUT YOURSELF? YOUR POWERS AND THE CHANGE YOU CAN EFFECT ON THIS WORLD HALTED?
DAVID.
ANTHONY.
POWELL.
THINK.

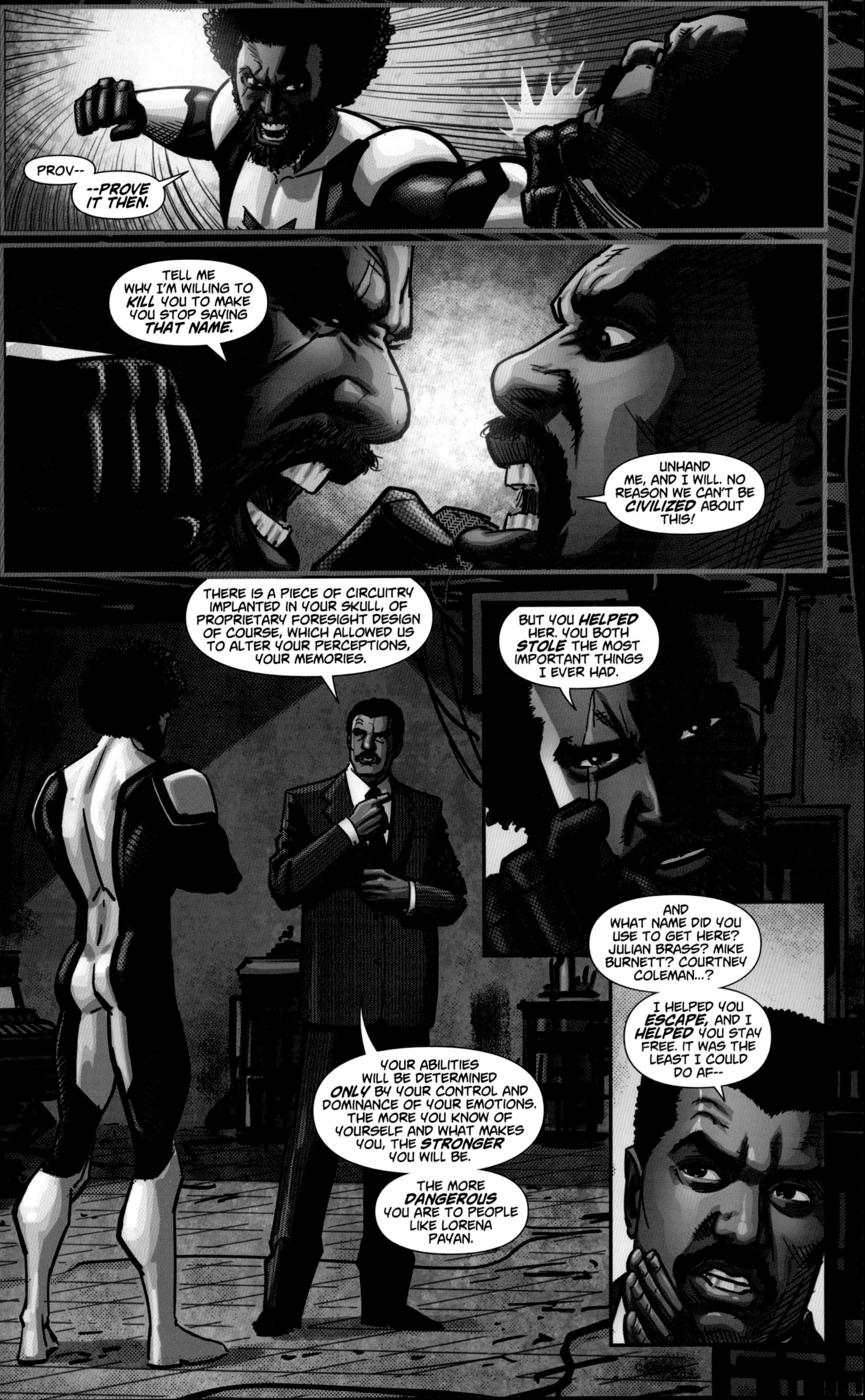
PROV--
--PROVE IT THEN.
TELL ME WHY I'M WILLING TO KILL YOU TO MAKE YOU STOP SAYING THAT NAME.
UNHAND ME, AND I WILL. NO REASON WE CAN'T BE CIVILIZED ABOUT THIS!
THERE IS A PIECE OF CIRCUITRY IMPLANTED IN YOUR SKULL, OF PROPRIETARY FORESIGHT DESIGN OF COURSE, WHICH ALLOWED US TO ALTER YOUR PERCEPTIONS, YOUR MEMORIES.
YOUR ABILITIES WILL BE DETERMINED ONLY BY YOUR CONTROL AND DOMINANCE OF YOUR EMOTIONS. THE MORE YOU KNOW OF YOURSELF AND WHAT MAKES YOU, THE STRONGER YOU WILL BE.
THE MORE DANGEROUS YOU ARE TO PEOPLE LIKE LORENA PAYAN.
BUT YOU HELPED HER. YOU BOTH STOLE THE MOST IMPORTANT THINGS I EVER HAD.
AND WHAT NAME DID YOU USE TO GET HERE? JULIAN BRASS? MIKE BURNETT? COURTNEY COLEMAN...?
I HELPED YOU ESCAPE, AND I HELPED YOU STAY FREE. IT WAS THE LEAST I COULD DO AF--

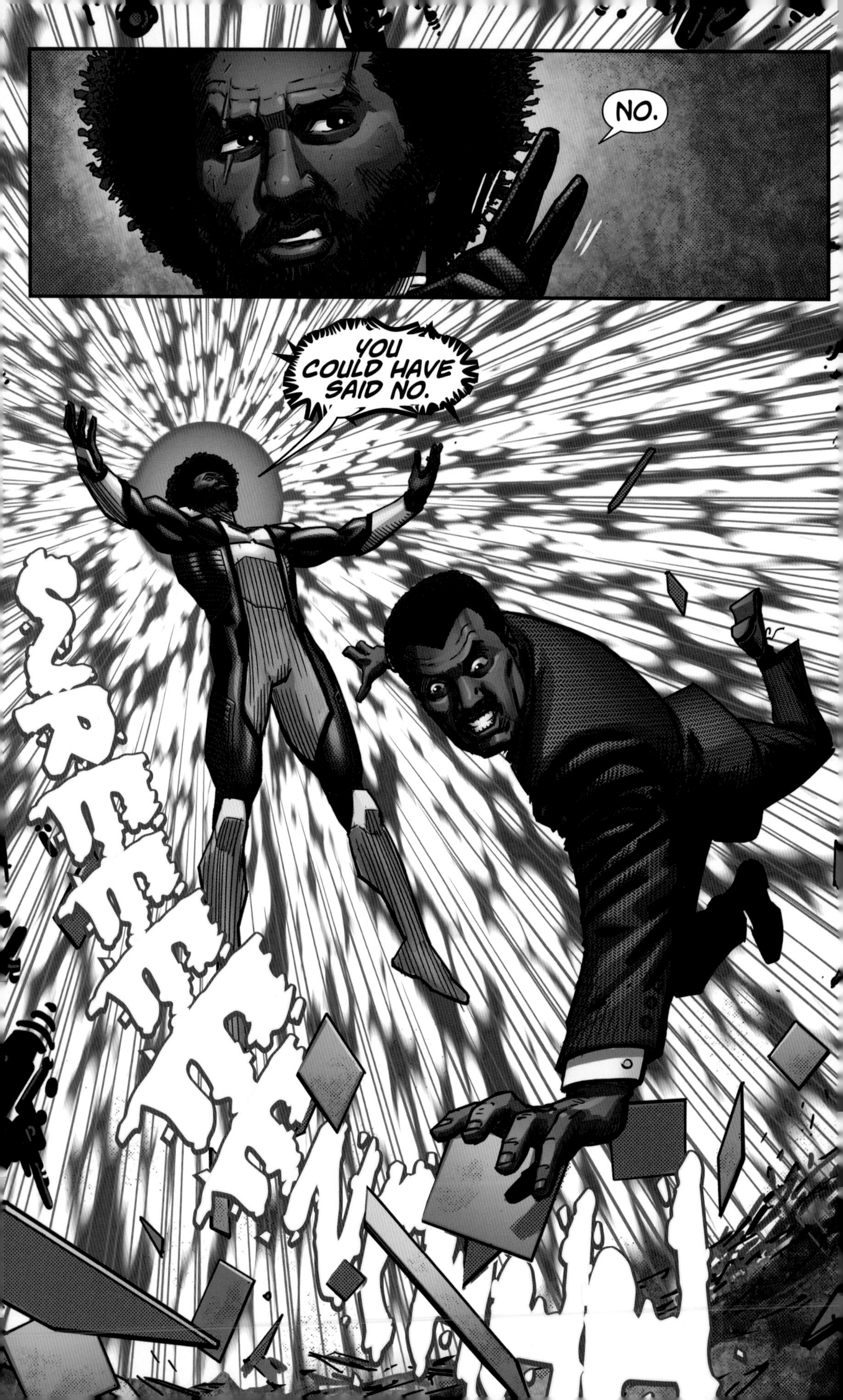
NO.
YOU COULD HAVE SAID NO.

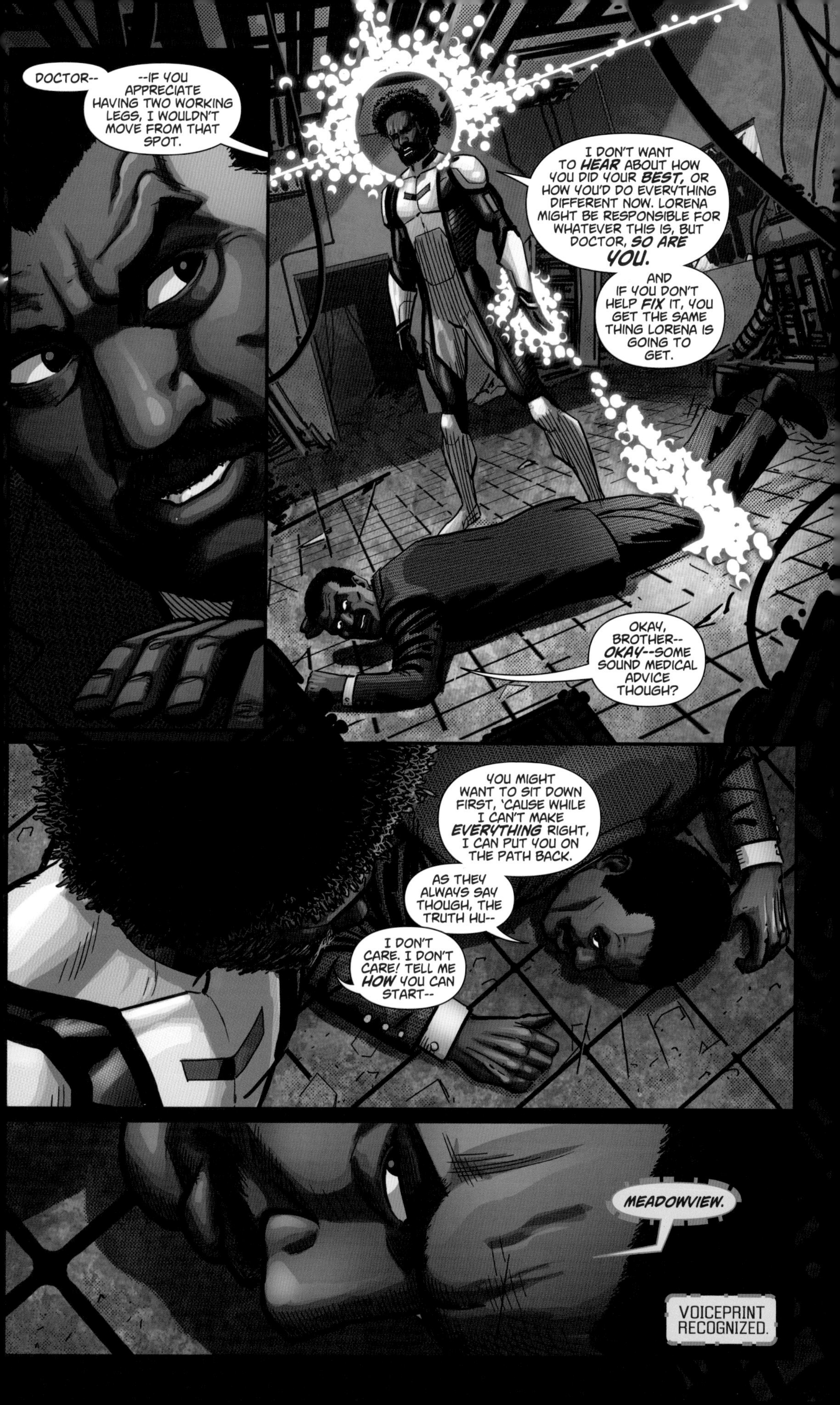
DOCTOR--
--IF YOU APPRECIATE HAVING TWO WORKING LEGS, I WOULDN'T MOVE FROM THAT SPOT.
I DON'T WANT TO HEAR ABOUT HOW YOU DID YOUR BEST, OR HOW YOU'D DO EVERYTHING DIFFERENT NOW. LORENA MIGHT BE RESPONSIBLE FOR WHATEVER THIS IS, BUT DOCTOR, SO ARE YOU.
AND IF YOU DON'T HELP FIX IT, YOU GET THE SAME THING LORENA IS GOING TO GET.
OKAY, BROTHER--OKAY--SOME SOUND MEDICAL ADVICE THOUGH?
YOU MIGHT WANT TO SIT DOWN FIRST, 'CAUSE WHILE I CAN'T MAKE EVERYTHING RIGHT, I CAN PUT YOU ON THE PATH BACK.
AS THEY ALWAYS SAY THOUGH, THE TRUTH HU--
I DON'T CARE. I DON'T CARE! TELL ME HOW YOU CAN START--
MEADOWVIEW.
VOICEPRINT RECOGNIZED.

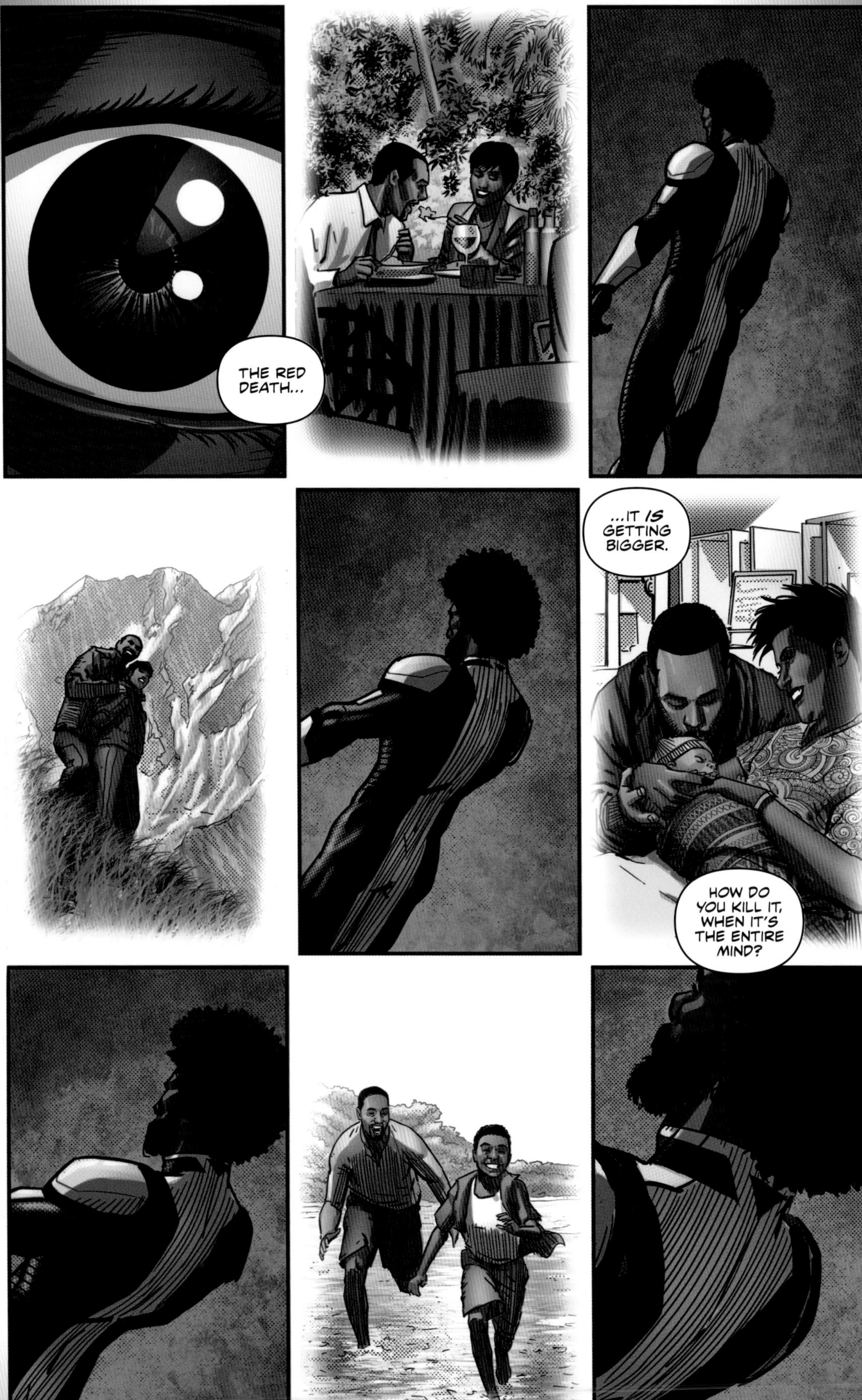
THE RED DEATH...
...IT IS GETTING BIGGER.
HOW DO YOU KILL IT, WHEN IT'S THE ENTIRE MIND?

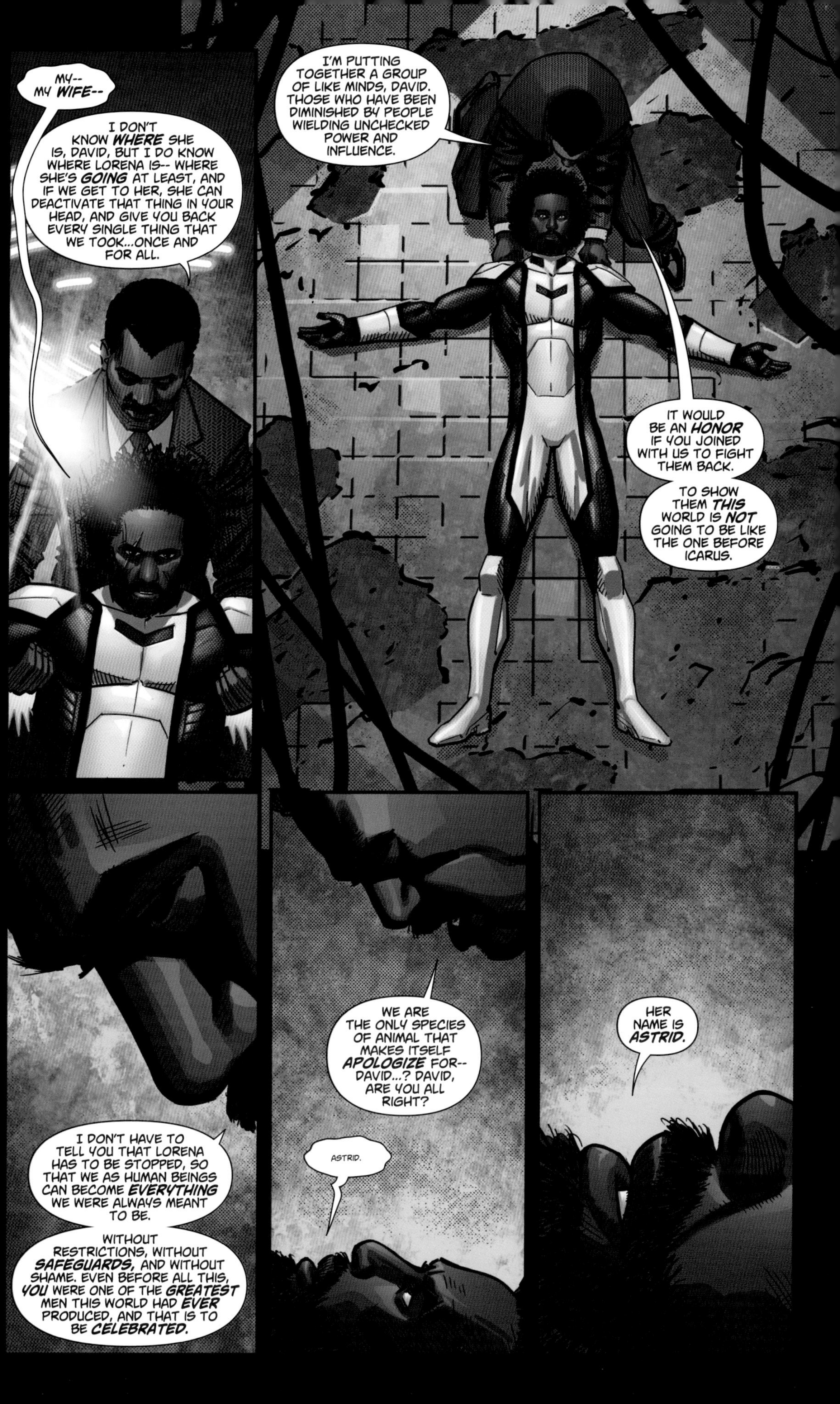
MY--
MY WIFE--
I DON'T KNOW WHERE SHE IS, DAVID, BUT I DO KNOW WHERE LORENA IS-- WHERE SHE'S GOING AT LEAST, AND IF WE GET TO HER, SHE CAN DEACTIVATE THAT THING IN YOUR HEAD, AND GIVE YOU BACK EVERY SINGLE THING THAT WE TOOK...ONCE AND FOR ALL.
I'M PUTTING TOGETHER A GROUP OF LIKE MINDS, DAVID. THOSE WHO HAVE BEEN DIMINISHED BY PEOPLE WIELDING UNCHECKED POWER AND INFLUENCE.
IT WOULD BE AN HONOR IF YOU JOINED WITH US TO FIGHT THEM BACK.
TO SHOW THEM THIS WORLD IS NOT GOING TO BE LIKE THE ONE BEFORE ICARUS.
I DON'T HAVE TO TELL YOU THAT LORENA HAS TO BE STOPPED, SO THAT WE AS HUMAN BEINGS CAN BECOME EVERYTHING WE WERE ALWAYS MEANT TO BE.
WITHOUT RESTRICTIONS, WITHOUT SAFEGUARDS, AND WITHOUT SHAME. EVEN BEFORE ALL THIS, YOU WERE ONE OF THE GREATEST MEN THIS WORLD HAD EVER PRODUCED, AND THAT IS TO BE CELEBRATED.
WE ARE THE ONLY SPECIES OF ANIMAL THAT MAKES ITSELF APOLOGIZE FOR-- DAVID...? DAVID, ARE YOU ALL RIGHT?
ASTRID.
HER NAME IS ASTRID.

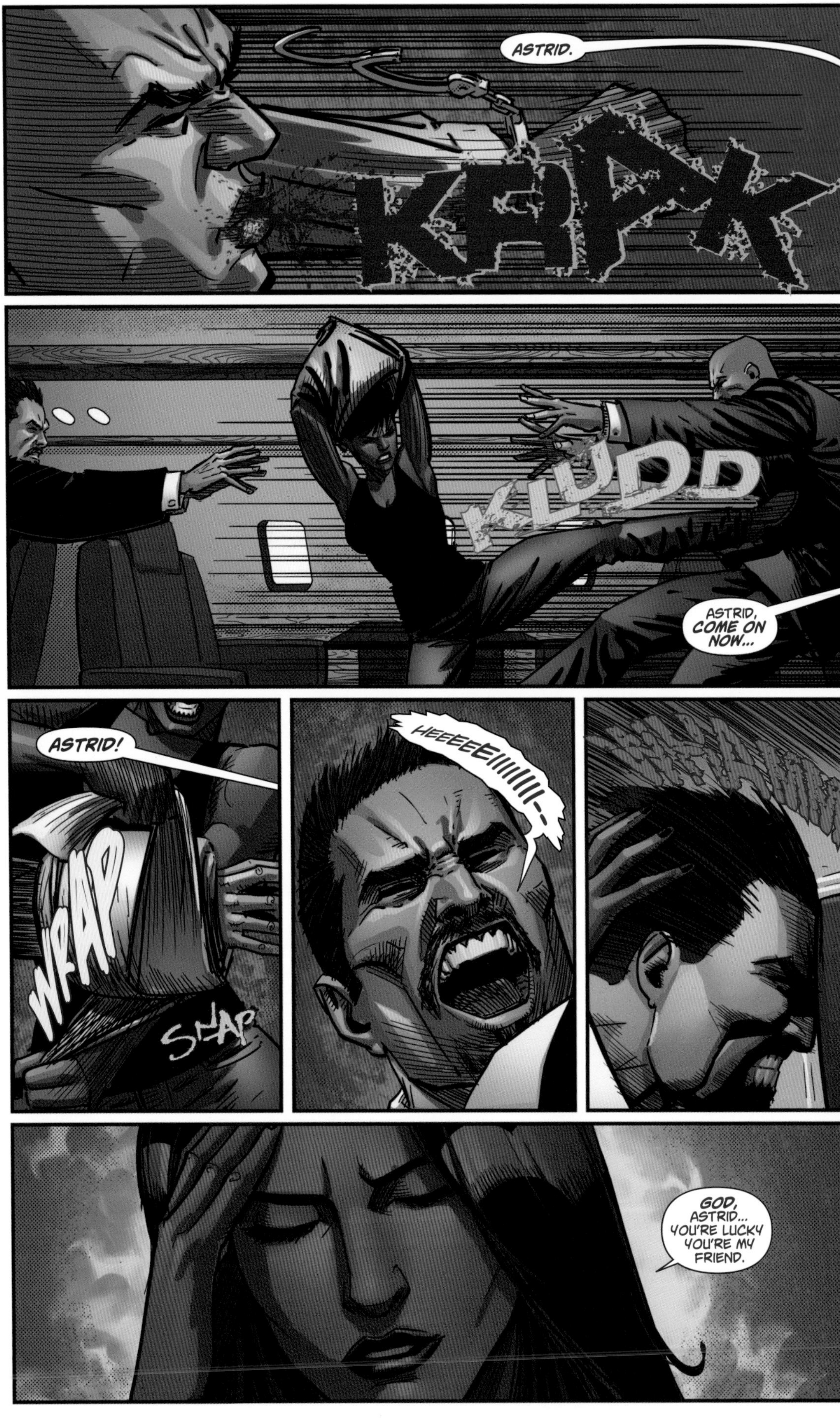
ASTRID.
KRAK
...
KLUDD
ASTRID, COME ON NOW...
ASTRID!
WRAP
SNAP
HEEEEE!!!!!!!--
GOD, ASTRID... YOU'RE LUCKY YOU'RE MY FRIEND.

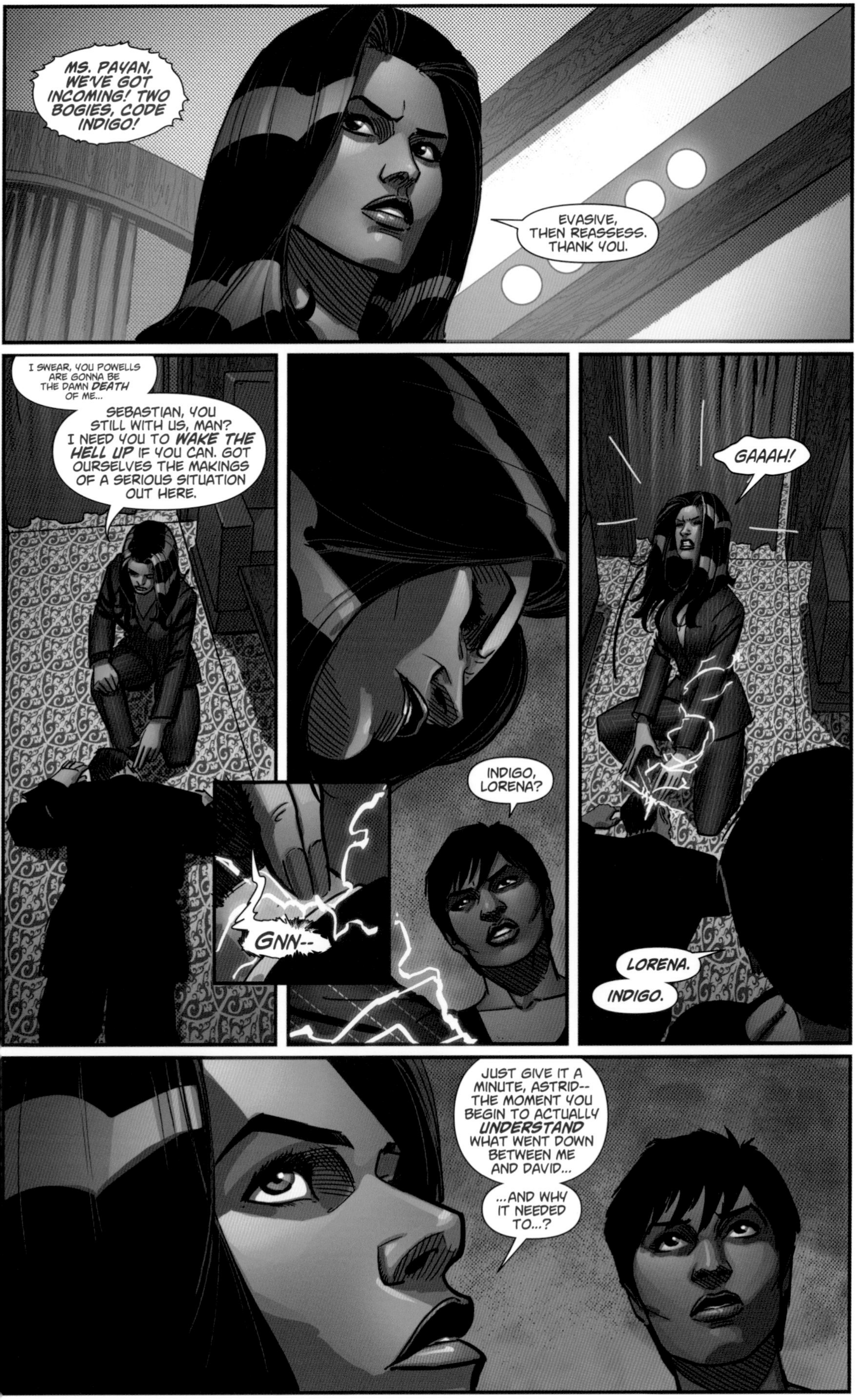
MS. PAYAN, WE'VE GOT INCOMING! TWO BOGIES, CODE INDIGO!
EVASIVE, THEN REASSESS. THANK YOU.
I SWEAR, YOU POWELLS ARE GONNA BE THE DAMN DEATH OF ME...
SEBASTIAN, YOU STILL WITH US, MAN? I NEED YOU TO WAKE THE HELL UP IF YOU CAN. GOT OURSELVES THE MAKINGS OF A SERIOUS SITUATION OUT HERE.
GNN--
INDIGO, LORENA?
GAAAH!
LORENA.
INDIGO.
JUST GIVE IT A MINUTE, ASTRID-- THE MOMENT YOU BEGIN TO ACTUALLY UNDERSTAND WHAT WENT DOWN BETWEEN ME AND DAVID...
...AND WHY IT NEEDED TO...?

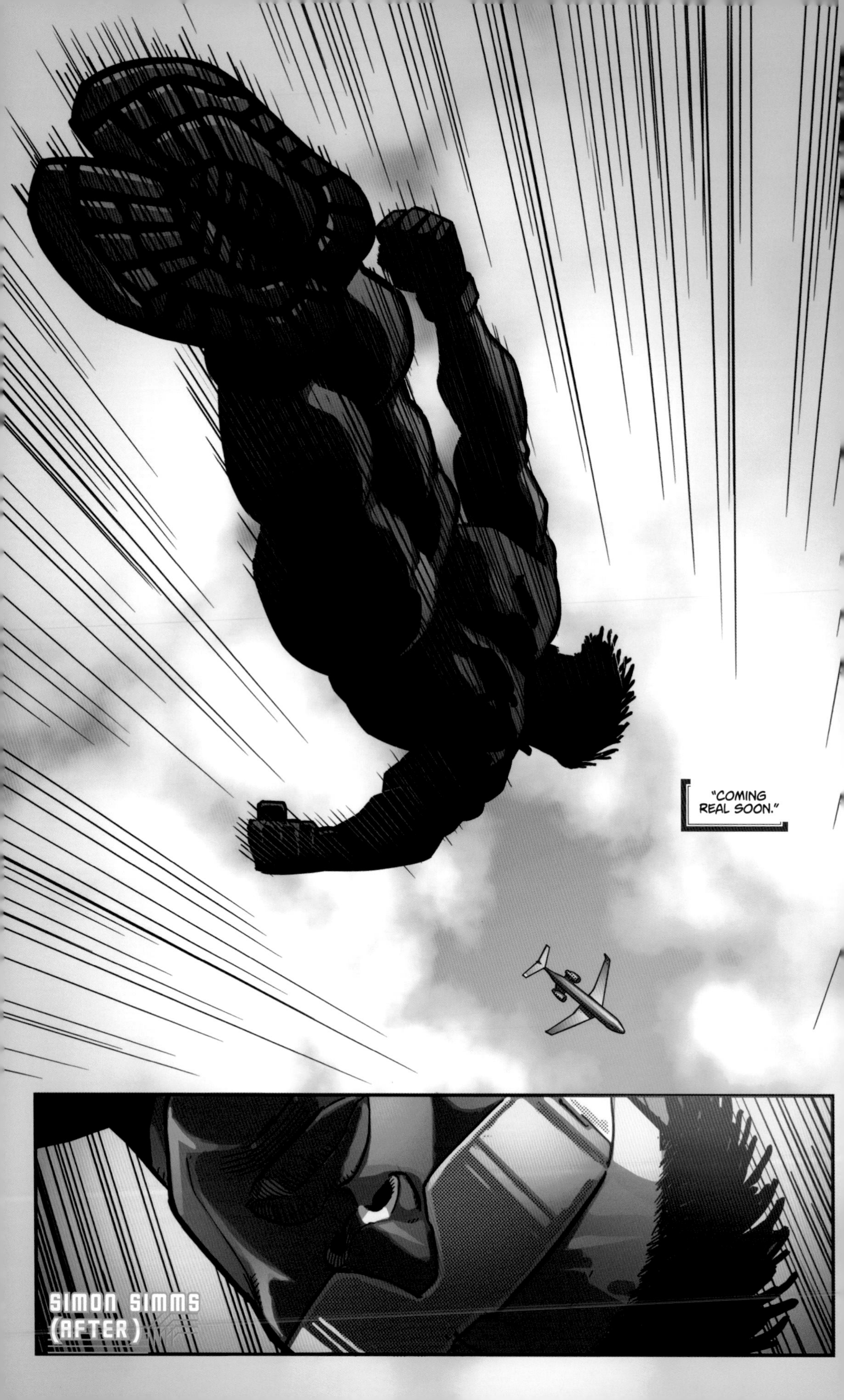
"COMING REAL SOON."
SIMON SIMMS (AFTER)

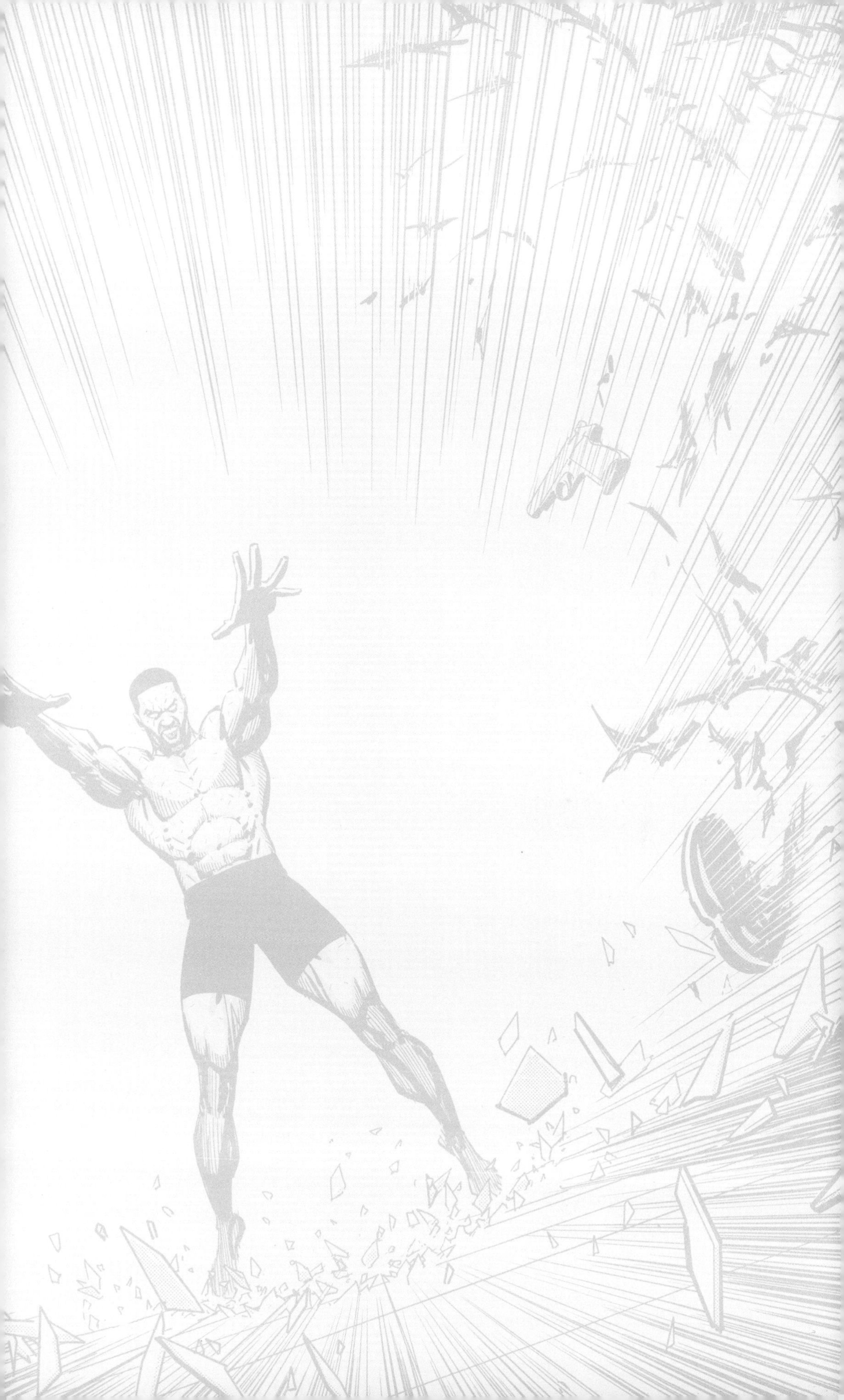

CHAPTER THREE

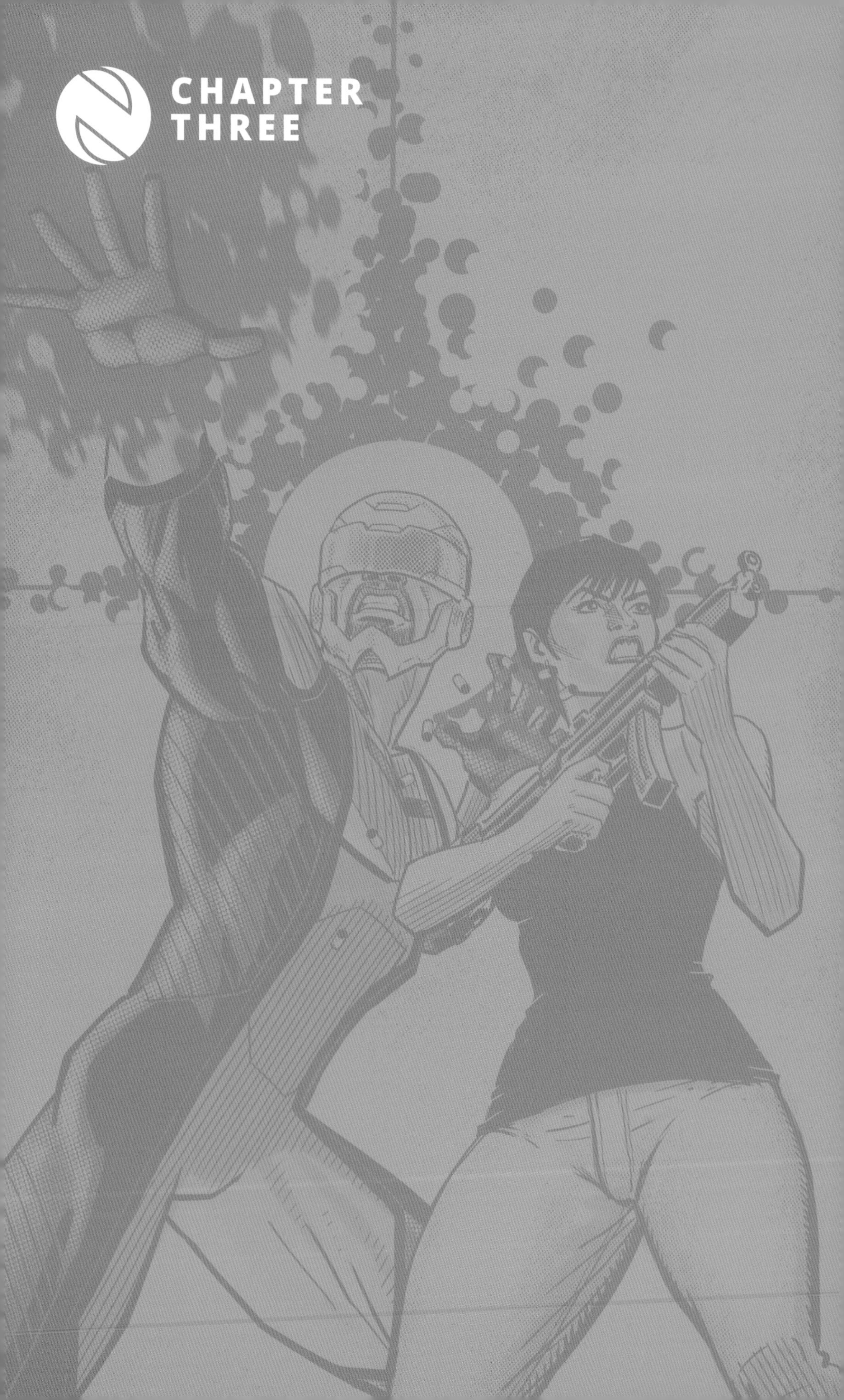

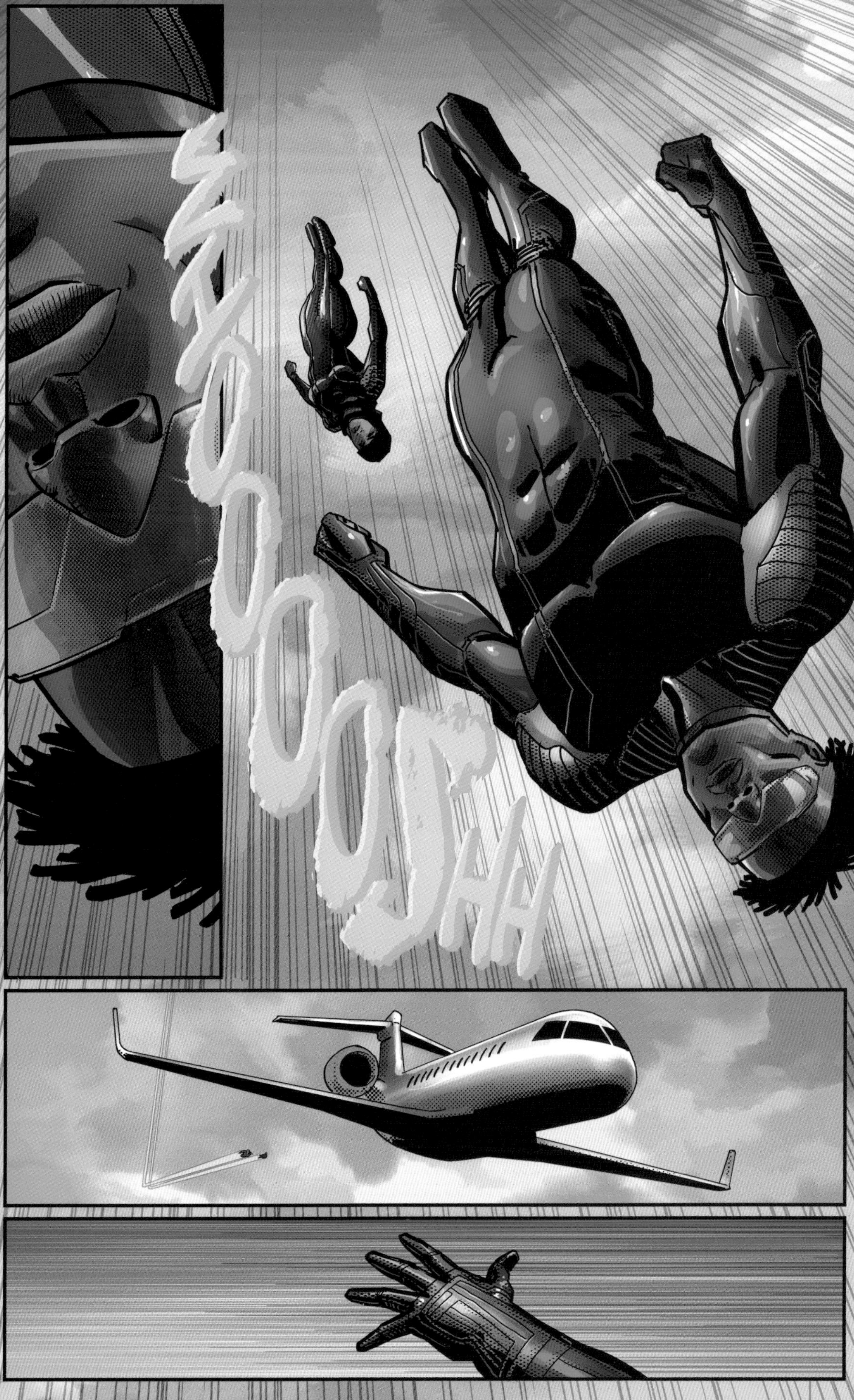

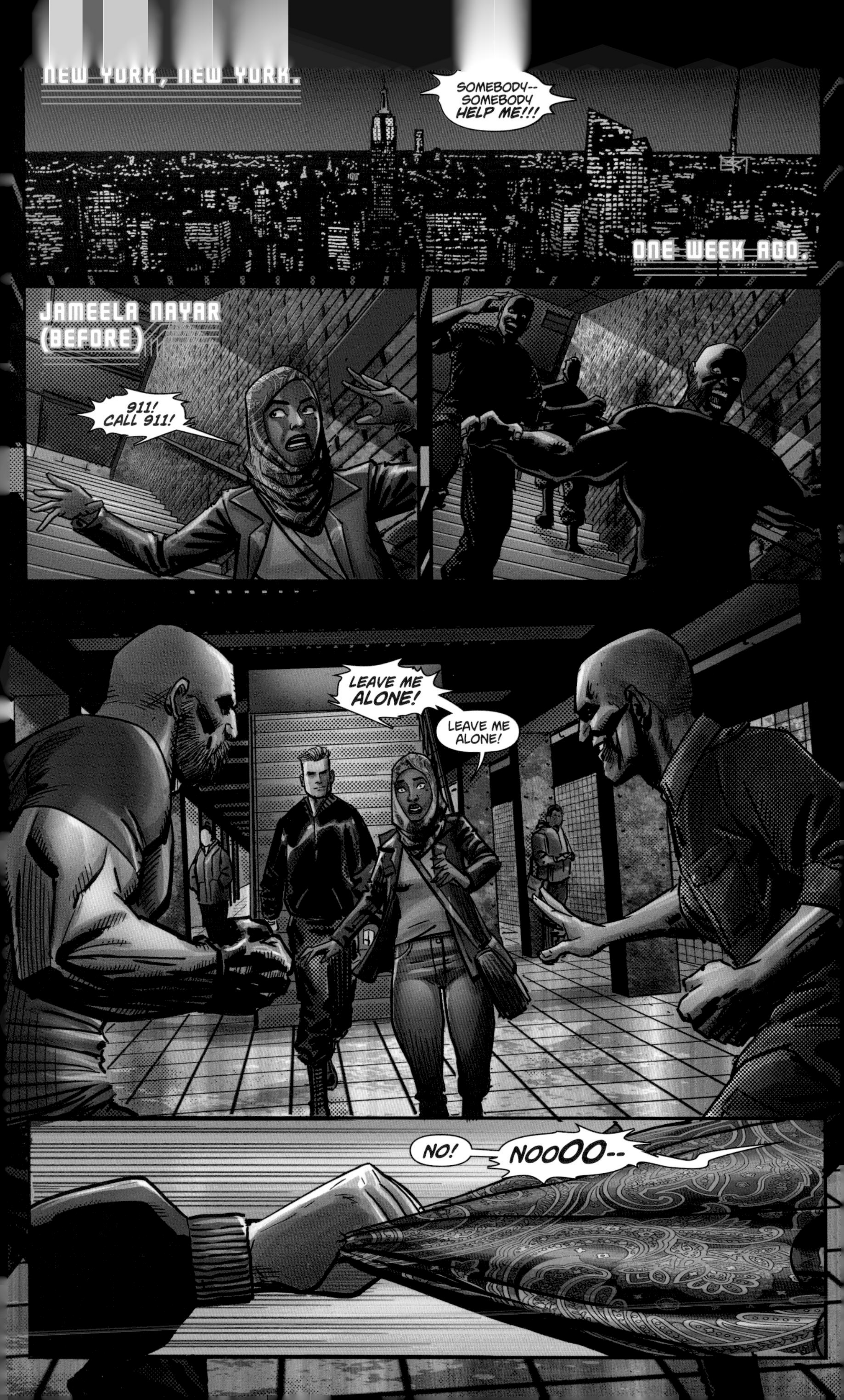
NEW YORK, NEW YORK.
SOMEBODY-- SOMEBODY HELP ME!!!
ONE WEEK AGO.
JAMEELA NAYAR (BEFORE)
911! CALL 911!
LEAVE ME ALONE!
LEAVE ME ALONE!
NO!
NOOOO--

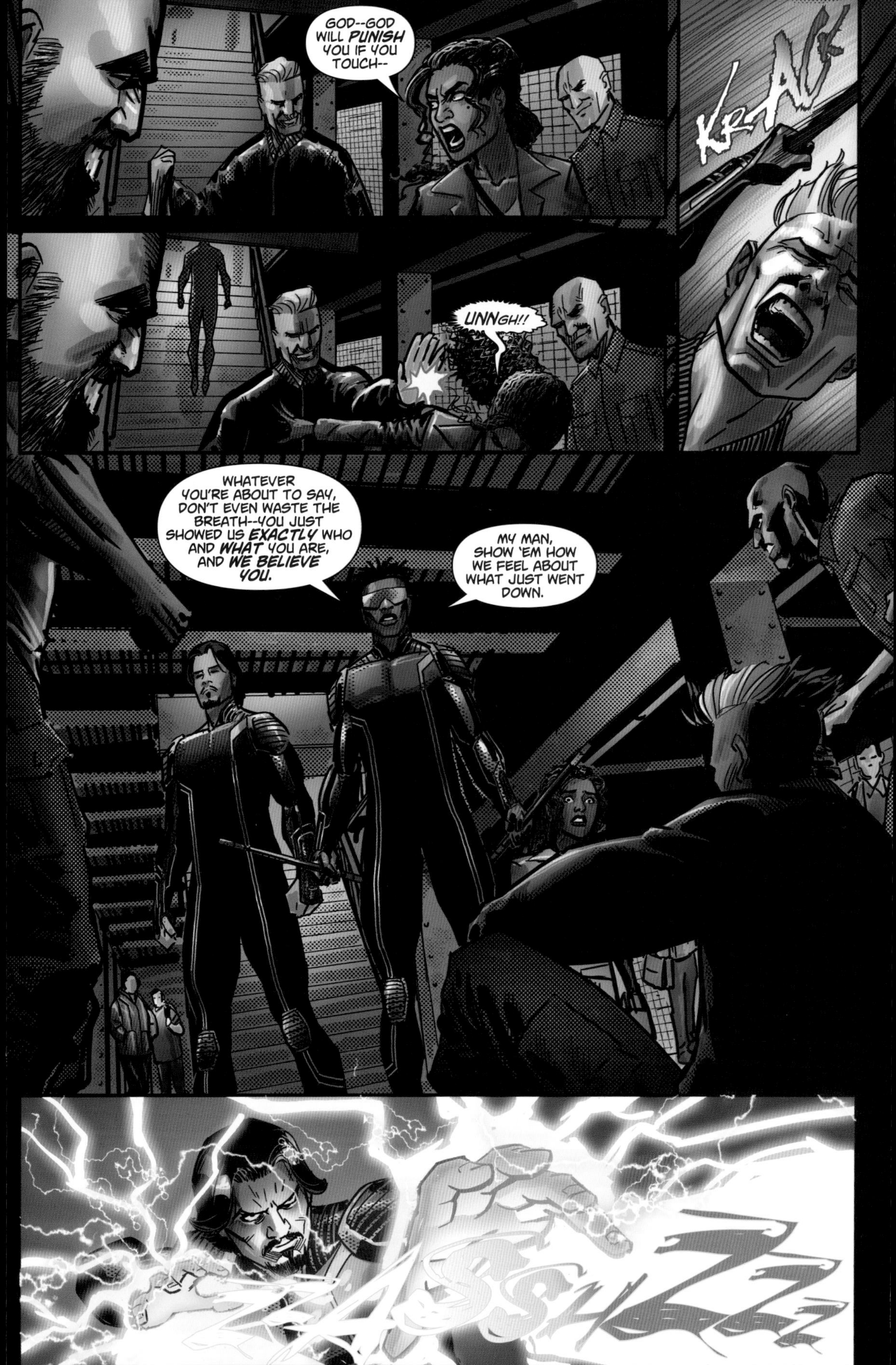
GOD--GOD WILL PUNISH YOU IF YOU TOUCH--
KRAK
UNNGH!!
WHATEVER YOU'RE ABOUT TO SAY, DON'T EVEN WASTE THE BREATH--YOU JUST SHOWED US EXACTLY WHO AND WHAT YOU ARE, AND WE BELIEVE YOU.
MY MAN, SHOW 'EM HOW WE FEEL ABOUT WHAT JUST WENT DOWN.
ZZASSHZZ

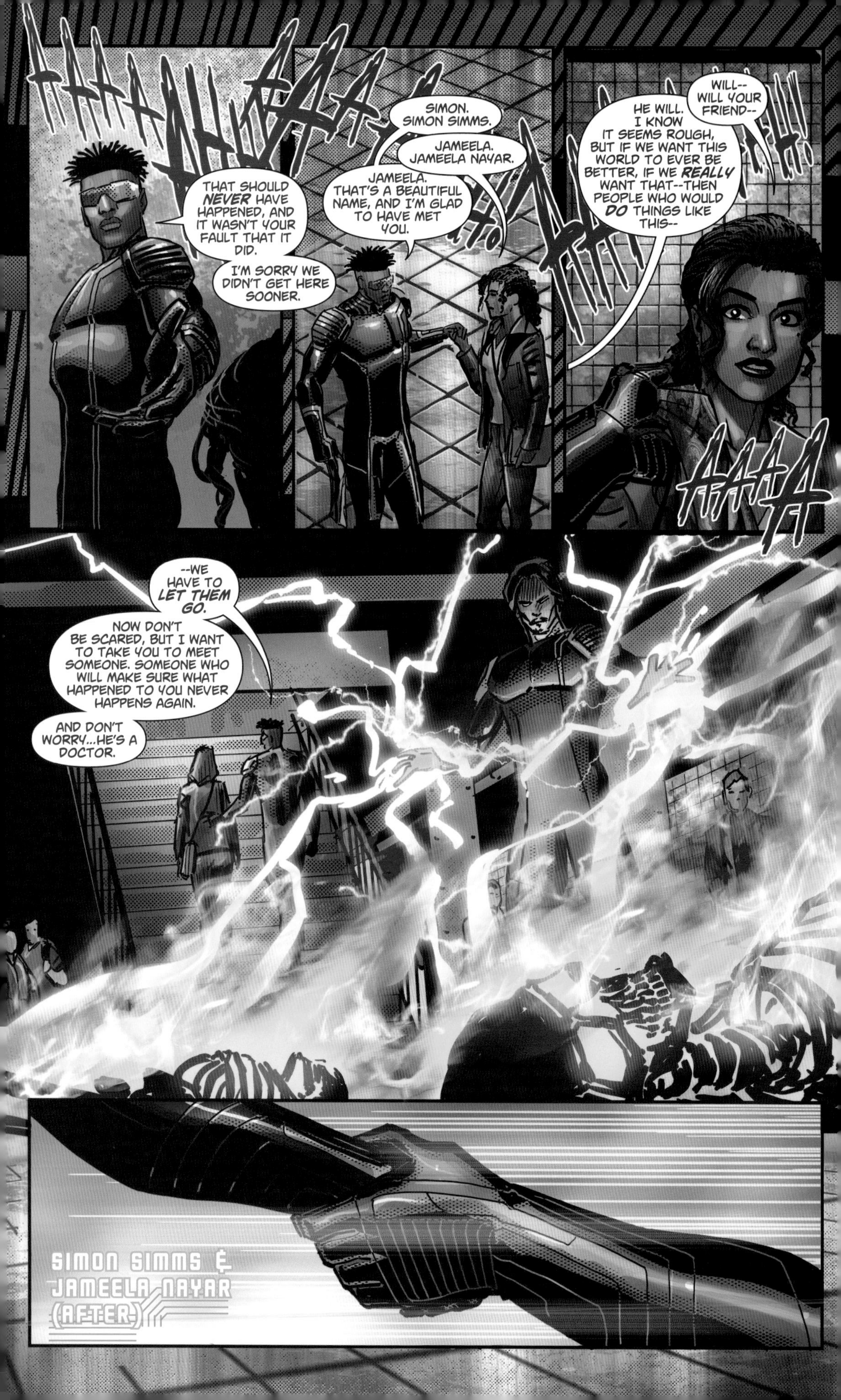

THAT SHOULD NEVER HAVE HAPPENED, AND IT WASN'T YOUR FAULT THAT IT DID.
I'M SORRY WE DIDN'T GET HERE SOONER.
SIMON. SIMON SIMMS.
JAMEELA. JAMEELA NAYAR.
JAMEELA. THAT'S A BEAUTIFUL NAME, AND I'M GLAD TO HAVE MET YOU.
WILL-- WILL YOUR FRIEND--
HE WILL. I KNOW IT SEEMS ROUGH, BUT IF WE WANT THIS WORLD TO EVER BE BETTER, IF WE REALLY WANT THAT--THEN PEOPLE WHO WOULD DO THINGS LIKE THIS--
AAAA
--WE HAVE TO LET THEM GO.
NOW DON'T BE SCARED, BUT I WANT TO TAKE YOU TO MEET SOMEONE. SOMEONE WHO WILL MAKE SURE WHAT HAPPENED TO YOU NEVER HAPPENS AGAIN.
AND DON'T WORRY...HE'S A DOCTOR.
SIMON SIMMS &
JAMEELA NAYAR
(AFTER)

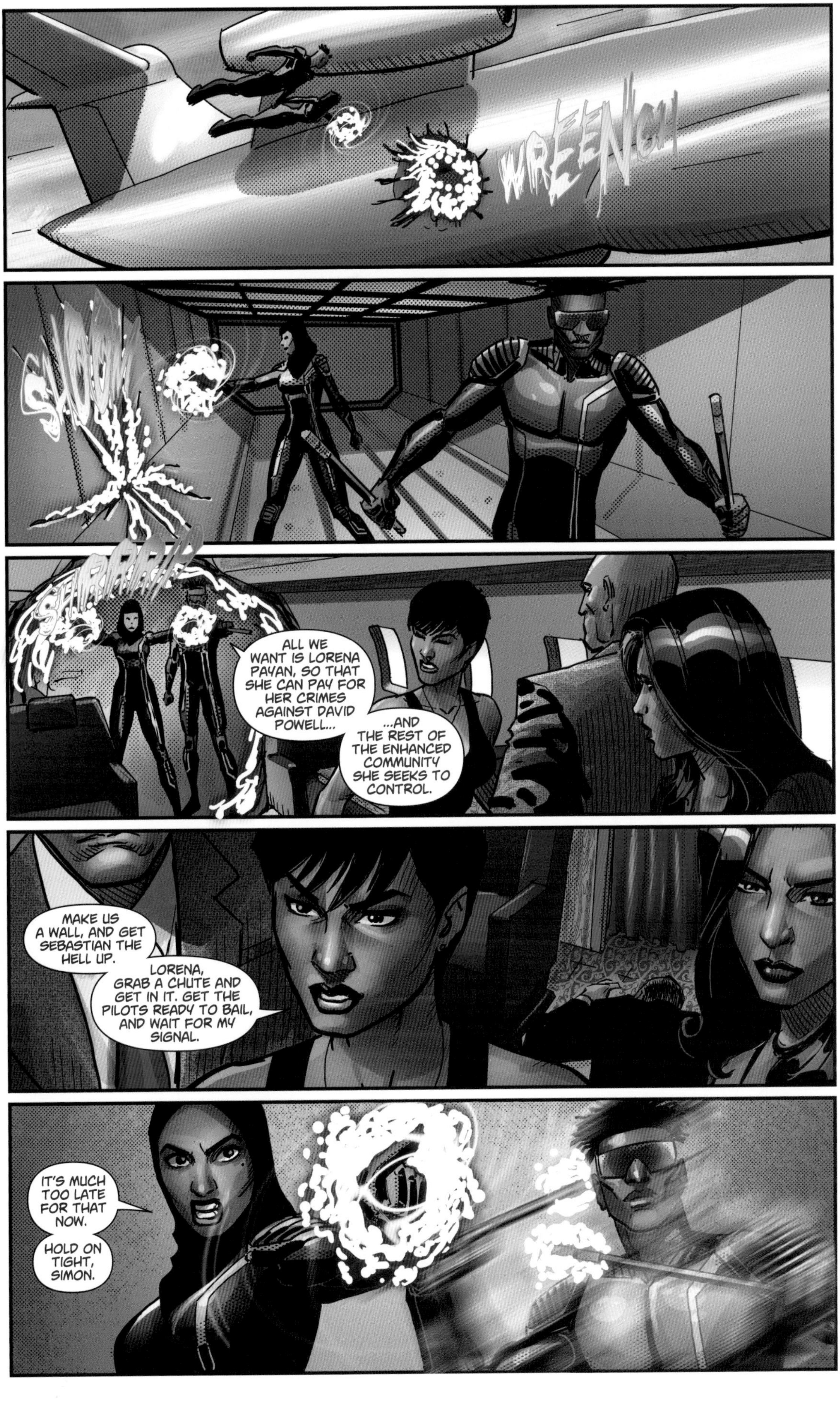
WREENCH
SHOOM
SHRRRRIP
ALL WE WANT IS LORENA PAYAN, SO THAT SHE CAN PAY FOR HER CRIMES AGAINST DAVID POWELL...
...AND THE REST OF THE ENHANCED COMMUNITY SHE SEEKS TO CONTROL.
MAKE US A WALL, AND GET SEBASTIAN THE HELL UP.
LORENA, GRAB A CHUTE AND GET IN IT. GET THE PILOTS READY TO BAIL, AND WAIT FOR MY SIGNAL.
IT'S MUCH TOO LATE FOR THAT NOW.
HOLD ON TIGHT, SIMON.

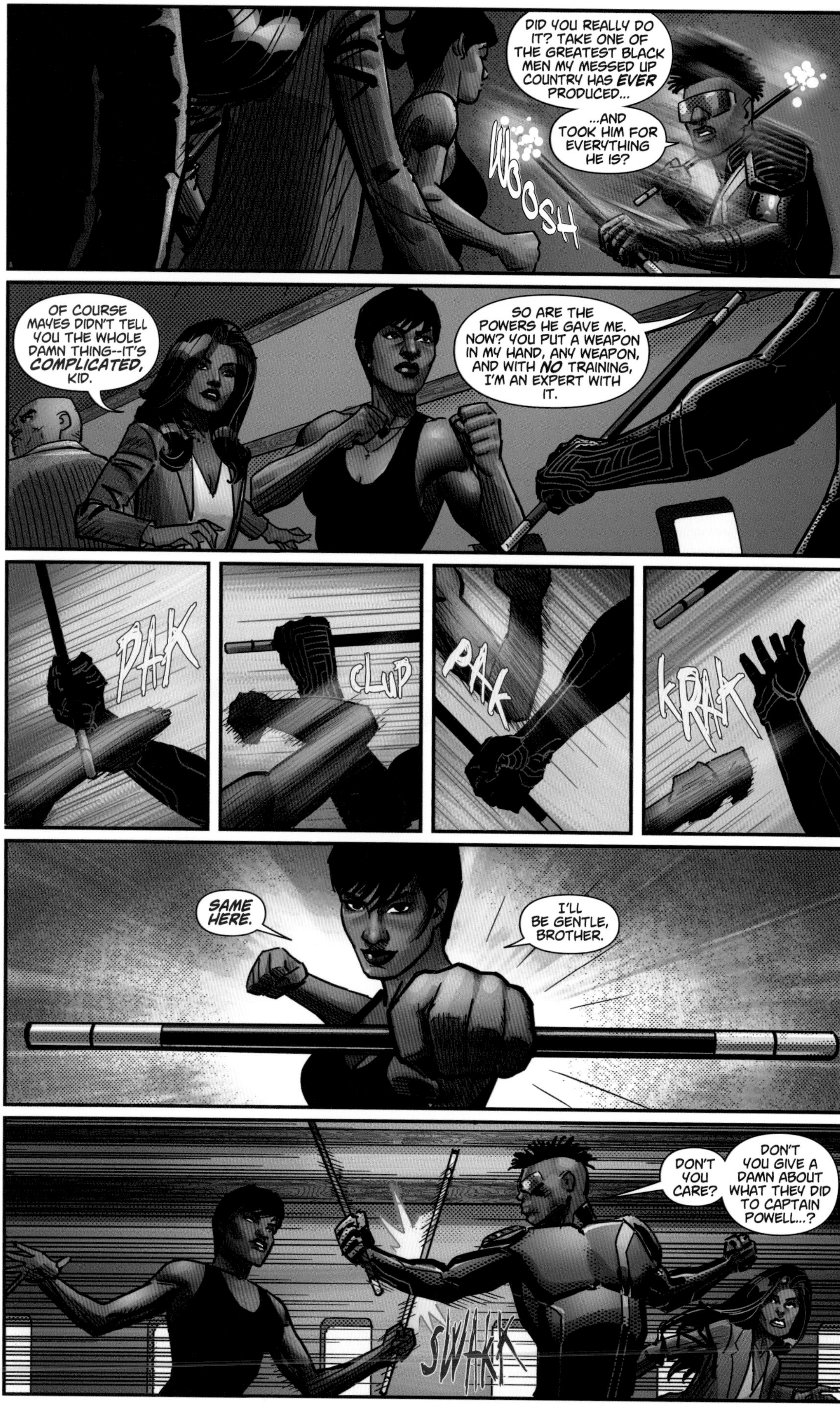
DID YOU REALLY DO IT? TAKE ONE OF THE GREATEST BLACK MEN MY MESSED UP COUNTRY HAS *EVER* PRODUCED...
...AND TOOK HIM FOR EVERYTHING HE IS?
WOOSH
OF COURSE MAYES DIDN'T TELL YOU THE WHOLE DAMN THING--IT'S *COMPLICATED,* KID.
SO ARE THE POWERS HE GAVE ME. NOW? YOU PUT A WEAPON IN MY HAND, ANY WEAPON, AND WITH *NO* TRAINING, I'M AN EXPERT WITH IT.
PAK
CLUP
PAK
KRAK
SAME HERE.
I'LL BE GENTLE, BROTHER.
DON'T YOU CARE?
DON'T YOU GIVE A DAMN ABOUT WHAT THEY DID TO CAPTAIN POWELL...?
SWAKK

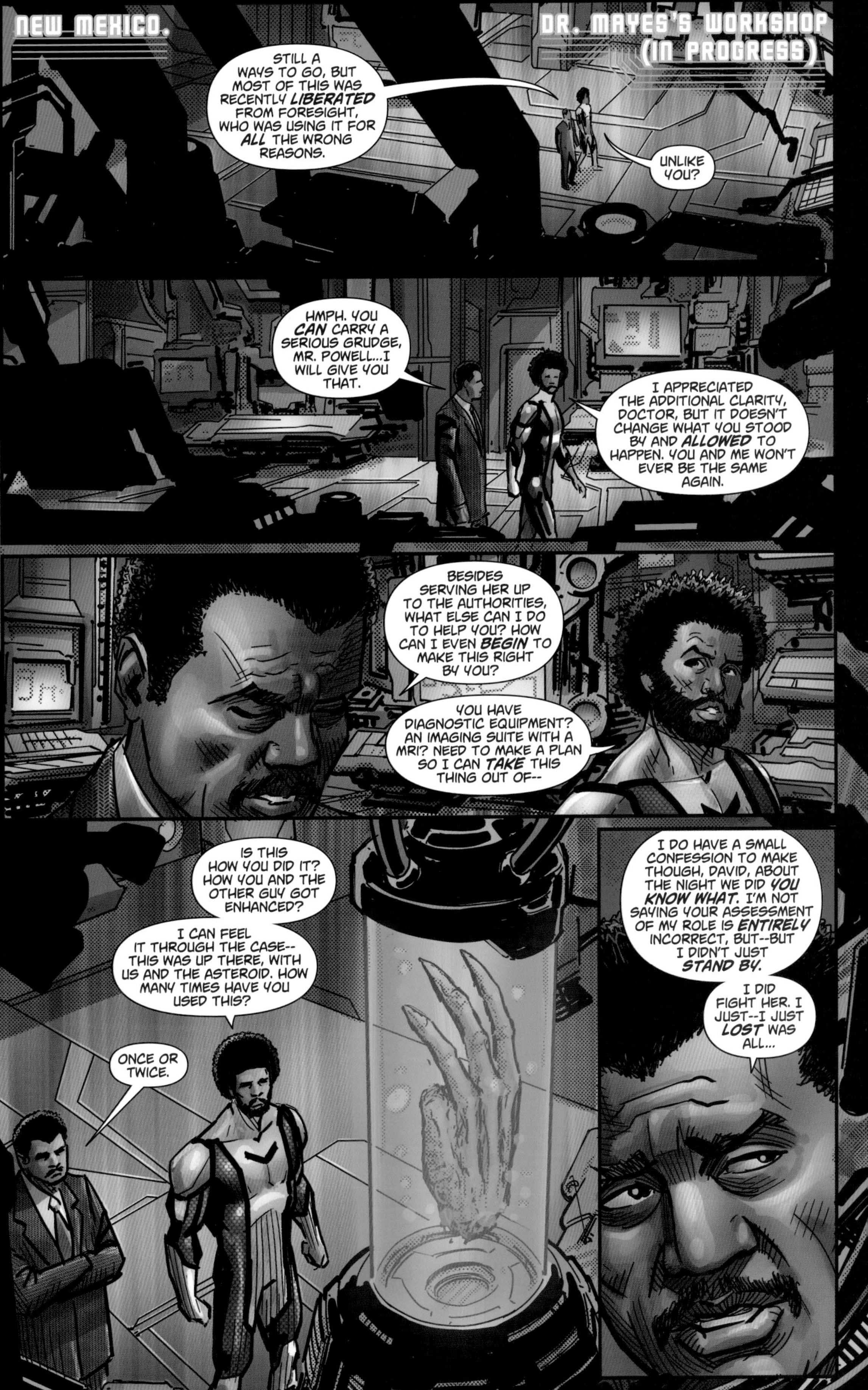

NEW MEXICO.
DR. MAYES'S WORKSHOP (IN PROGRESS)
STILL A WAYS TO GO, BUT MOST OF THIS WAS RECENTLY LIBERATED FROM FORESIGHT, WHO WAS USING IT FOR ALL THE WRONG REASONS.
UNLIKE YOU?
HMPH. YOU CAN CARRY A SERIOUS GRUDGE, MR. POWELL...I WILL GIVE YOU THAT.
I APPRECIATED THE ADDITIONAL CLARITY, DOCTOR, BUT IT DOESN'T CHANGE WHAT YOU STOOD BY AND ALLOWED TO HAPPEN. YOU AND ME WON'T EVER BE THE SAME AGAIN.
BESIDES SERVING HER UP TO THE AUTHORITIES, WHAT ELSE CAN I DO TO HELP YOU? HOW CAN I EVEN BEGIN TO MAKE THIS RIGHT BY YOU?
YOU HAVE DIAGNOSTIC EQUIPMENT? AN IMAGING SUITE WITH A MRI? NEED TO MAKE A PLAN SO I CAN TAKE THIS THING OUT OF--
IS THIS HOW YOU DID IT? HOW YOU AND THE OTHER GUY GOT ENHANCED?
I CAN FEEL IT THROUGH THE CASE-- THIS WAS UP THERE, WITH US AND THE ASTEROID. HOW MANY TIMES HAVE YOU USED THIS?
ONCE OR TWICE.
I DO HAVE A SMALL CONFESSION TO MAKE THOUGH, DAVID, ABOUT THE NIGHT WE DID YOU KNOW WHAT. I'M NOT SAYING YOUR ASSESSMENT OF MY ROLE IS ENTIRELY INCORRECT, BUT--BUT I DIDN'T JUST STAND BY.
I DID FIGHT HER. I JUST--I JUST LOST WAS ALL...

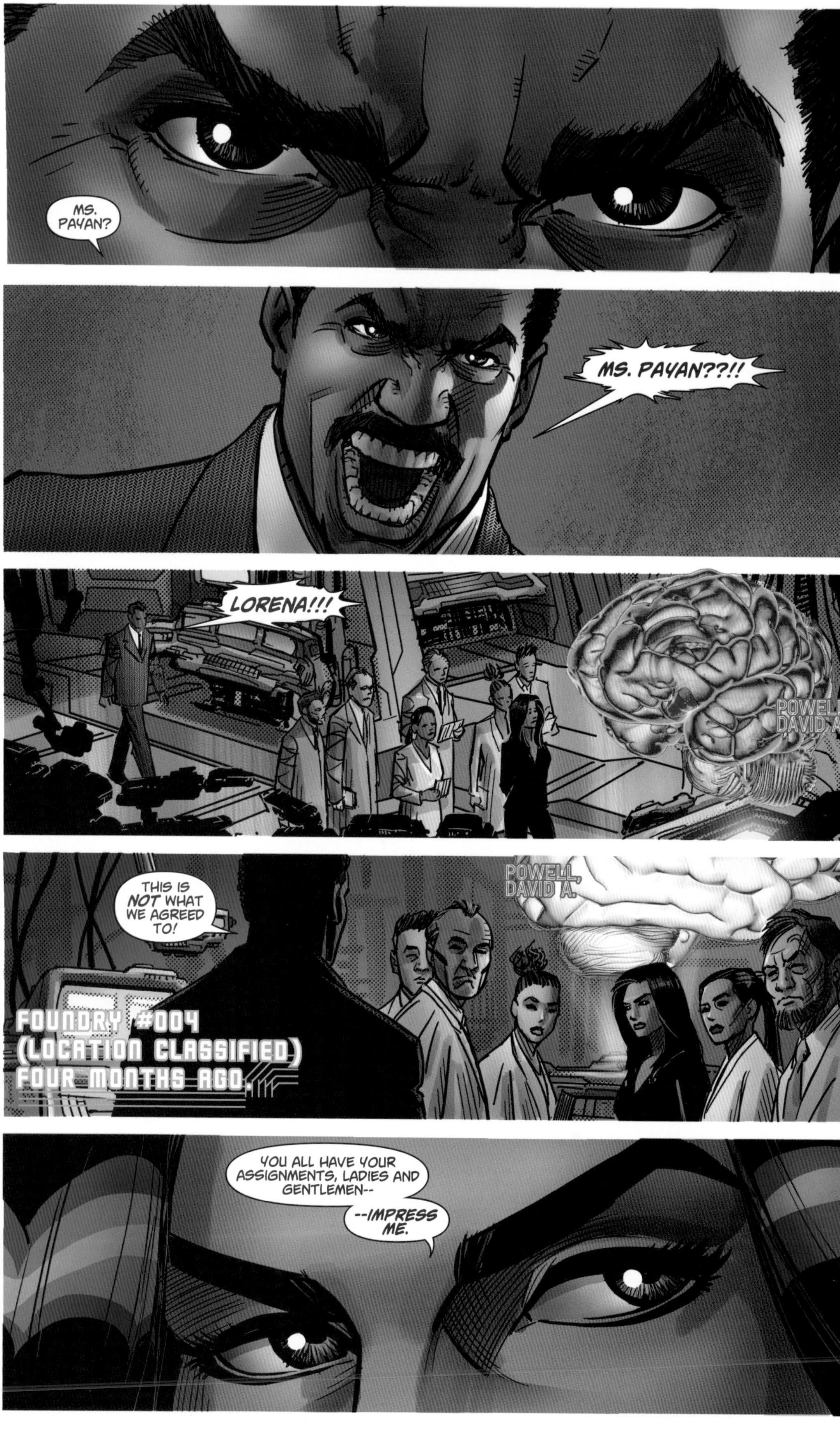

MS. PAYAN?
MS. PAYAN??!!
LORENA!!!
POWELL, DAVID A.
POWELL, DAVID A.
THIS IS NOT WHAT WE AGREED TO!
FOUNDRY #004 (LOCATION CLASSIFIED) FOUR MONTHS AGO.
YOU ALL HAVE YOUR ASSIGNMENTS, LADIES AND GENTLEMEN--
--IMPRESS ME.

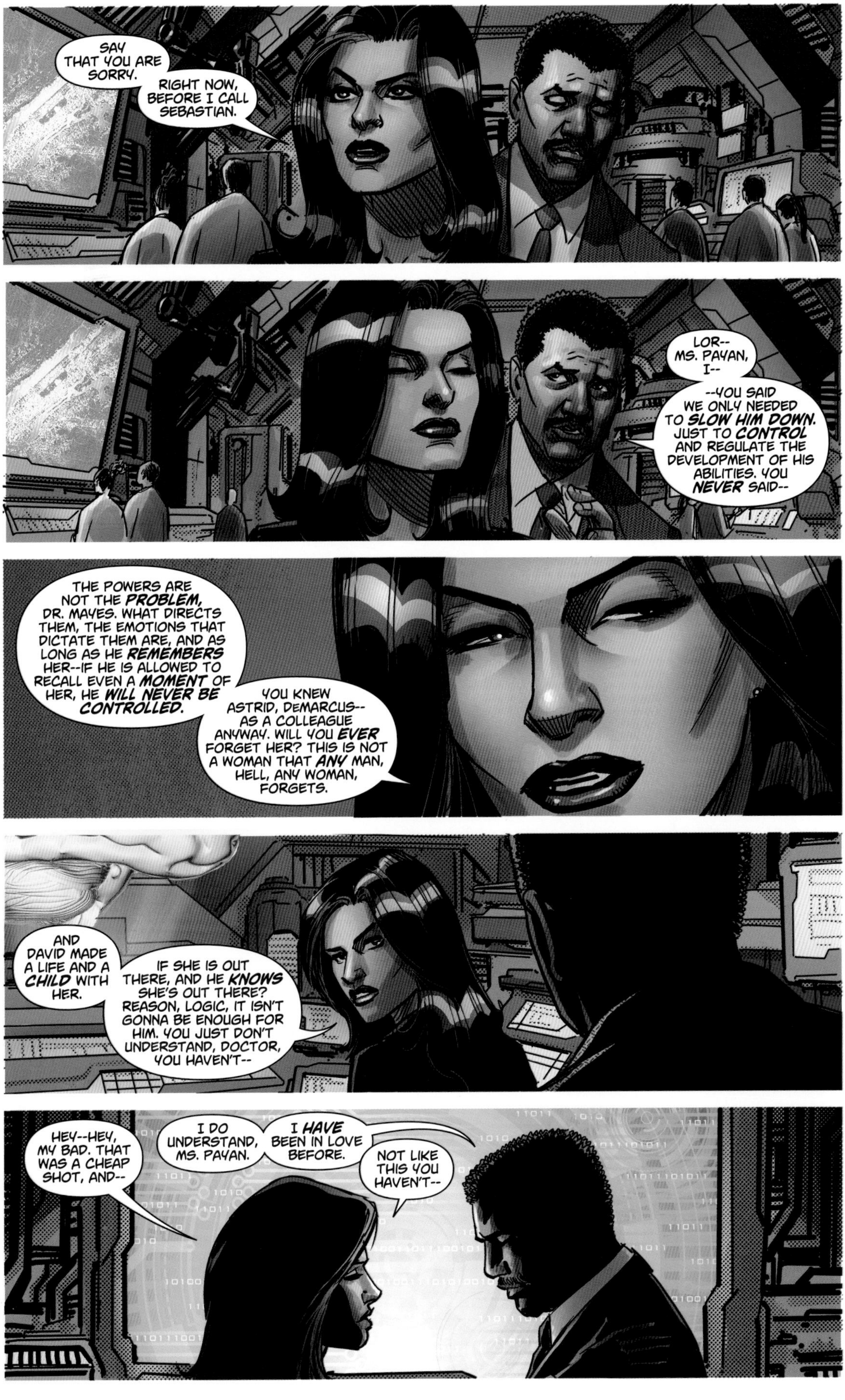
SAY THAT YOU ARE SORRY.
RIGHT NOW, BEFORE I CALL SEBASTIAN.
LOR-- MS. PAYAN, I--
--YOU SAID WE ONLY NEEDED TO SLOW HIM DOWN. JUST TO CONTROL AND REGULATE THE DEVELOPMENT OF HIS ABILITIES. YOU NEVER SAID--
THE POWERS ARE NOT THE PROBLEM, DR. MAYES. WHAT DIRECTS THEM, THE EMOTIONS THAT DICTATE THEM ARE, AND AS LONG AS HE REMEMBERS HER--IF HE IS ALLOWED TO RECALL EVEN A MOMENT OF HER, HE WILL NEVER BE CONTROLLED.
YOU KNEW ASTRID, DEMARCUS-- AS A COLLEAGUE ANYWAY. WILL YOU EVER FORGET HER? THIS IS NOT A WOMAN THAT ANY MAN, HELL, ANY WOMAN, FORGETS.
AND DAVID MADE A LIFE AND A CHILD WITH HER.
IF SHE IS OUT THERE, AND HE KNOWS SHE'S OUT THERE? REASON, LOGIC, IT ISN'T GONNA BE ENOUGH FOR HIM. YOU JUST DON'T UNDERSTAND, DOCTOR, YOU HAVEN'T--
HEY--HEY, MY BAD. THAT WAS A CHEAP SHOT, AND--
I DO UNDERSTAND, MS. PAYAN.
I HAVE BEEN IN LOVE BEFORE.
NOT LIKE THIS YOU HAVEN'T--

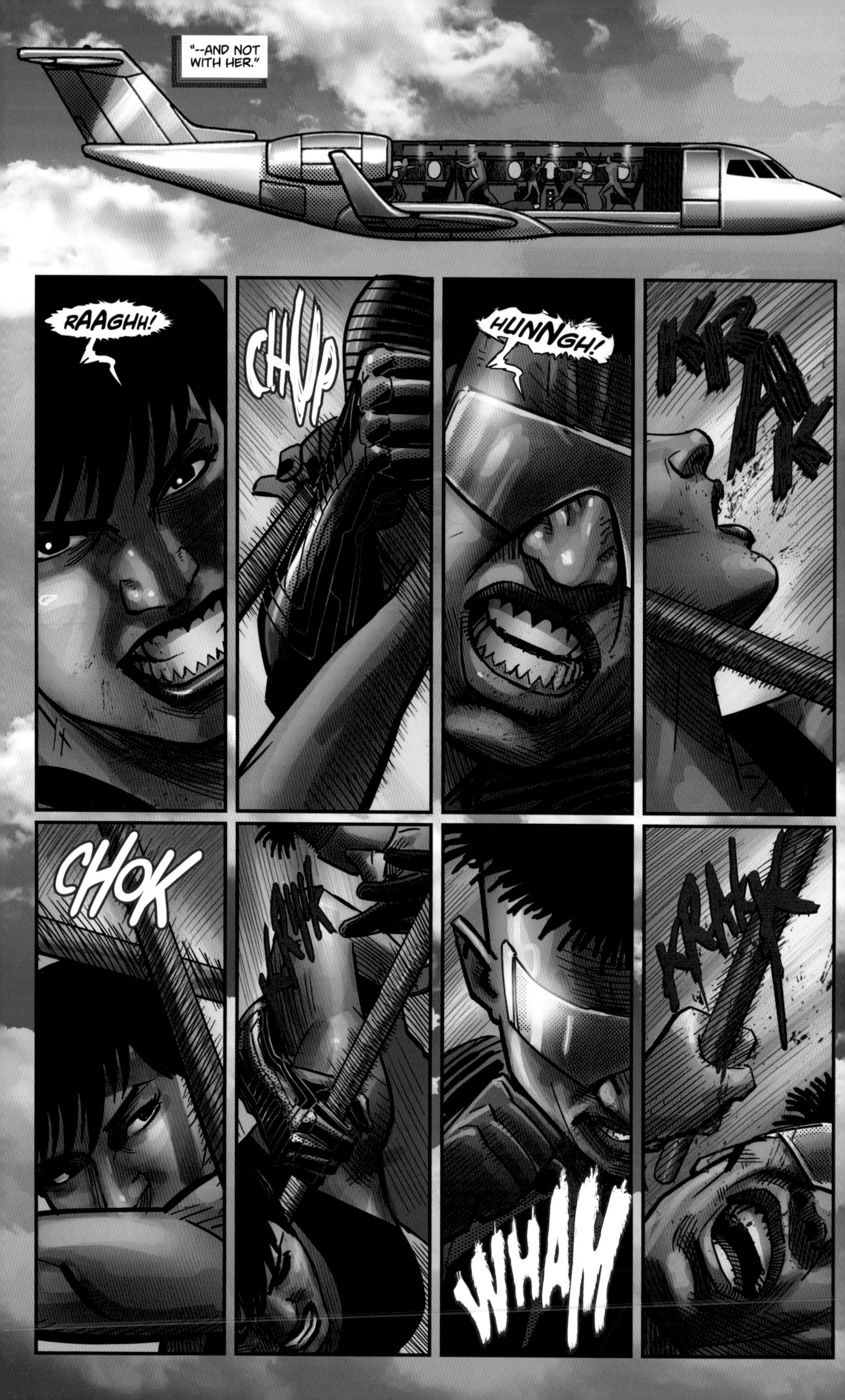
"--AND NOT WITH HER."
RAAGHH!
CHUP
HUNNGH!
CHOK
WHAM

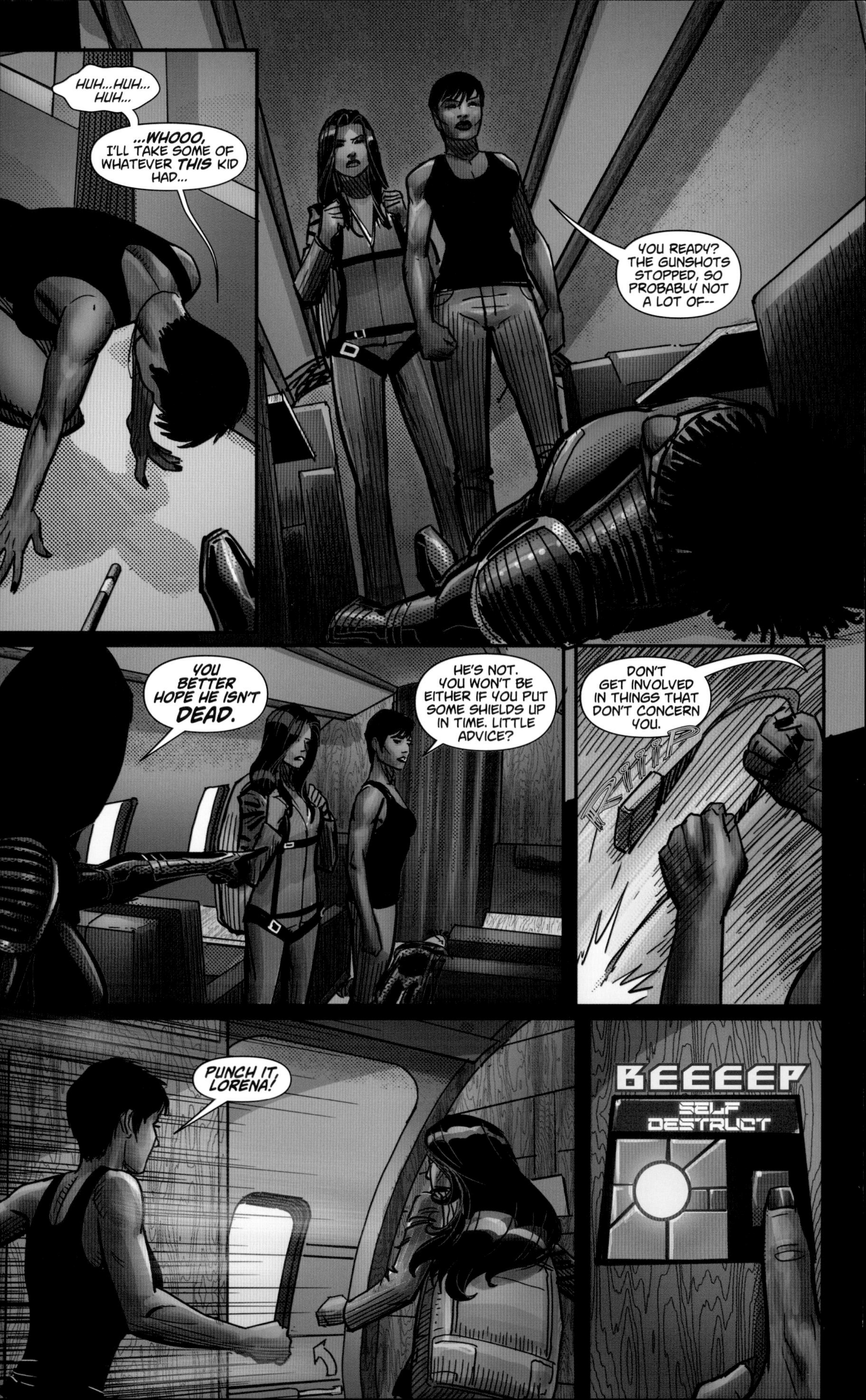
HUH...HUH... HUH...
...WHOOO, I'LL TAKE SOME OF WHATEVER THIS KID HAD...
YOU READY? THE GUNSHOTS STOPPED, SO PROBABLY NOT A LOT OF--
YOU BETTER HOPE HE ISN'T DEAD.
HE'S NOT. YOU WON'T BE EITHER IF YOU PUT SOME SHIELDS UP IN TIME. LITTLE ADVICE?
DON'T GET INVOLVED IN THINGS THAT DON'T CONCERN YOU.
RIIIIP
PUNCH IT, LORENA!
BEEEEP
SELF DESTRUCT

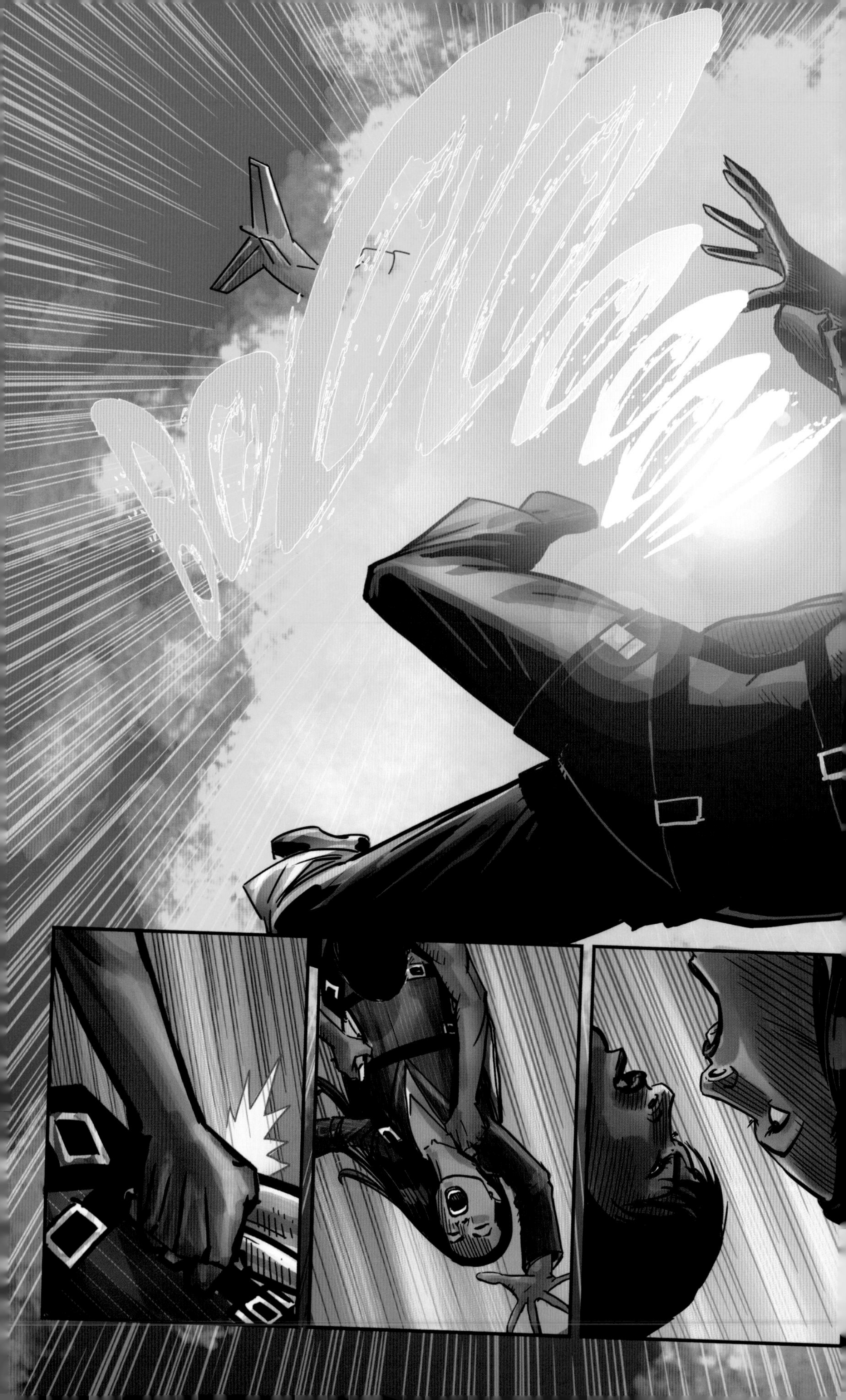

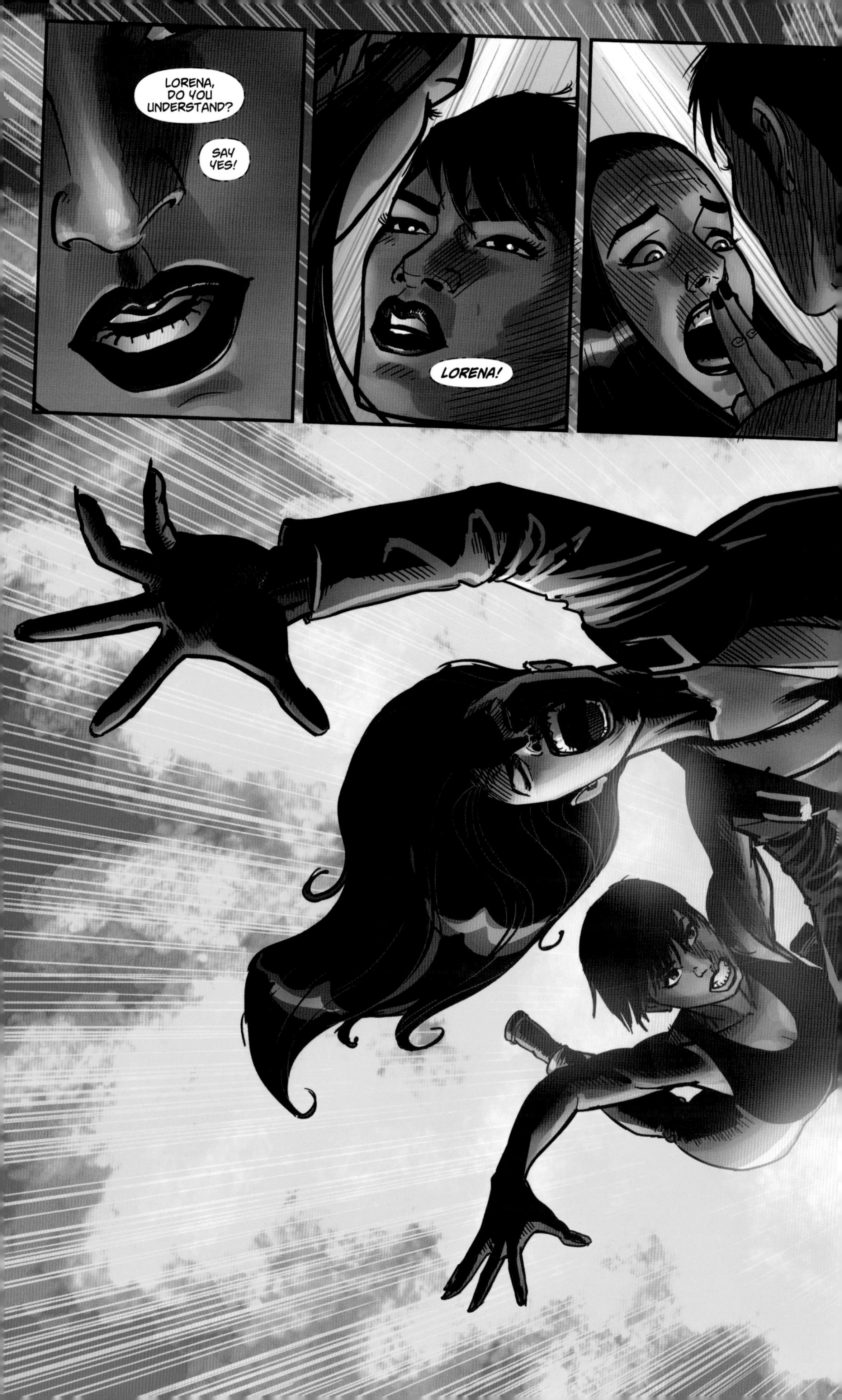
LORENA, DO YOU UNDERSTAND?
SAY YES!
LORENA!

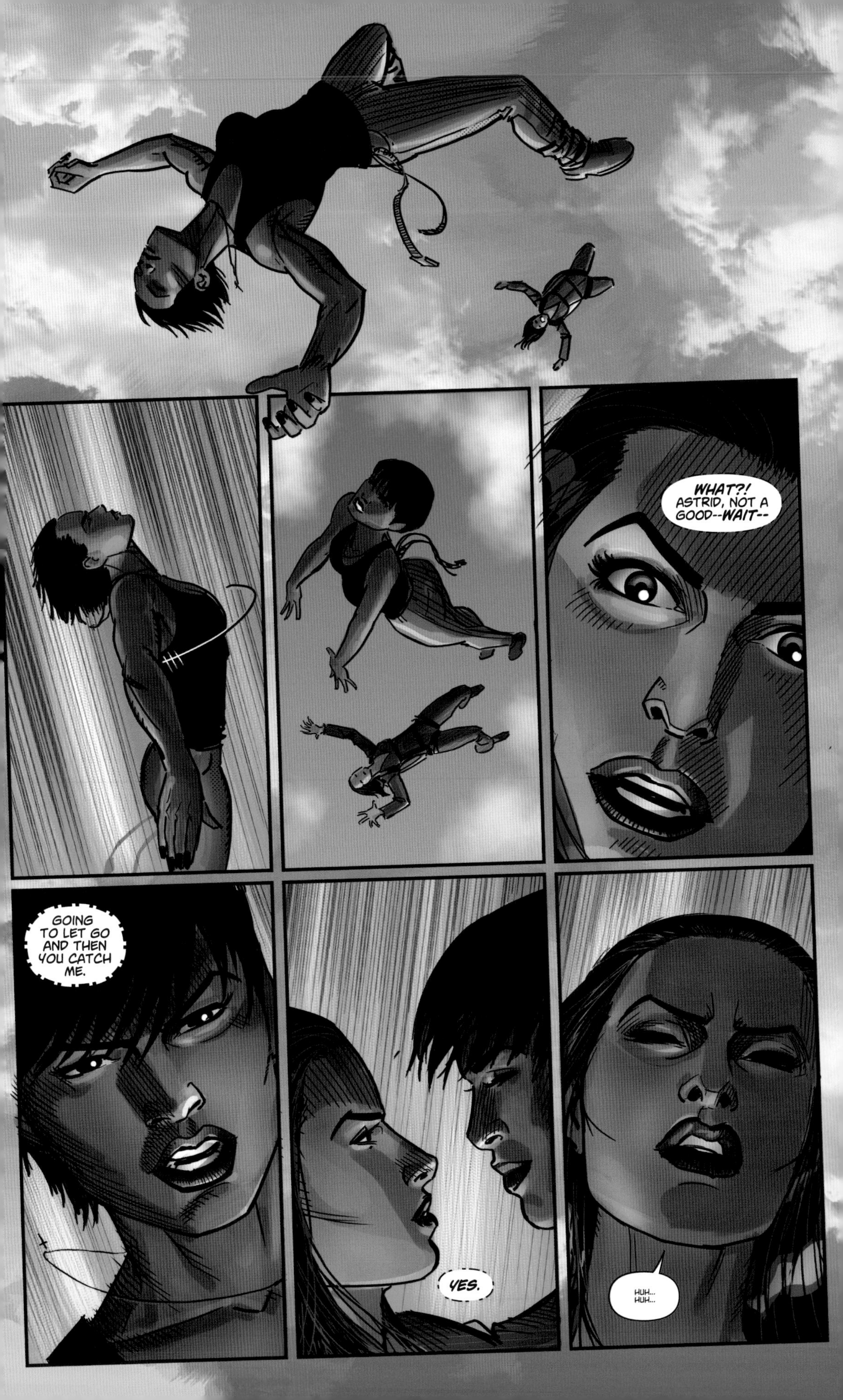
WHAT?! ASTRID, NOT A GOOD--WAIT--
GOING TO LET GO AND THEN YOU CATCH ME.
YES.
HUH... HUH...

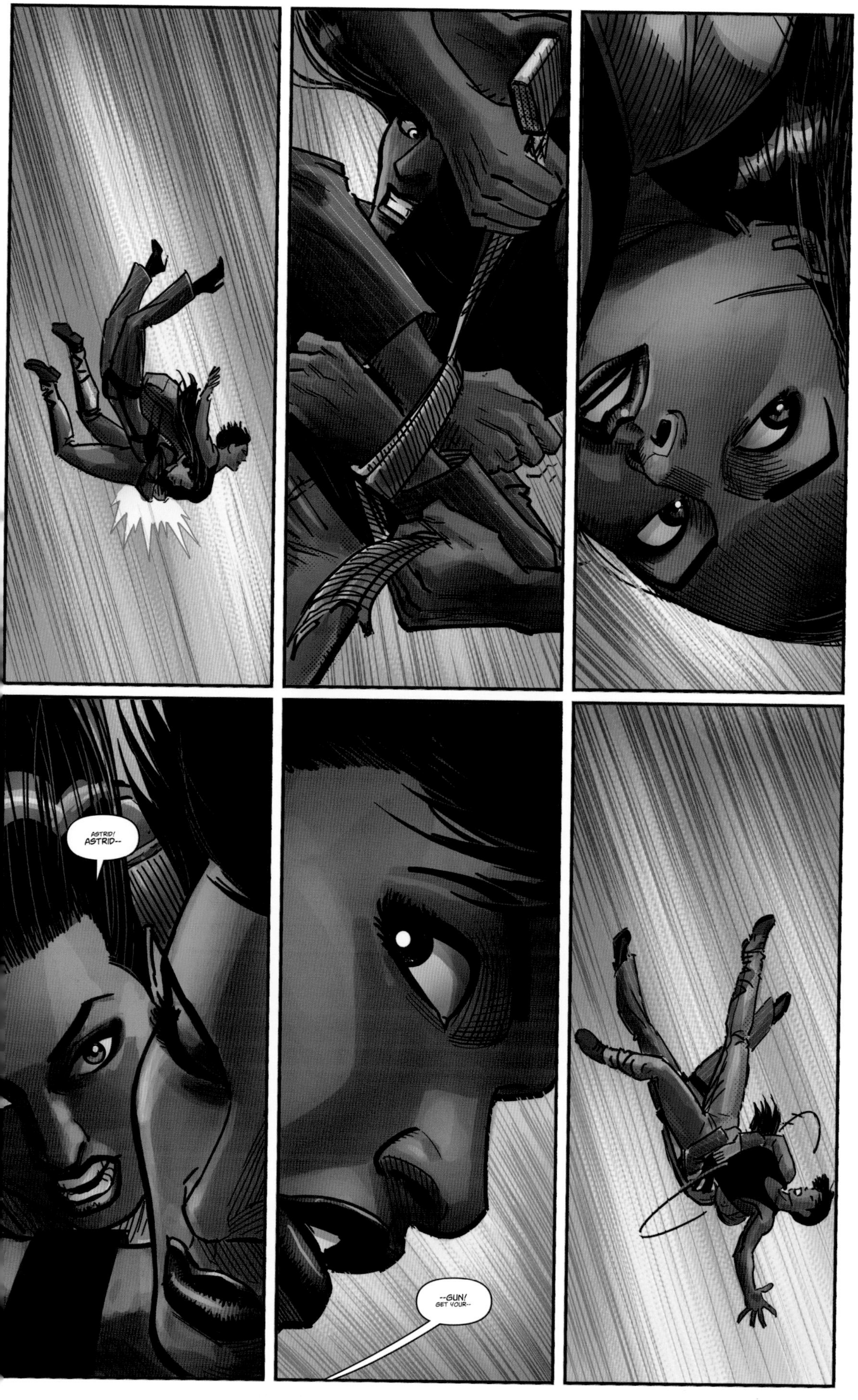
ASTRID! ASTRID--
--GUN! GET YOUR--

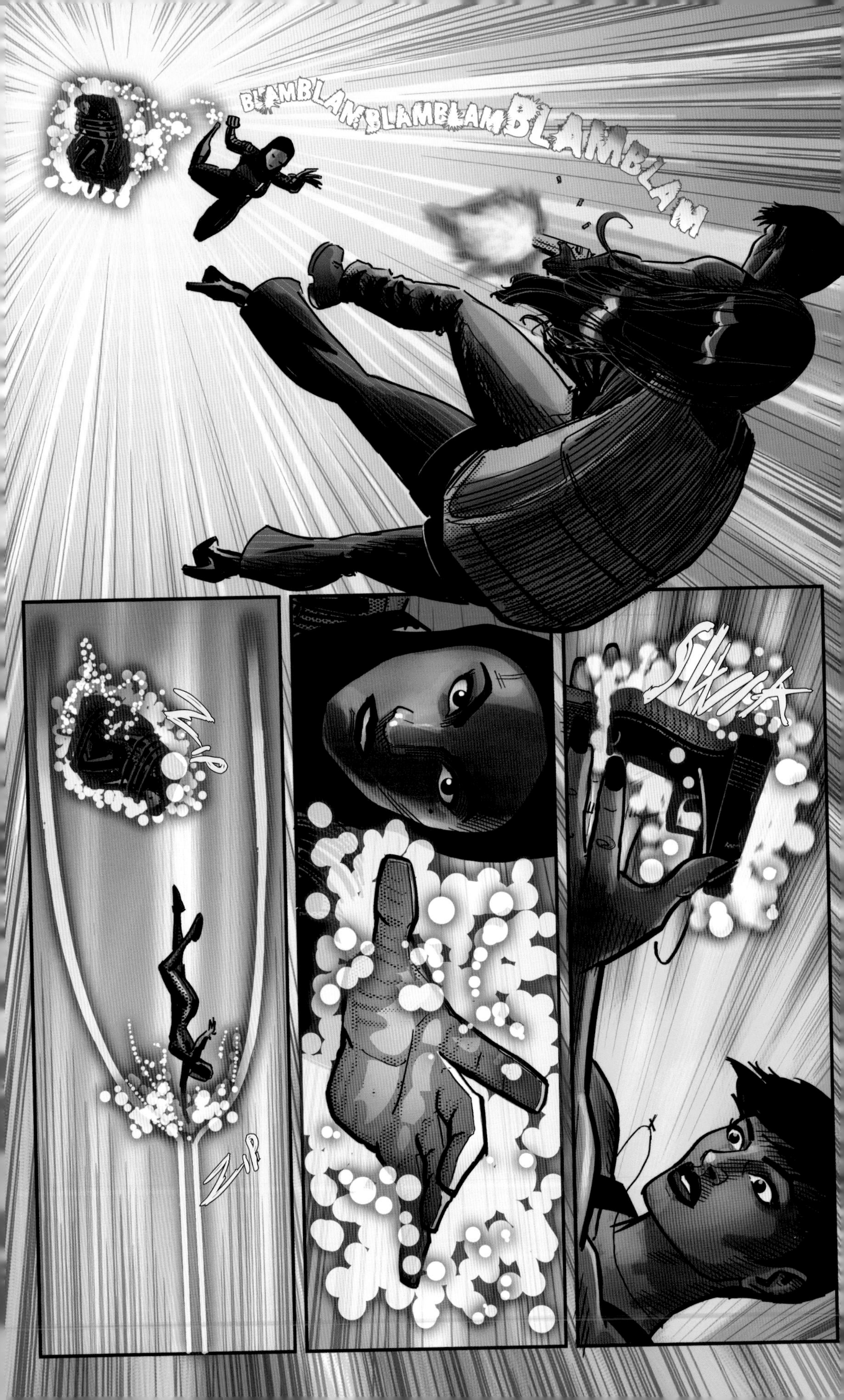
BLAMBLAMBLAMBLAMBLAMBLAM
ZIP
ZIP

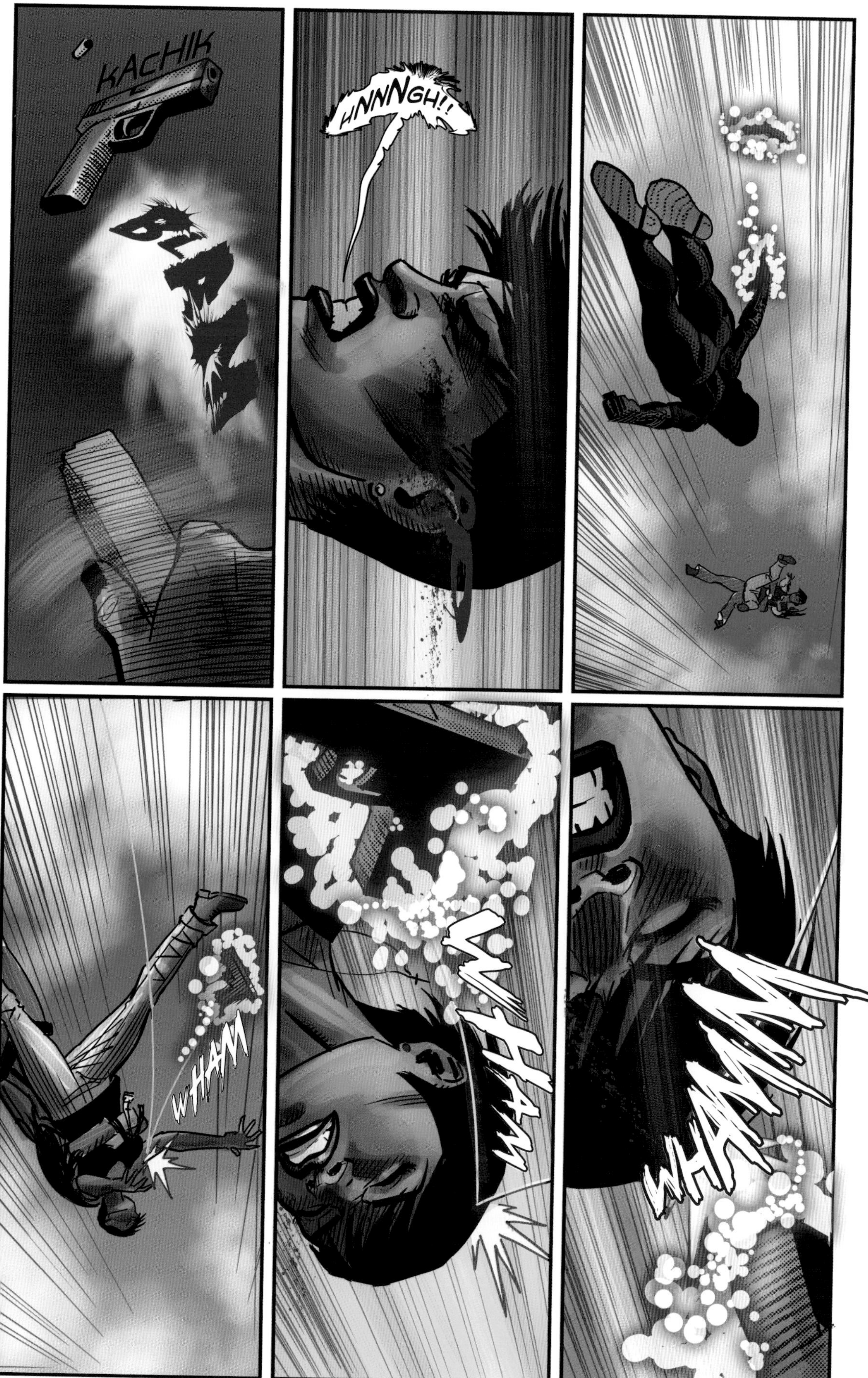
KACHIK
BLAM
UNNNGH!!
WHAM
WHAM
WHAM

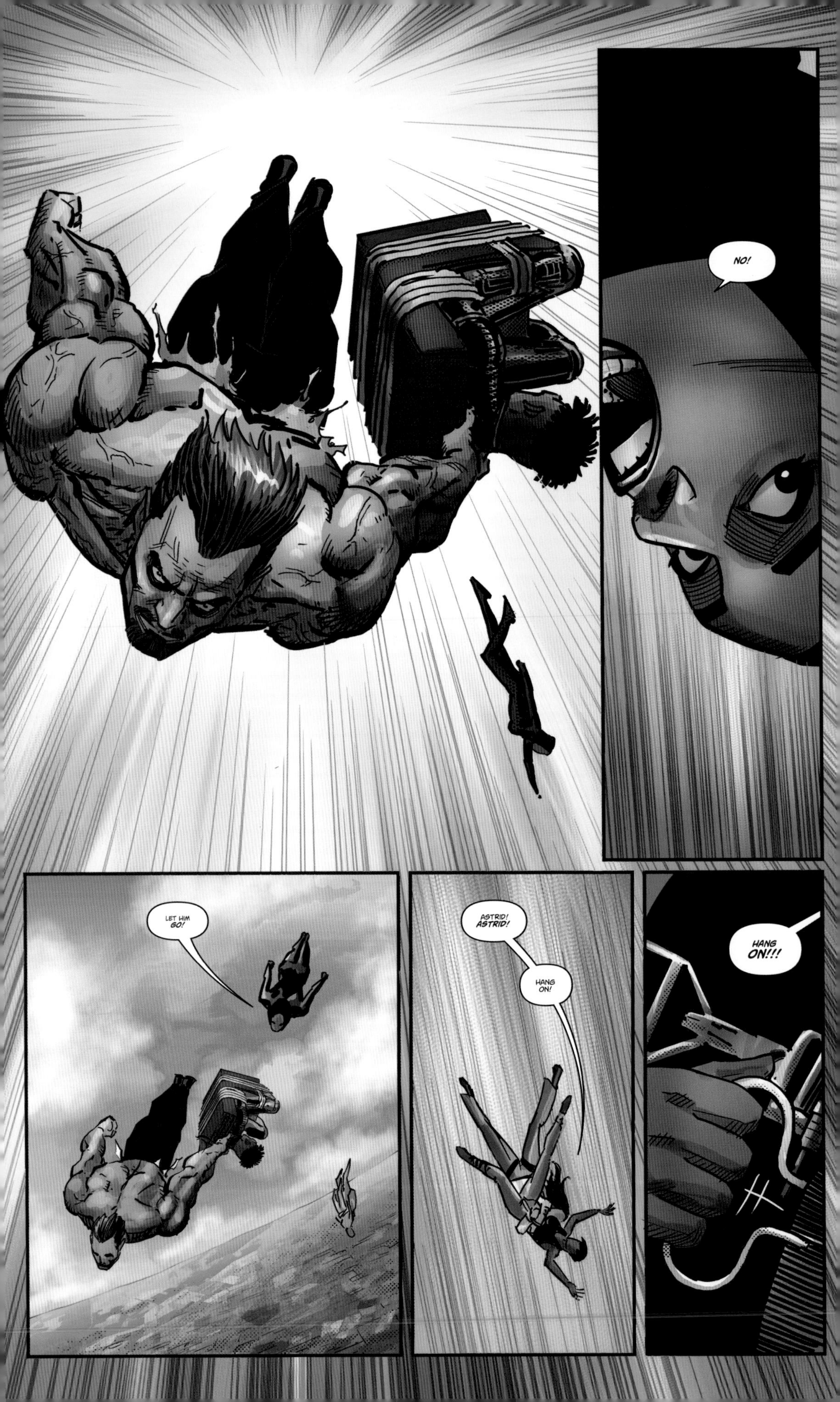
NO!
LET HIM GO!
ASTRID! ASTRID!
HANG ON!
HANG ON!!!

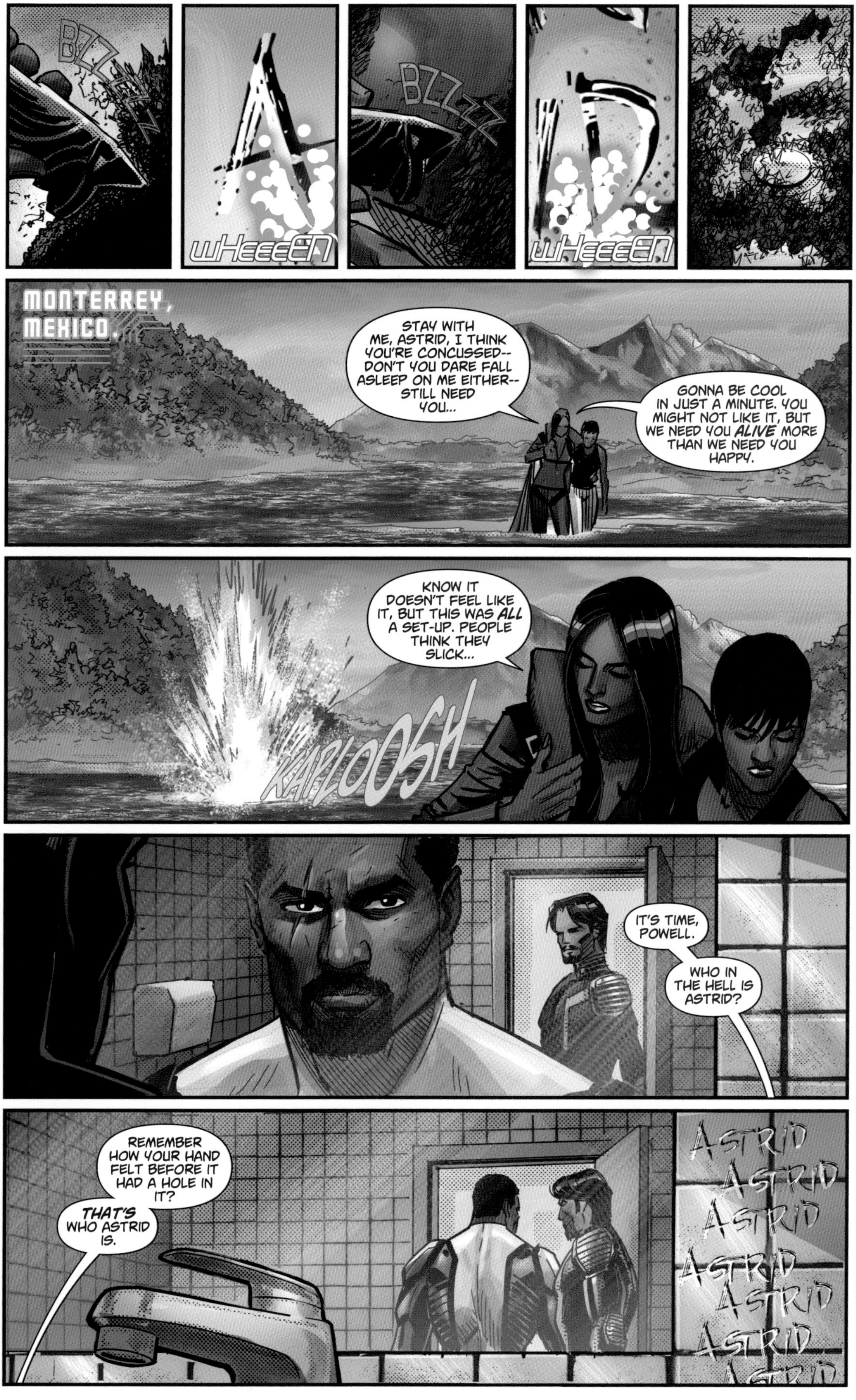
BZZZZZ
wHEEEEEN
BZZZZZ
wHEEEEEN
MONTERREY, MEXICO.
STAY WITH ME, ASTRID, I THINK YOU'RE CONCUSSED-- DON'T YOU DARE FALL ASLEEP ON ME EITHER-- STILL NEED YOU...
GONNA BE COOL IN JUST A MINUTE. YOU MIGHT NOT LIKE IT, BUT WE NEED YOU ALIVE MORE THAN WE NEED YOU HAPPY.
KNOW IT DOESN'T FEEL LIKE IT, BUT THIS WAS ALL A SET-UP. PEOPLE THINK THEY SLICK...
KAPLOOSH
IT'S TIME, POWELL.
WHO IN THE HELL IS ASTRID?
REMEMBER HOW YOUR HAND FELT BEFORE IT HAD A HOLE IN IT?
THAT'S WHO ASTRID IS.
ASTRID ASTRID ASTRID ASTRID ASTRID ASTRID

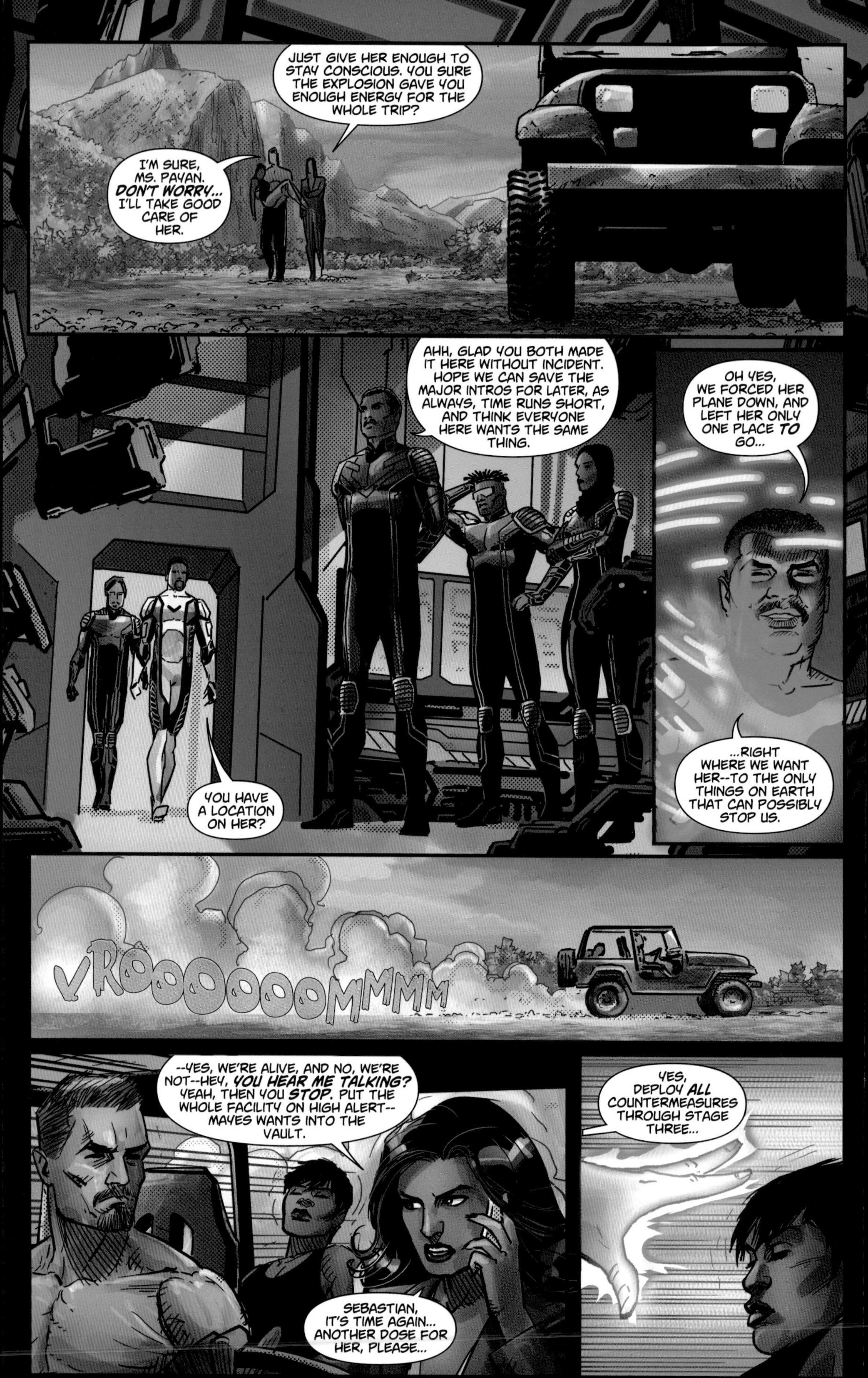
JUST GIVE HER ENOUGH TO STAY CONSCIOUS. YOU SURE THE EXPLOSION GAVE YOU ENOUGH ENERGY FOR THE WHOLE TRIP?
I'M SURE, MS. PAYAN. DON'T WORRY... I'LL TAKE GOOD CARE OF HER.
AHH, GLAD YOU BOTH MADE IT HERE WITHOUT INCIDENT. HOPE WE CAN SAVE THE MAJOR INTROS FOR LATER, AS ALWAYS, TIME RUNS SHORT, AND THINK EVERYONE HERE WANTS THE SAME THING.
YOU HAVE A LOCATION ON HER?
OH YES, WE FORCED HER PLANE DOWN, AND LEFT HER ONLY ONE PLACE TO GO...
...RIGHT WHERE WE WANT HER--TO THE ONLY THINGS ON EARTH THAT CAN POSSIBLY STOP US.
VROOOOOOOMMMMM
--YES, WE'RE ALIVE, AND NO, WE'RE NOT--HEY, YOU HEAR ME TALKING? YEAH, THEN YOU STOP. PUT THE WHOLE FACILITY ON HIGH ALERT-- MAYES WANTS INTO THE VAULT.
SEBASTIAN, IT'S TIME AGAIN... ANOTHER DOSE FOR HER, PLEASE...
YES, DEPLOY ALL COUNTERMEASURES THROUGH STAGE THREE...

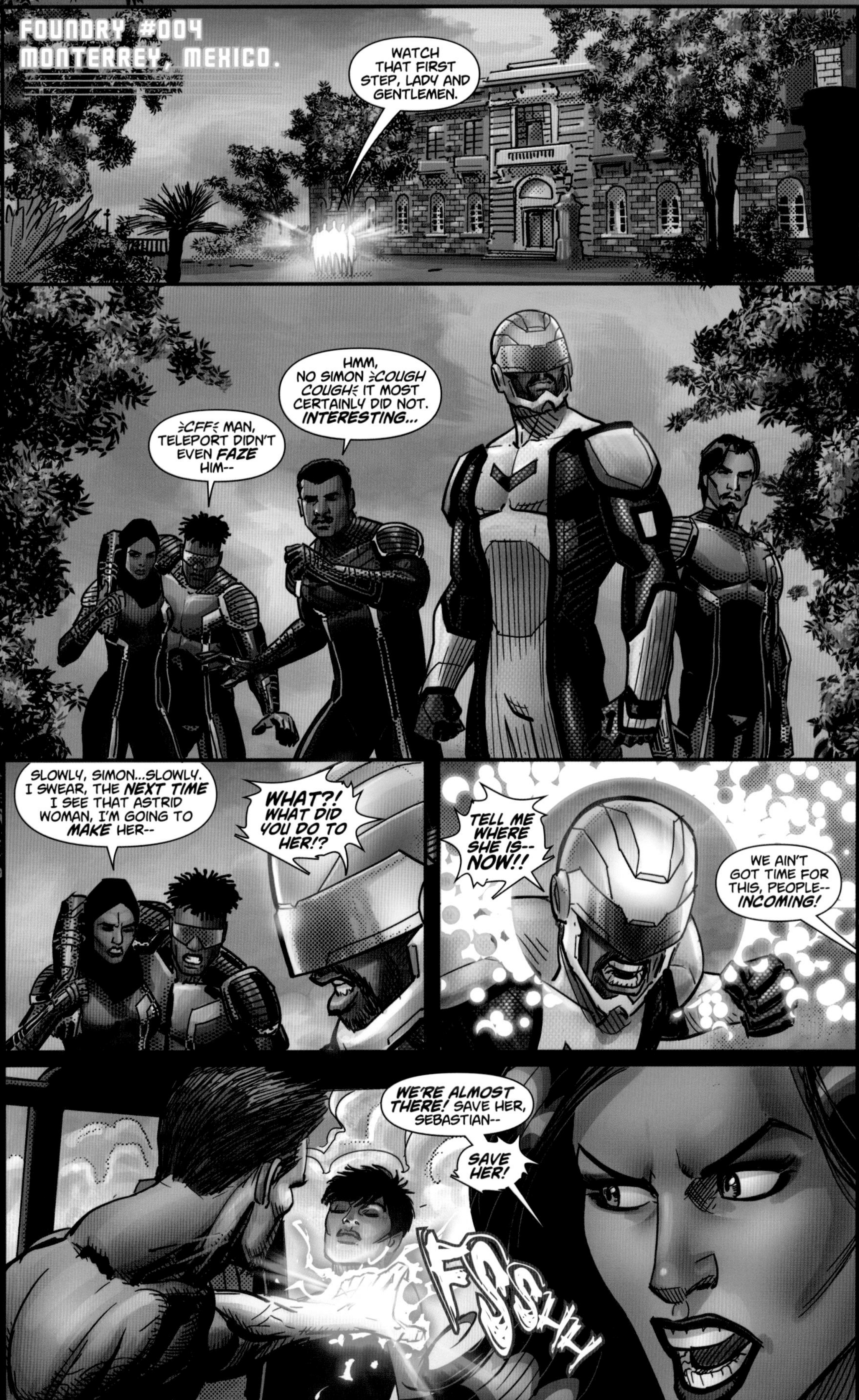
FOUNDRY #004
MONTERREY, MEXICO.
WATCH THAT FIRST STEP, LADY AND GENTLEMEN.
CFF MAN, TELEPORT DIDN'T EVEN FAZE HIM--
HMM, NO SIMON *COUGH COUGH* IT MOST CERTAINLY DID NOT. INTERESTING...
SLOWLY, SIMON...SLOWLY. I SWEAR, THE NEXT TIME I SEE THAT ASTRID WOMAN, I'M GOING TO MAKE HER--
WHAT?! WHAT DID YOU DO TO HER!?
TELL ME WHERE SHE IS-- NOW!!
WE AIN'T GOT TIME FOR THIS, PEOPLE-- INCOMING!
WE'RE ALMOST THERE! SAVE HER, SEBASTIAN--
SAVE HER!
FSSHH

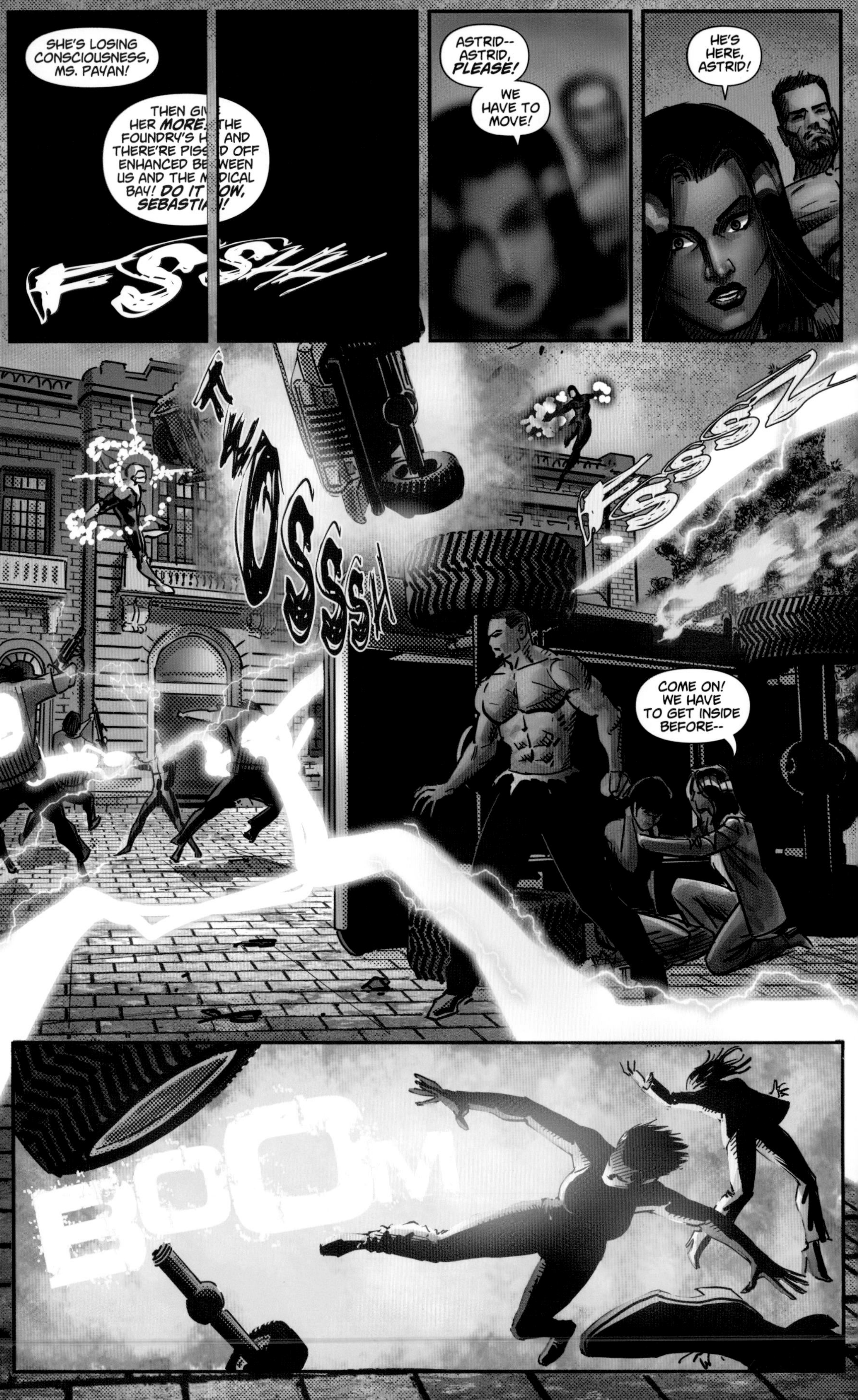
SHE'S LOSING CONSCIOUSNESS, MS. PAYAN!
THEN GIVE HER MORE! THE FOUNDRY'S HIT AND THERE'RE PISSED OFF ENHANCED BETWEEN US AND THE MEDICAL BAY! DO IT NOW, SEBASTIAN!
ASTRID-- ASTRID, PLEASE!
WE HAVE TO MOVE!
HE'S HERE, ASTRID!
FWOOSSSSH
COME ON! WE HAVE TO GET INSIDE BEFORE--
BOOM

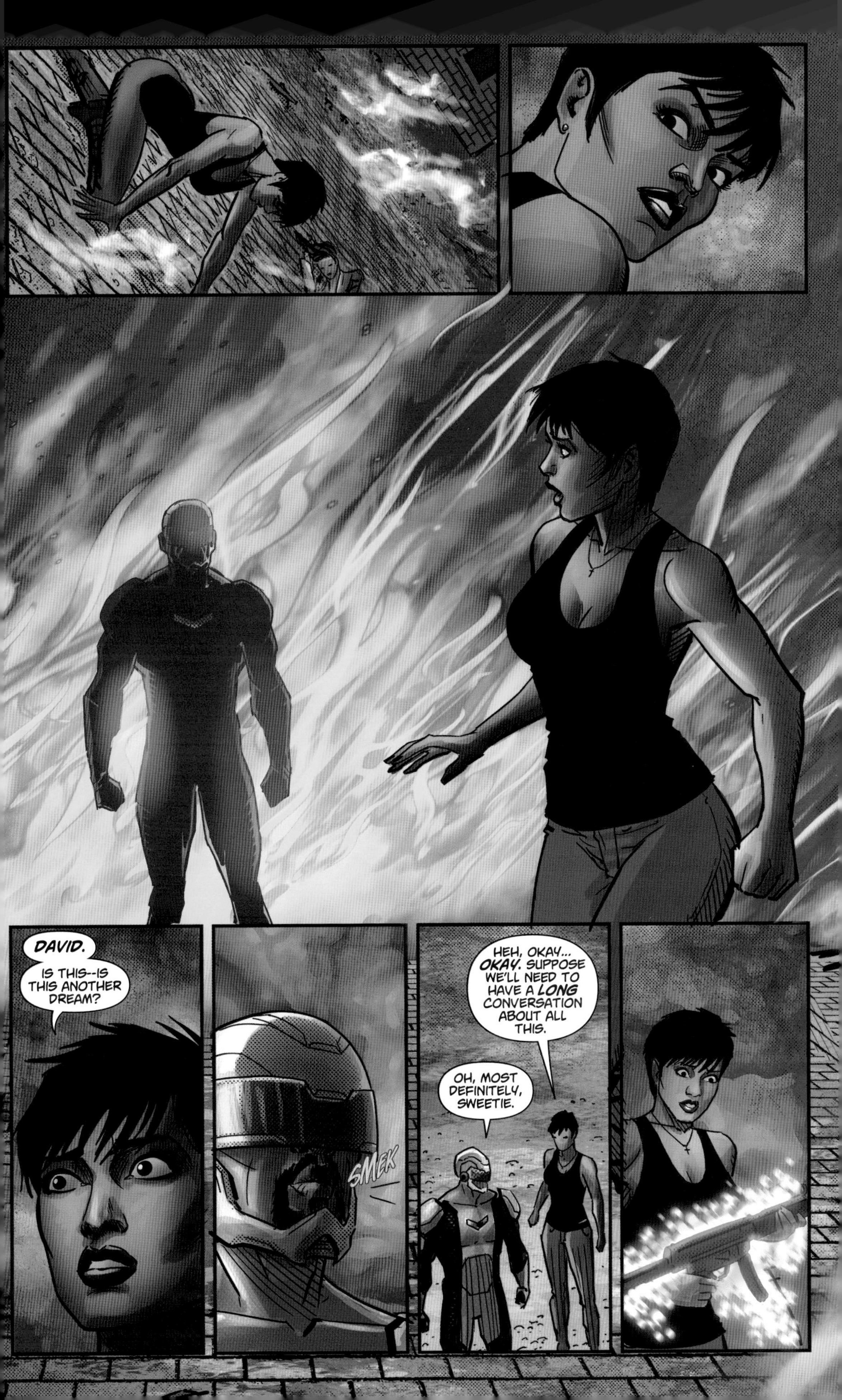

DAVID.
IS THIS--IS THIS ANOTHER DREAM?
SMEK
HEH, OKAY... OKAY. SUPPOSE WE'LL NEED TO HAVE A LONG CONVERSATION ABOUT ALL THIS.
OH, MOST DEFINITELY, SWEETIE.

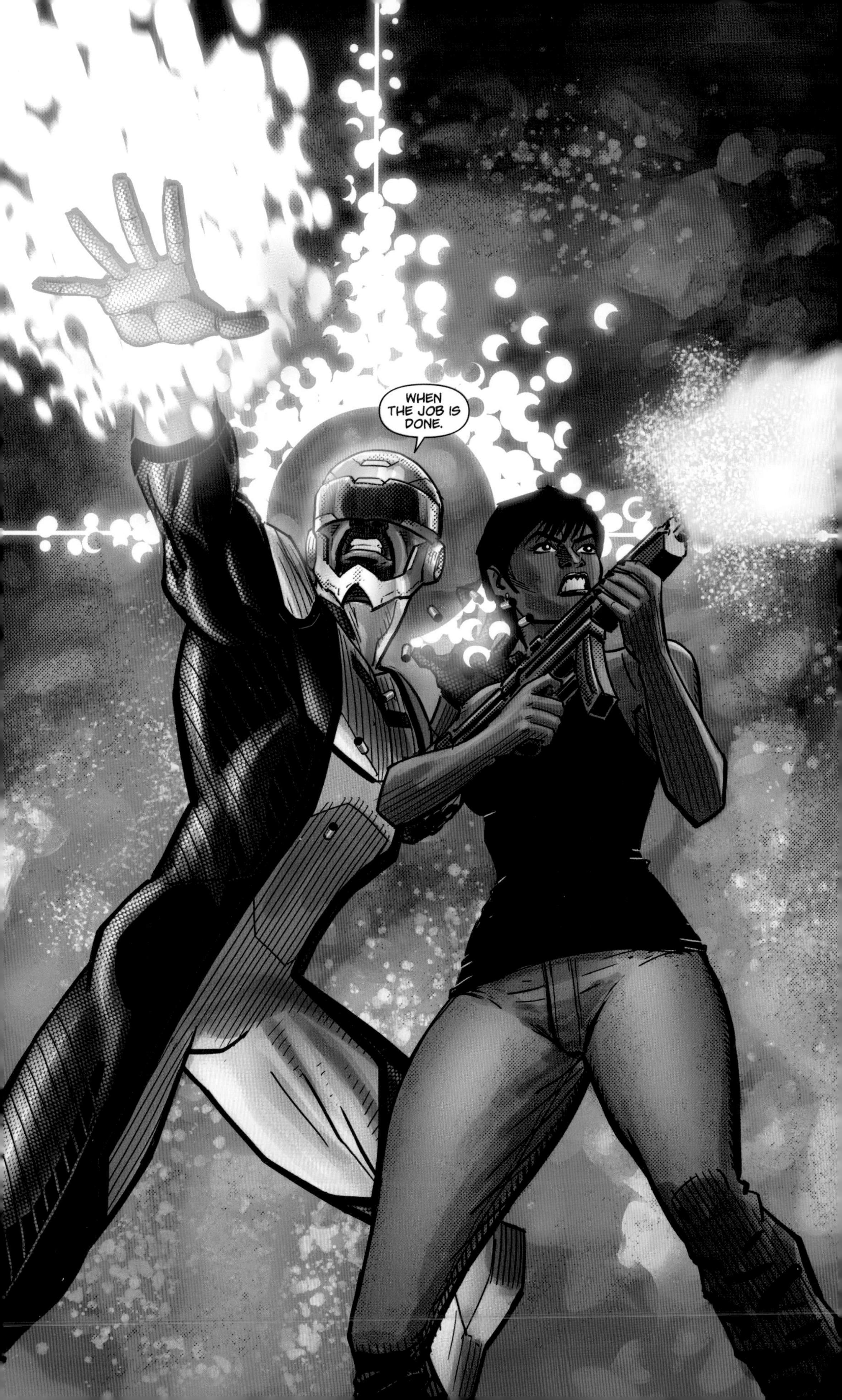
WHEN THE JOB IS DONE.

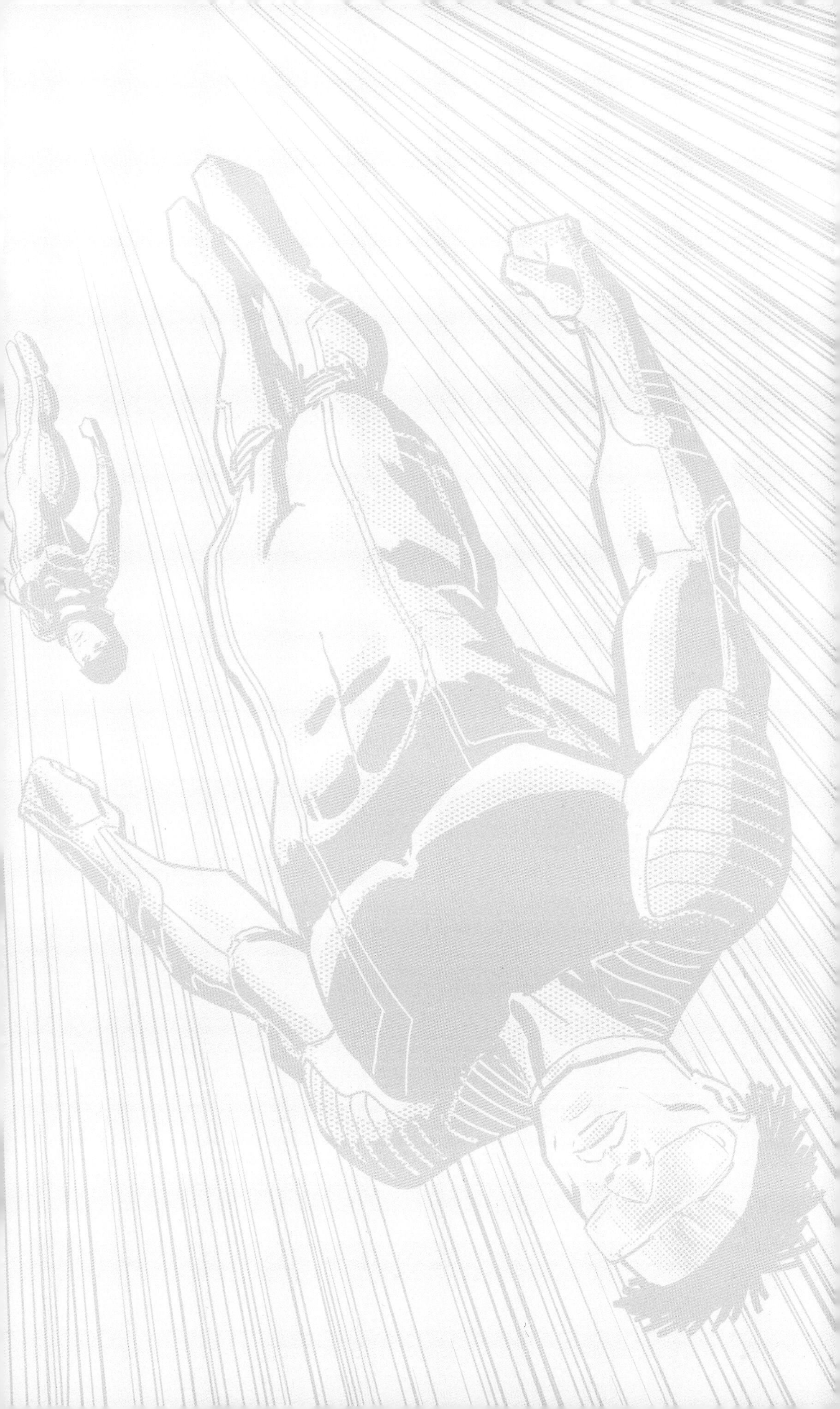

CHAPTER FOUR

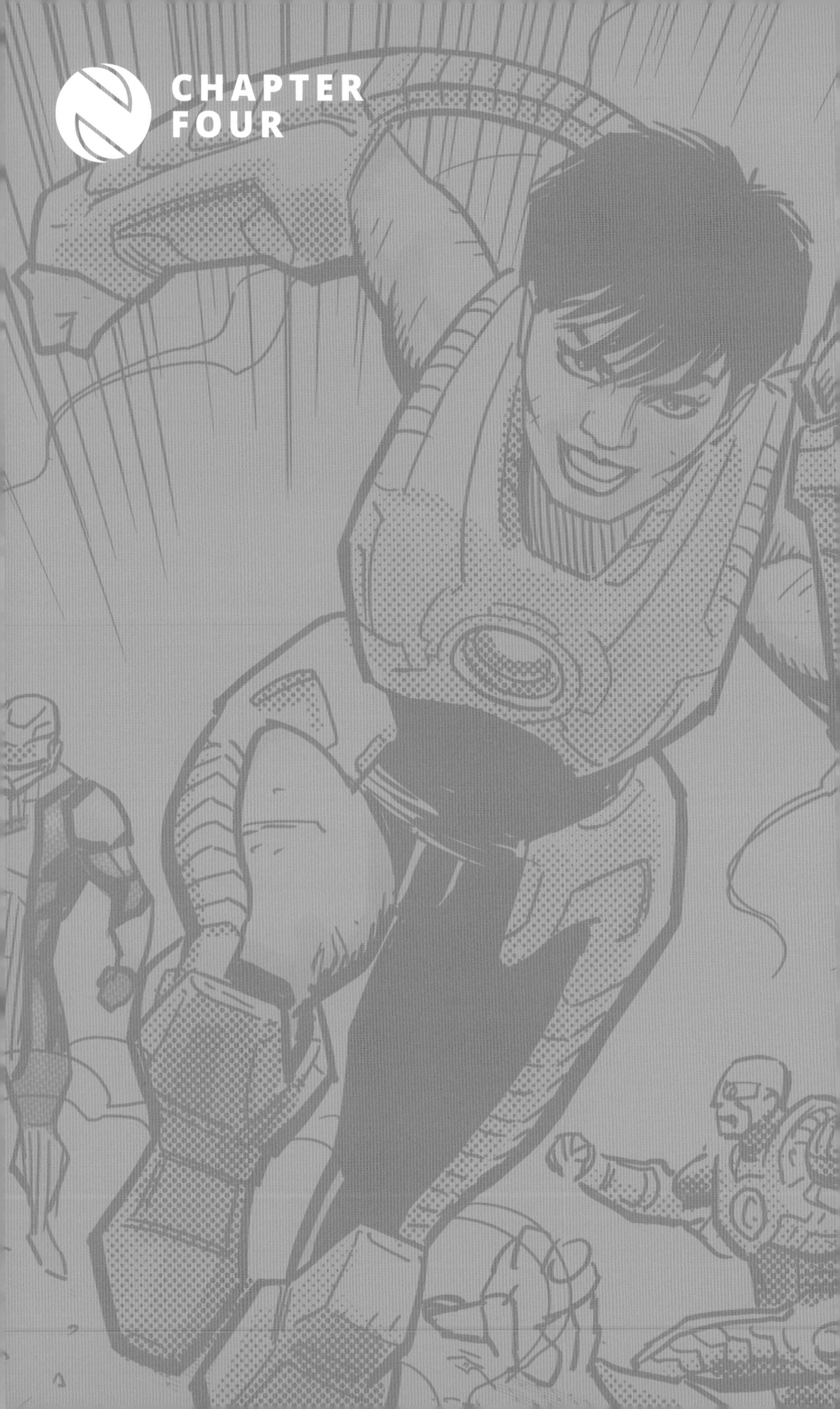

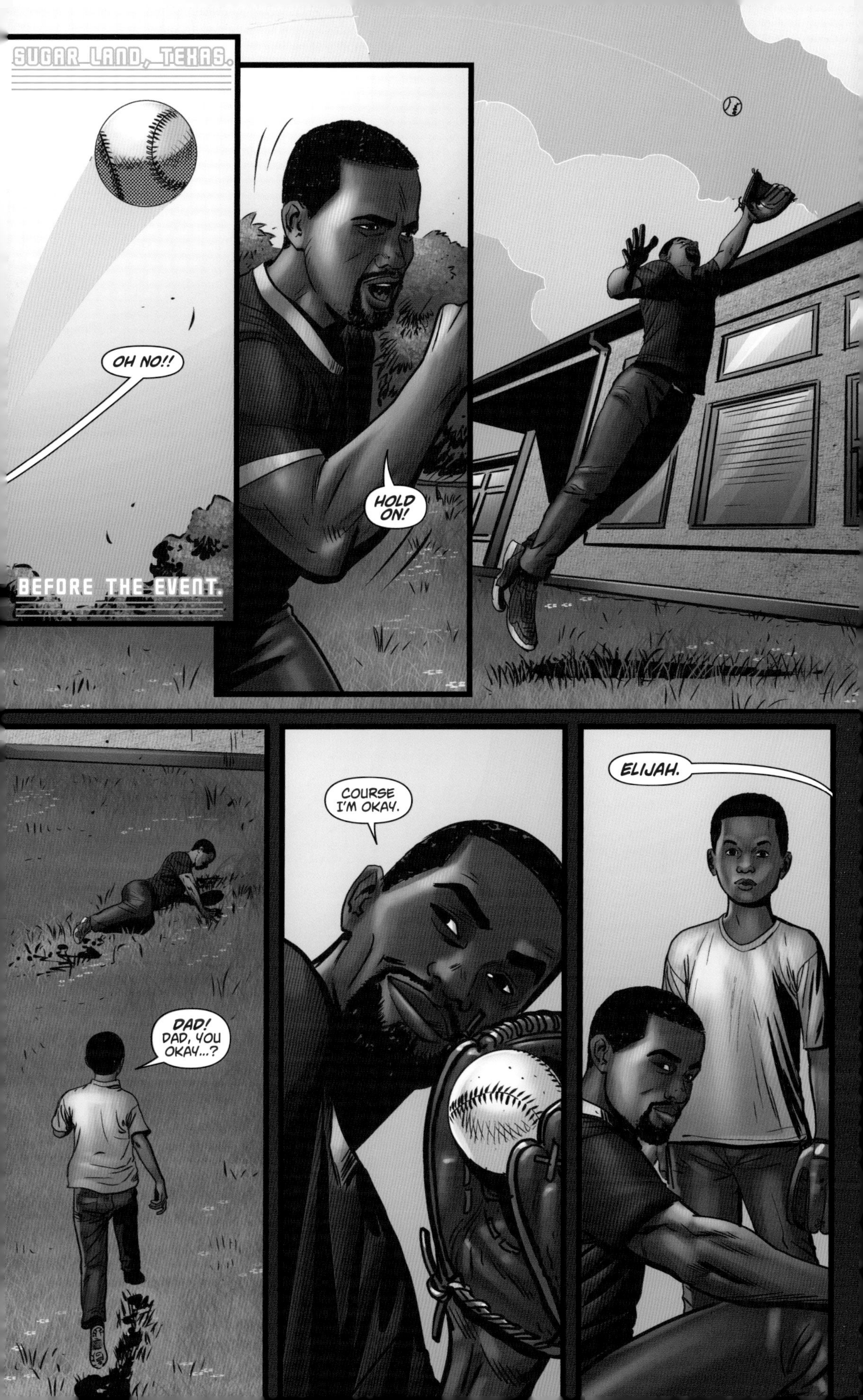
SUGAR LAND, TEXAS.
OH NO!!
BEFORE THE EVENT.
HOLD ON!
DAD! DAD, YOU OKAY...?
COURSE I'M OKAY.
ELIJAH.

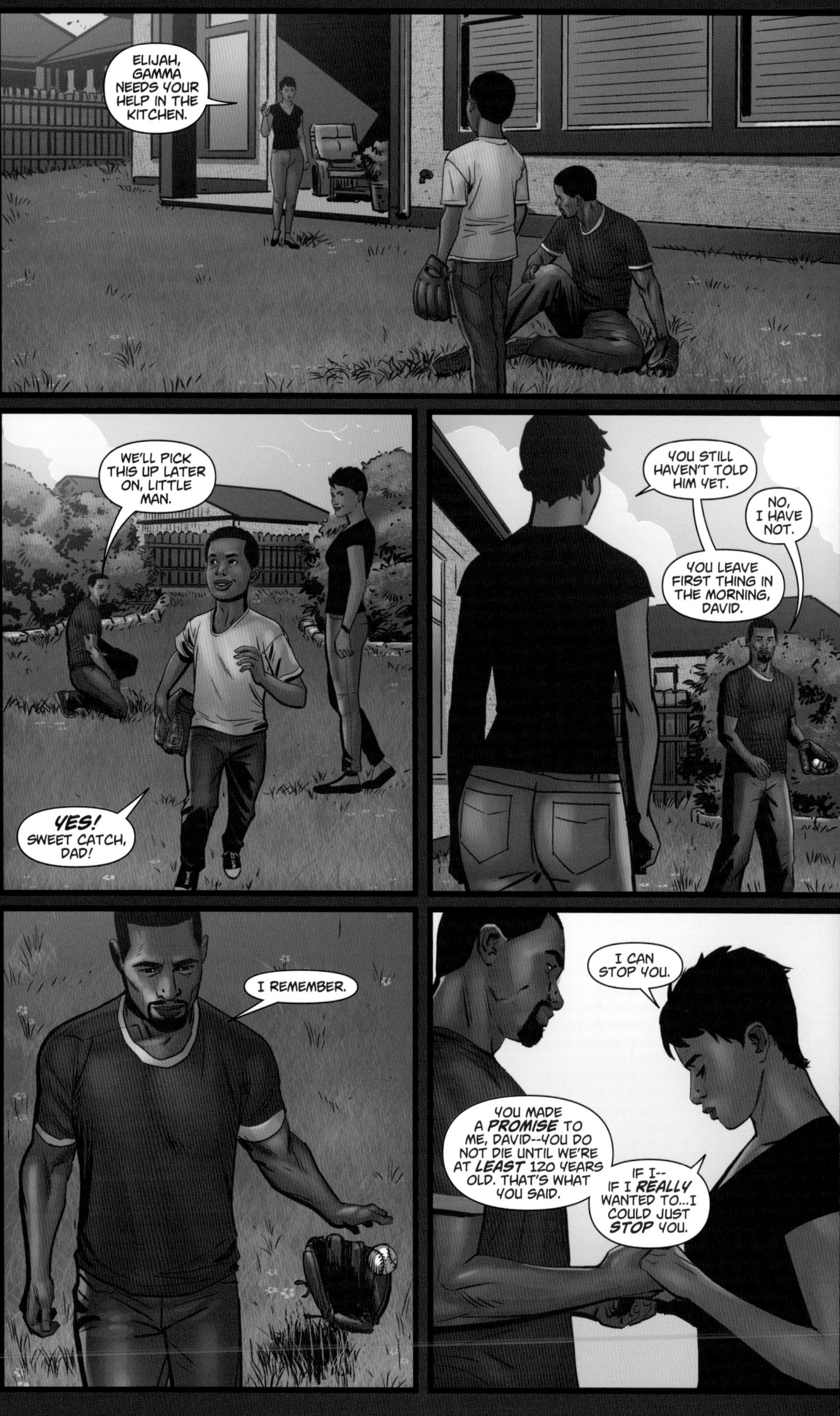
ELIJAH, GAMMA NEEDS YOUR HELP IN THE KITCHEN.
WE'LL PICK THIS UP LATER ON, LITTLE MAN.
YES! SWEET CATCH, DAD!
YOU STILL HAVEN'T TOLD HIM YET.
YOU LEAVE FIRST THING IN THE MORNING, DAVID.
NO, I HAVE NOT.
I REMEMBER.
I CAN STOP YOU.
YOU MADE A PROMISE TO ME, DAVID--YOU DO NOT DIE UNTIL WE'RE AT LEAST 120 YEARS OLD. THAT'S WHAT YOU SAID.
IF I-- IF I REALLY WANTED TO...I COULD JUST STOP YOU.

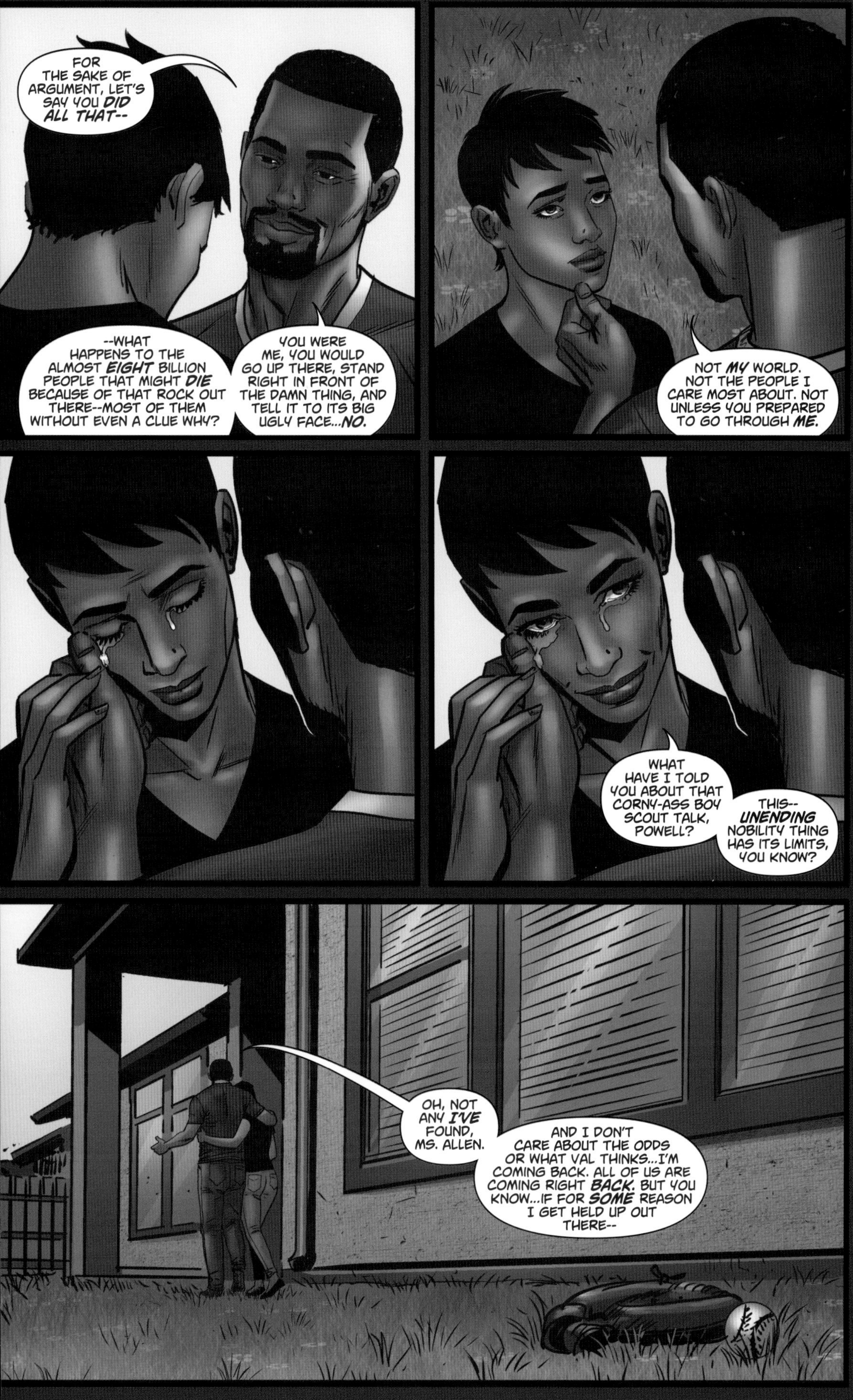
FOR THE SAKE OF ARGUMENT, LET'S SAY YOU DID ALL THAT--
--WHAT HAPPENS TO THE ALMOST EIGHT BILLION PEOPLE THAT MIGHT DIE BECAUSE OF THAT ROCK OUT THERE--MOST OF THEM WITHOUT EVEN A CLUE WHY?
YOU WERE ME, YOU WOULD GO UP THERE, STAND RIGHT IN FRONT OF THE DAMN THING, AND TELL IT TO ITS BIG UGLY FACE...NO.
NOT MY WORLD. NOT THE PEOPLE I CARE MOST ABOUT. NOT UNLESS YOU PREPARED TO GO THROUGH ME.
WHAT HAVE I TOLD YOU ABOUT THAT CORNY-ASS BOY SCOUT TALK, POWELL?
THIS-- UNENDING NOBILITY THING HAS ITS LIMITS, YOU KNOW?
OH, NOT ANY I'VE FOUND, MS. ALLEN.
AND I DON'T CARE ABOUT THE ODDS OR WHAT VAL THINKS...I'M COMING BACK. ALL OF US ARE COMING RIGHT BACK. BUT YOU KNOW...IF FOR SOME REASON I GET HELD UP OUT THERE--

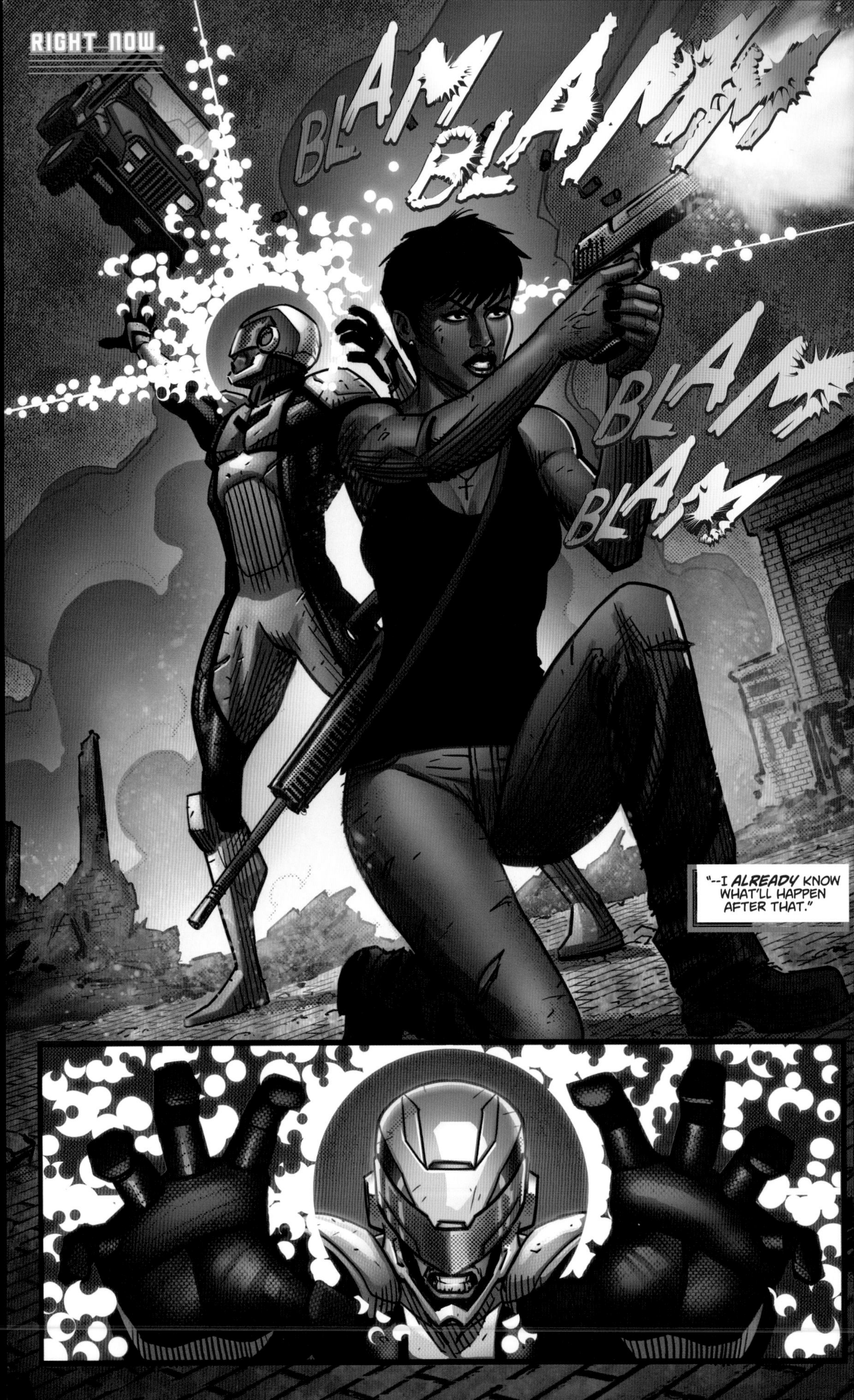
RIGHT NOW.
BLAM
BLAM
BLAM
BLAM
"--I ALREADY KNOW WHAT'LL HAPPEN AFTER THAT."

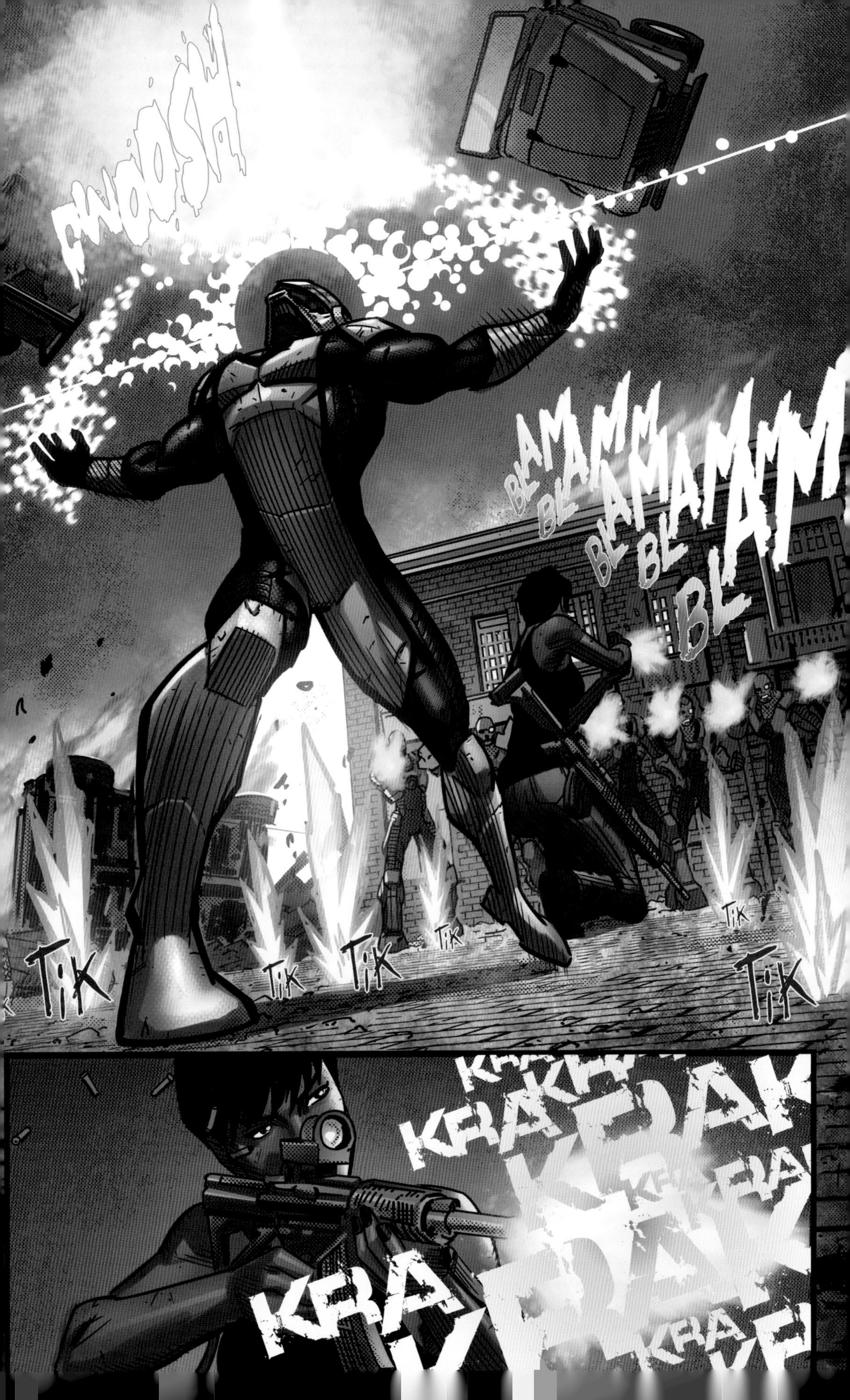

FWOOSH
BLAMM
BLAMM
BLAMM
BLAM
TIK
TIK
TIK
TIK
TIK
TIK
KRAKAK
KRAK

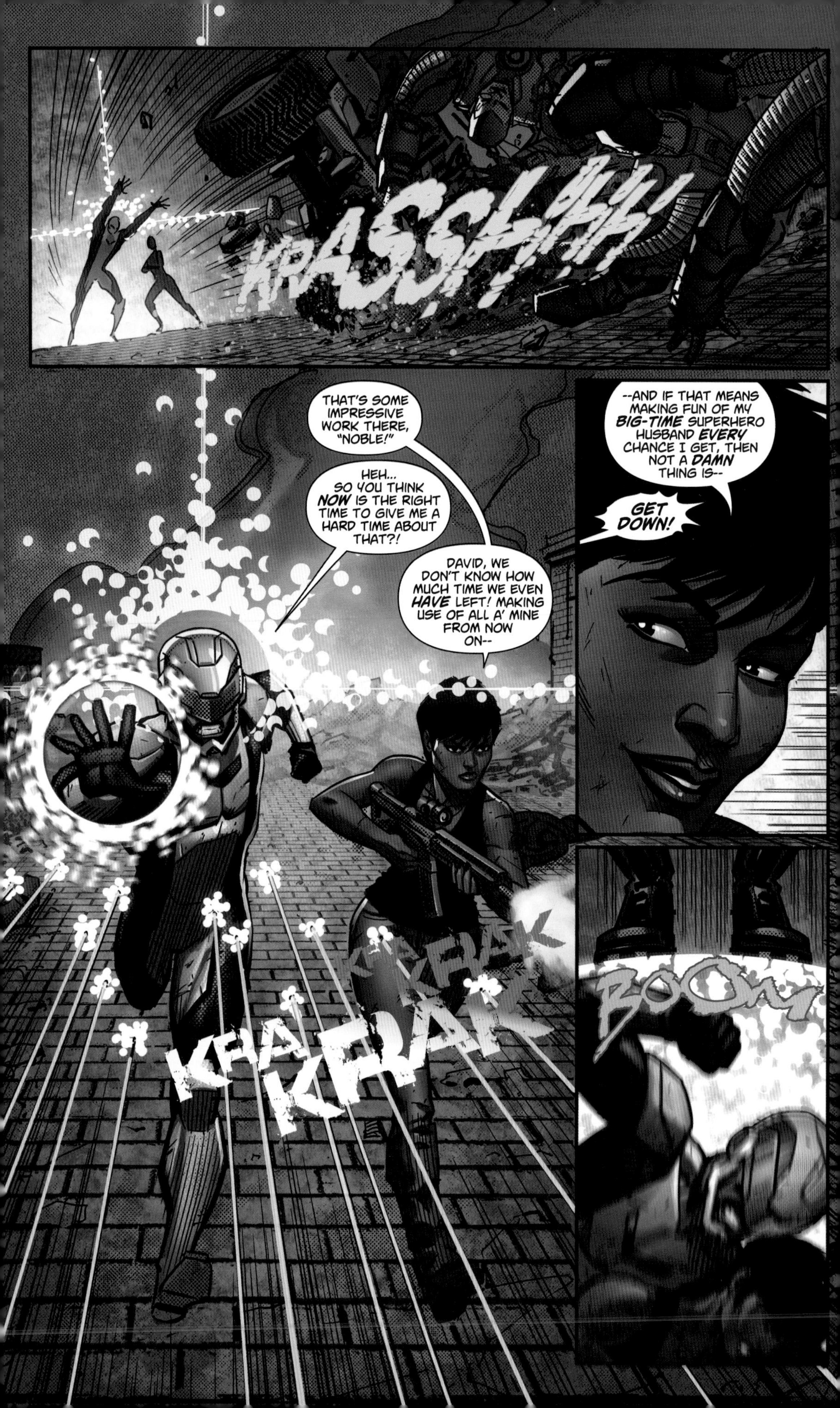
KRASSHHH
THAT'S SOME IMPRESSIVE WORK THERE, "NOBLE!"
HEH... SO YOU THINK NOW IS THE RIGHT TIME TO GIVE ME A HARD TIME ABOUT THAT?!
DAVID, WE DON'T KNOW HOW MUCH TIME WE EVEN HAVE LEFT! MAKING USE OF ALL A' MINE FROM NOW ON--
KRAK KRAK
KRAK KRAK
--AND IF THAT MEANS MAKING FUN OF MY BIG-TIME SUPERHERO HUSBAND EVERY CHANCE I GET, THEN NOT A DAMN THING IS--
GET DOWN!
BOOM

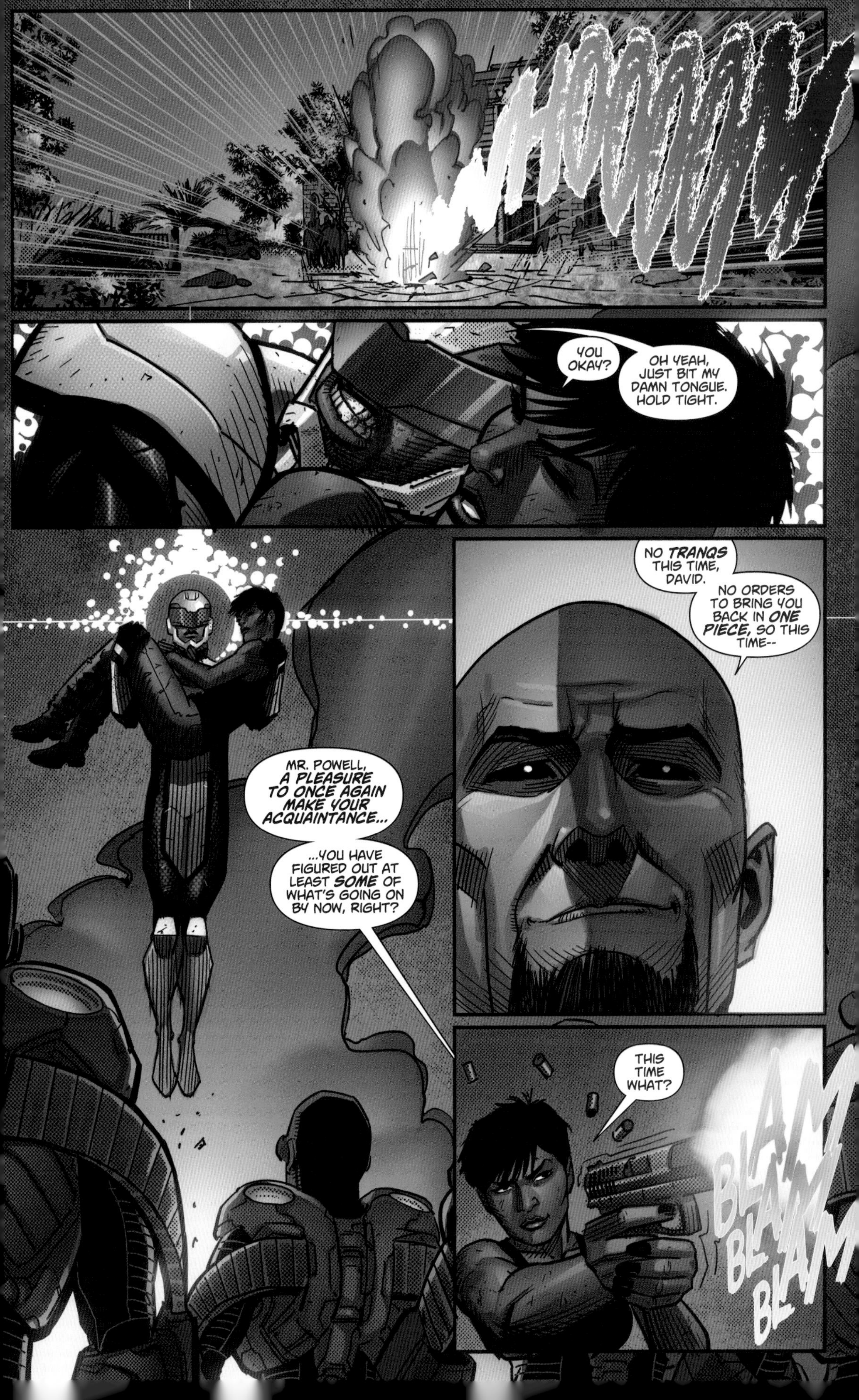

WHOOOOM
YOU OKAY?
OH YEAH, JUST BIT MY DAMN TONGUE. HOLD TIGHT.
MR. POWELL, A PLEASURE TO ONCE AGAIN MAKE YOUR ACQUAINTANCE...
...YOU HAVE FIGURED OUT AT LEAST SOME OF WHAT'S GOING ON BY NOW, RIGHT?
NO TRANQS THIS TIME, DAVID.
NO ORDERS TO BRING YOU BACK IN ONE PIECE, SO THIS TIME--
THIS TIME WHAT?
BLAM BLAM BLAM BLAM

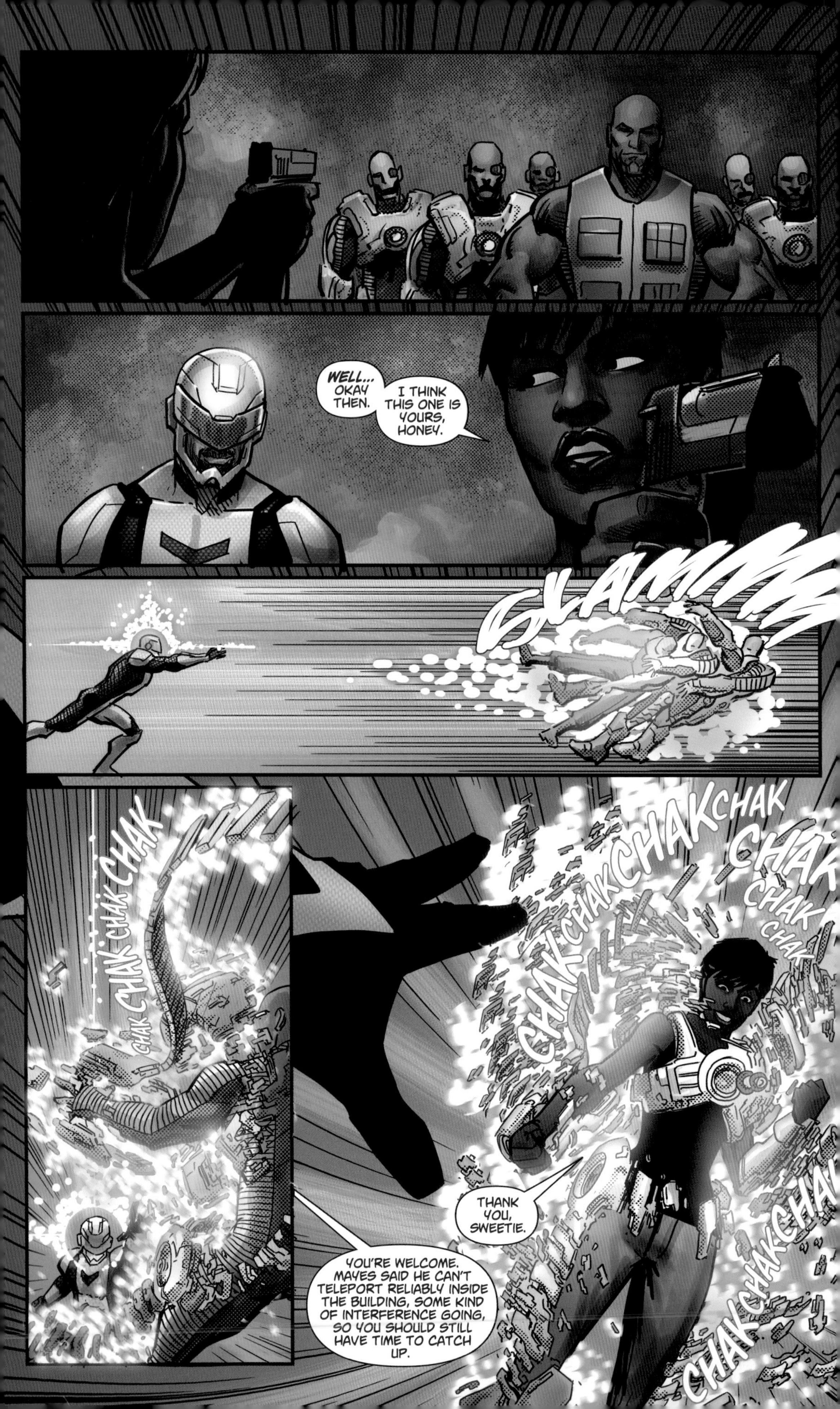
WELL... OKAY THEN.
I THINK THIS ONE IS YOURS, HONEY.
SLAMMM
CHAK CHAK CHAK CHAK CHAK
CHAK CHAK CHAK CHAK CHAK CHAK CHAK CHAK
THANK YOU, SWEETIE.
YOU'RE WELCOME. MAYES SAID HE CAN'T TELEPORT RELIABLY INSIDE THE BUILDING, SOME KIND OF INTERFERENCE GOING, SO YOU SHOULD STILL HAVE TIME TO CATCH UP.
CHAKCHAKCHAK

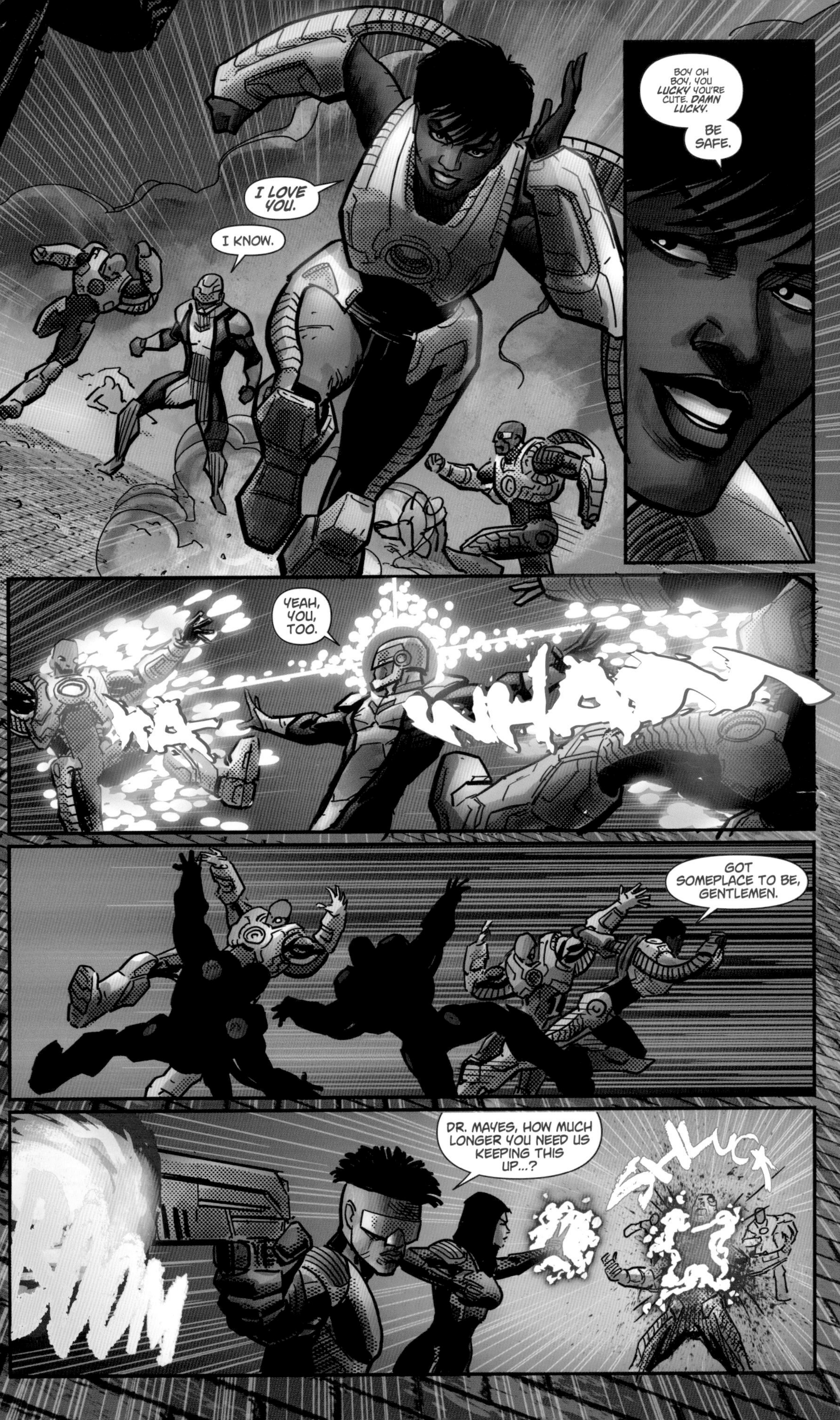
I LOVE YOU.
I KNOW.
BOY OH BOY, YOU LUCKY YOU'RE CUTE. DAMN LUCKY.
BE SAFE.
YEAH, YOU, TOO.
THA
WHAT
GOT SOMEPLACE TO BE, GENTLEMEN.
DR. MAYES, HOW MUCH LONGER YOU NEED US KEEPING THIS UP...?
SHUCK
BUUM

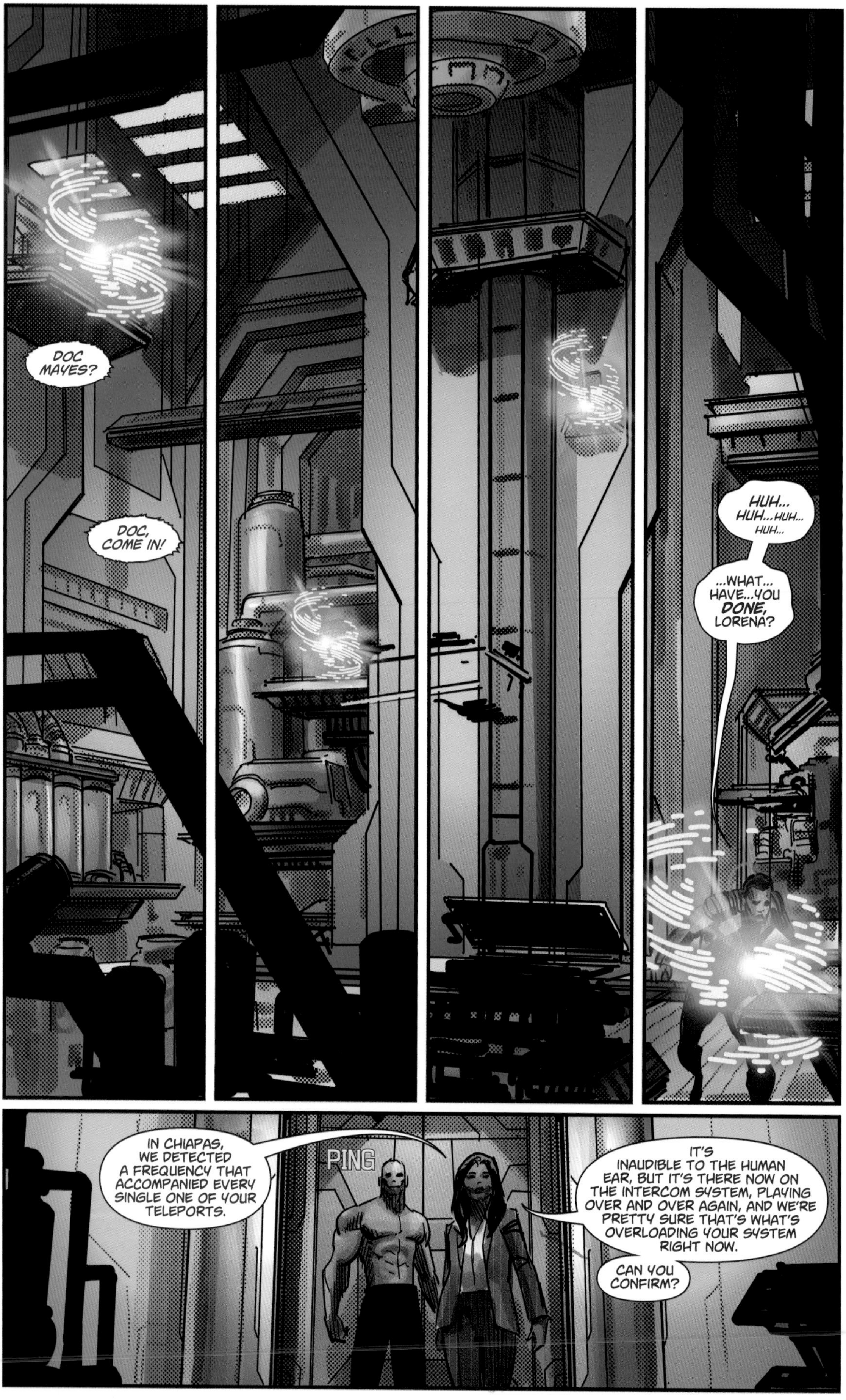
DOC MAYES?
DOC, COME IN!
HUH... HUH...HUH... HUH...
...WHAT... HAVE...YOU DONE, LORENA?
IN CHIAPAS, WE DETECTED A FREQUENCY THAT ACCOMPANIED EVERY SINGLE ONE OF YOUR TELEPORTS.
PING
IT'S INAUDIBLE TO THE HUMAN EAR, BUT IT'S THERE NOW ON THE INTERCOM SYSTEM, PLAYING OVER AND OVER AGAIN, AND WE'RE PRETTY SURE THAT'S WHAT'S OVERLOADING YOUR SYSTEM RIGHT NOW.
CAN YOU CONFIRM?

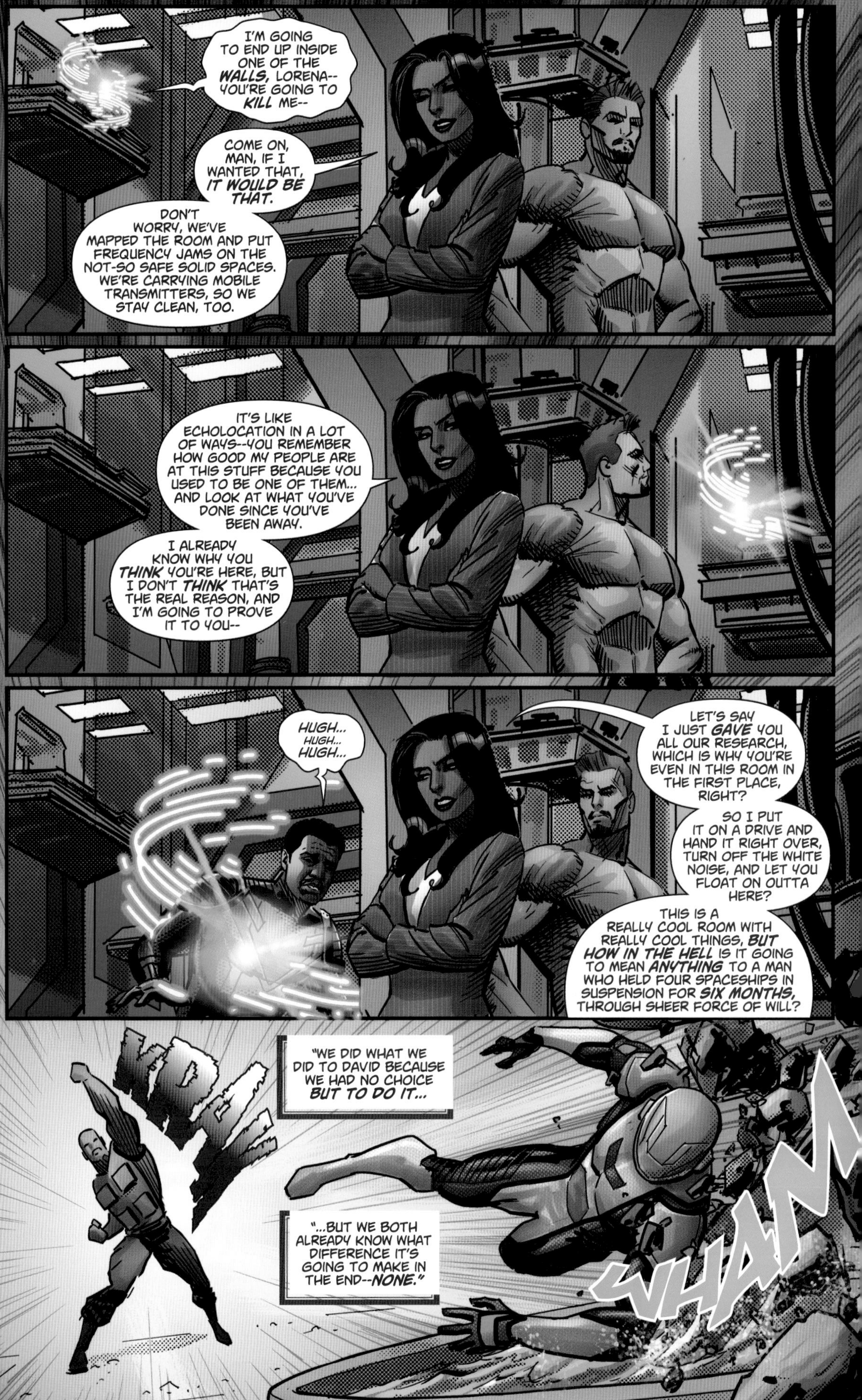
I'M GOING TO END UP INSIDE ONE OF THE WALLS, LORENA-- YOU'RE GOING TO KILL ME--
COME ON, MAN, IF I WANTED THAT, IT WOULD BE THAT.
DON'T WORRY, WE'VE MAPPED THE ROOM AND PUT FREQUENCY JAMS ON THE NOT-SO SAFE SOLID SPACES. WE'RE CARRYING MOBILE TRANSMITTERS, SO WE STAY CLEAN, TOO.
IT'S LIKE ECHOLOCATION IN A LOT OF WAYS--YOU REMEMBER HOW GOOD MY PEOPLE ARE AT THIS STUFF BECAUSE YOU USED TO BE ONE OF THEM... AND LOOK AT WHAT YOU'VE DONE SINCE YOU'VE BEEN AWAY.
I ALREADY KNOW WHY YOU THINK YOU'RE HERE, BUT I DON'T THINK THAT'S THE REAL REASON, AND I'M GOING TO PROVE IT TO YOU--
HUGH... HUGH... HUGH...
LET'S SAY I JUST GAVE YOU ALL OUR RESEARCH, WHICH IS WHY YOU'RE EVEN IN THIS ROOM IN THE FIRST PLACE, RIGHT?
SO I PUT IT ON A DRIVE AND HAND IT RIGHT OVER, TURN OFF THE WHITE NOISE, AND LET YOU FLOAT ON OUTTA HERE?
THIS IS A REALLY COOL ROOM WITH REALLY COOL THINGS, BUT HOW IN THE HELL IS IT GOING TO MEAN ANYTHING TO A MAN WHO HELD FOUR SPACESHIPS IN SUSPENSION FOR SIX MONTHS, THROUGH SHEER FORCE OF WILL?
"WE DID WHAT WE DID TO DAVID BECAUSE WE HAD NO CHOICE BUT TO DO IT...
"...BUT WE BOTH ALREADY KNOW WHAT DIFFERENCE IT'S GOING TO MAKE IN THE END--NONE."
WHAM

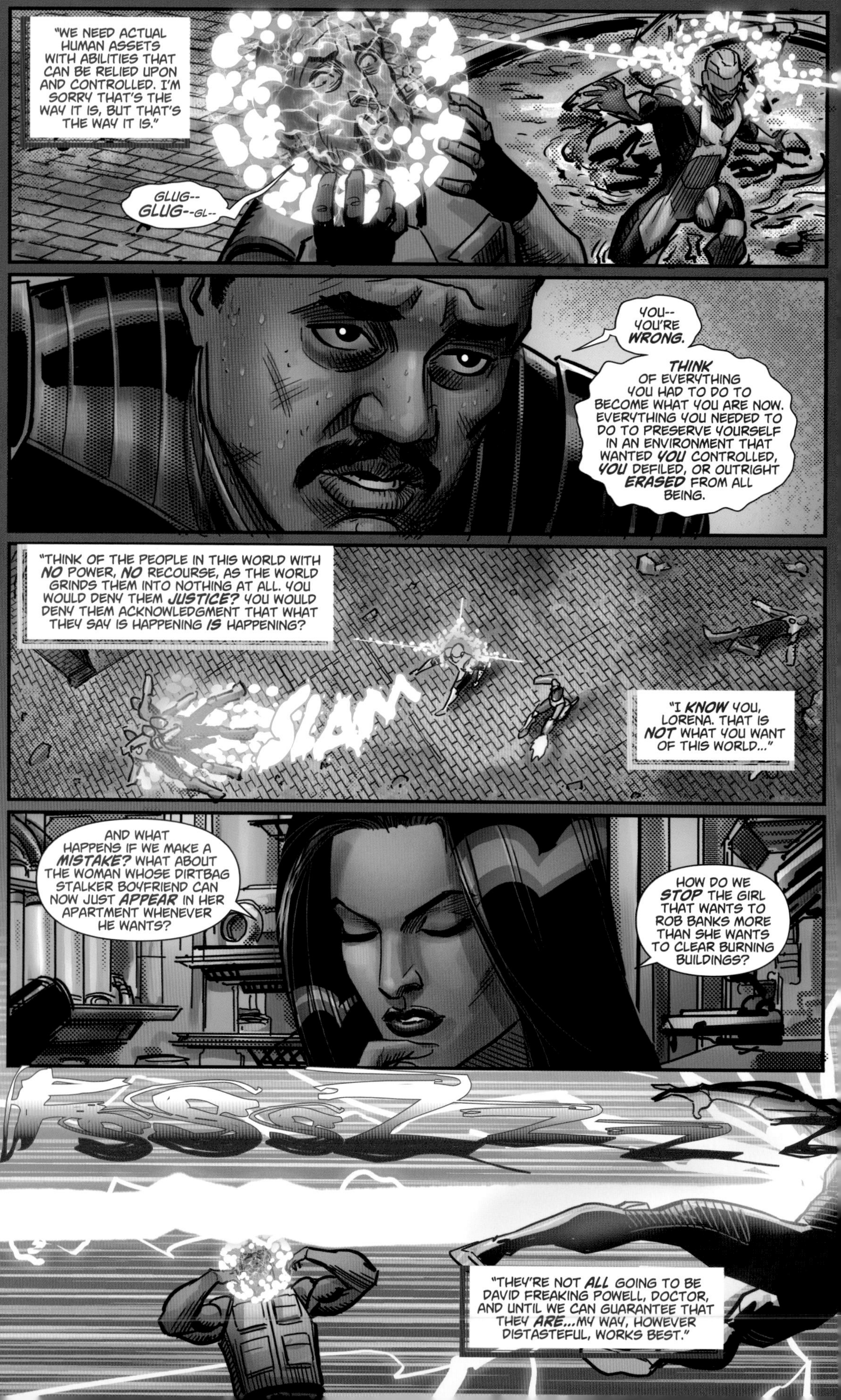
"WE NEED ACTUAL HUMAN ASSETS WITH ABILITIES THAT CAN BE RELIED UPON AND CONTROLLED. I'M SORRY THAT'S THE WAY IT IS, BUT THAT'S THE WAY IT IS."
GLUG-- GLUG--GL--
YOU-- YOU'RE WRONG.
THINK OF EVERYTHING YOU HAD TO DO TO BECOME WHAT YOU ARE NOW. EVERYTHING YOU NEEDED TO DO TO PRESERVE YOURSELF IN AN ENVIRONMENT THAT WANTED YOU CONTROLLED, YOU DEFILED, OR OUTRIGHT ERASED FROM ALL BEING.
"THINK OF THE PEOPLE IN THIS WORLD WITH NO POWER, NO RECOURSE, AS THE WORLD GRINDS THEM INTO NOTHING AT ALL. YOU WOULD DENY THEM JUSTICE? YOU WOULD DENY THEM ACKNOWLEDGMENT THAT WHAT THEY SAY IS HAPPENING IS HAPPENING?
SLAM
"I KNOW YOU, LORENA. THAT IS NOT WHAT YOU WANT OF THIS WORLD..."
AND WHAT HAPPENS IF WE MAKE A MISTAKE? WHAT ABOUT THE WOMAN WHOSE DIRTBAG STALKER BOYFRIEND CAN NOW JUST APPEAR IN HER APARTMENT WHENEVER HE WANTS?
HOW DO WE STOP THE GIRL THAT WANTS TO ROB BANKS MORE THAN SHE WANTS TO CLEAR BURNING BUILDINGS?
FSSZ
"THEY'RE NOT ALL GOING TO BE DAVID FREAKING POWELL, DOCTOR, AND UNTIL WE CAN GUARANTEE THAT THEY ARE...MY WAY, HOWEVER DISTASTEFUL, WORKS BEST."

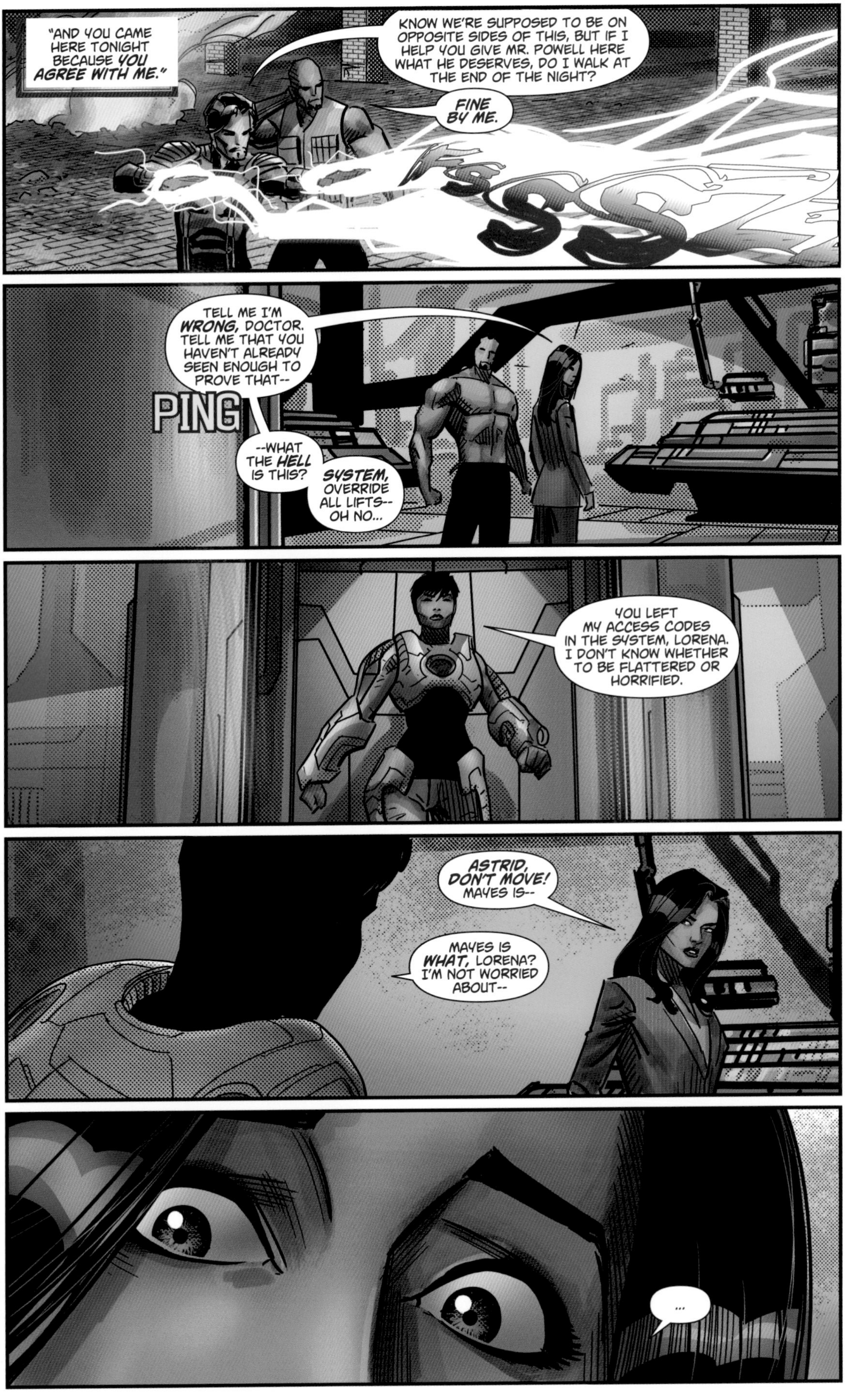
"AND YOU CAME HERE TONIGHT BECAUSE YOU AGREE WITH ME."
KNOW WE'RE SUPPOSED TO BE ON OPPOSITE SIDES OF THIS, BUT IF I HELP YOU GIVE MR. POWELL HERE WHAT HE DESERVES, DO I WALK AT THE END OF THE NIGHT?
FINE BY ME.
FSSSS
TELL ME I'M WRONG, DOCTOR. TELL ME THAT YOU HAVEN'T ALREADY SEEN ENOUGH TO PROVE THAT--
PING
--WHAT THE HELL IS THIS?
SYSTEM, OVERRIDE ALL LIFTS-- OH NO...
YOU LEFT MY ACCESS CODES IN THE SYSTEM, LORENA. I DON'T KNOW WHETHER TO BE FLATTERED OR HORRIFIED.
ASTRID, DON'T MOVE! MAYES IS--
MAYES IS WHAT, LORENA? I'M NOT WORRIED ABOUT--
...

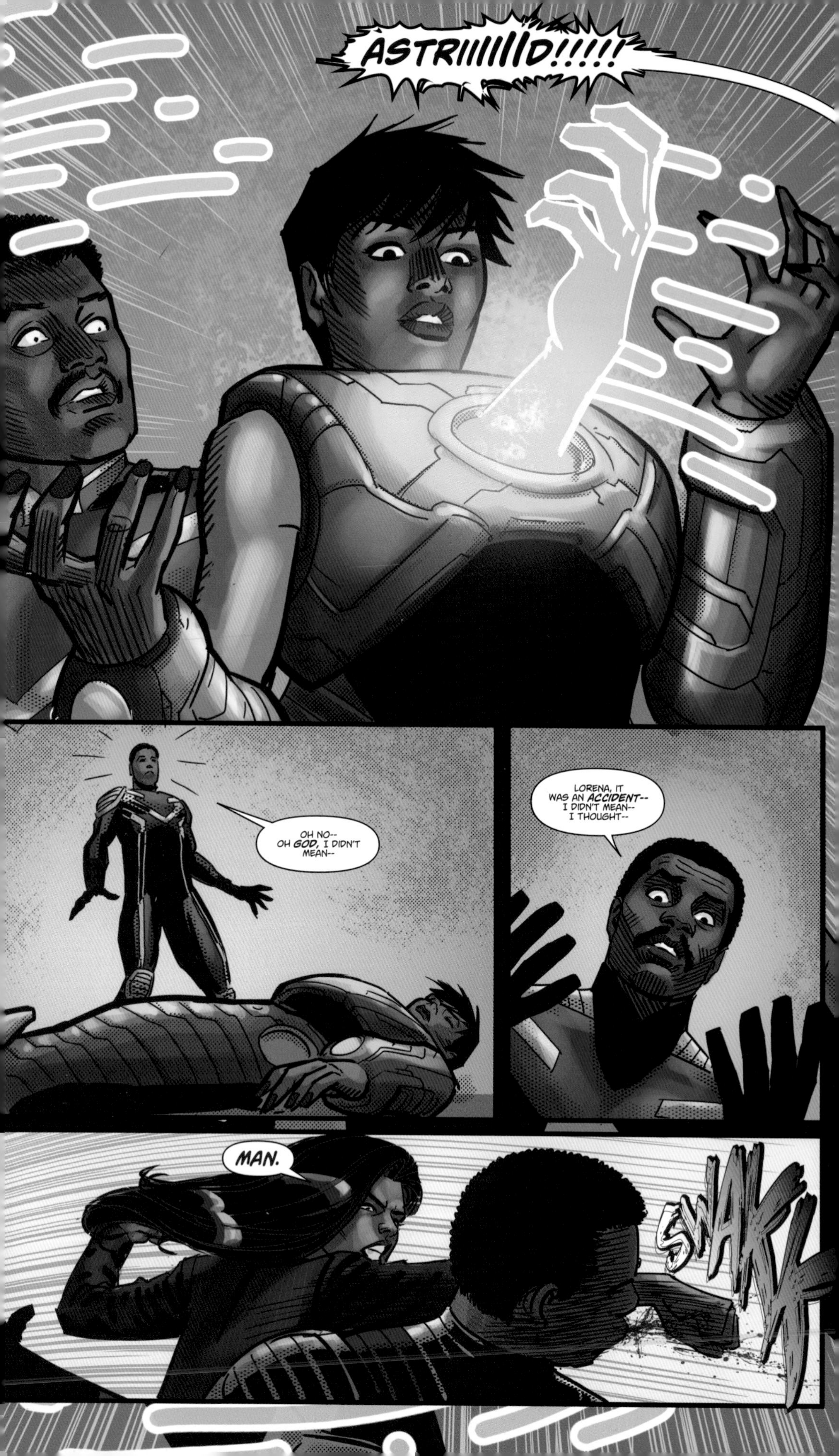
ASTRIIIIIIID!!!!!
OH NO-- OH GOD, I DIDN'T MEAN--
LORENA, IT WAS AN ACCIDENT-- I DIDN'T MEAN-- I THOUGHT--
MAN.
SWAKK

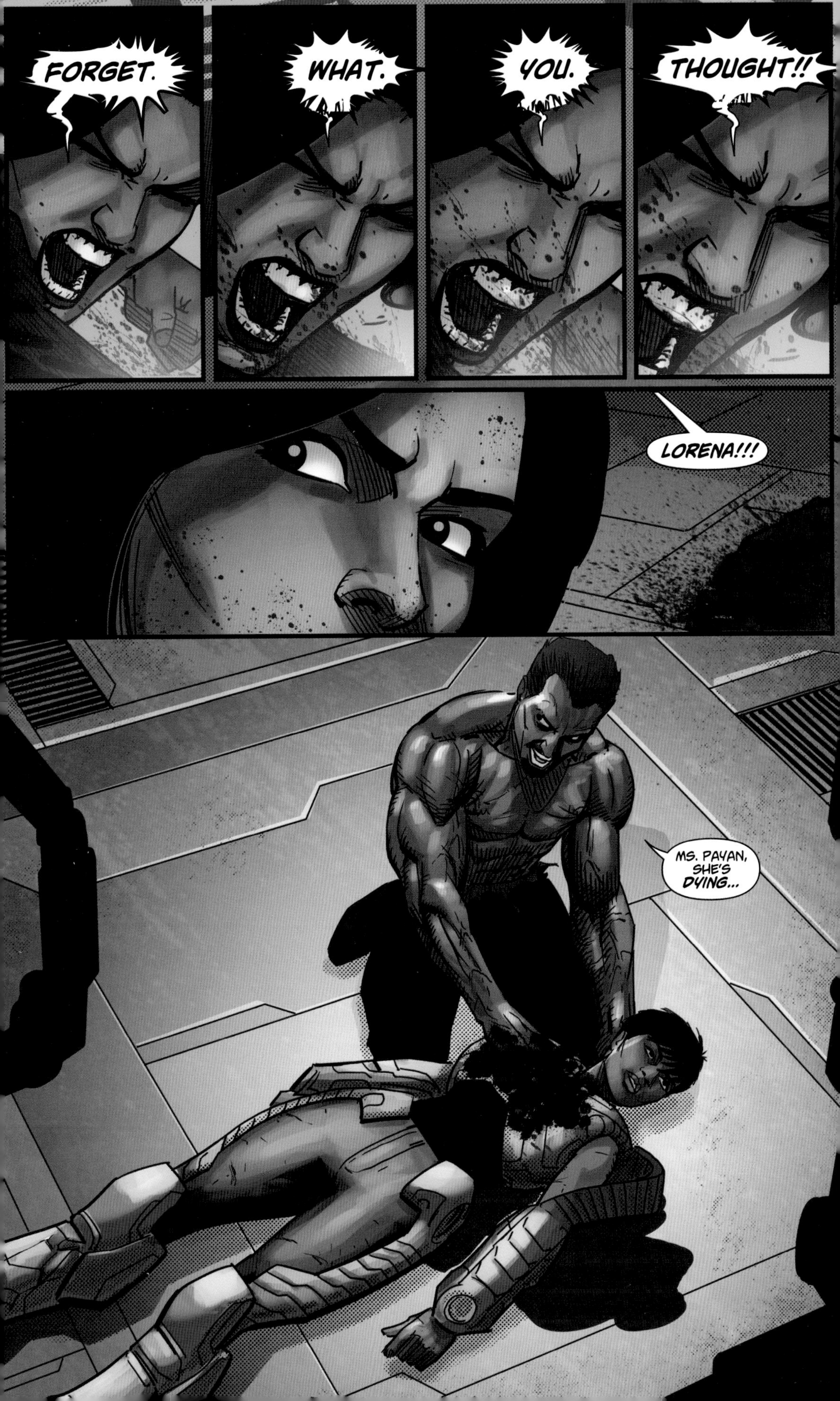
FORGET.
WHAT.
YOU.
THOUGHT!!
LORENA!!!
MS. PAYAN, SHE'S DYING...

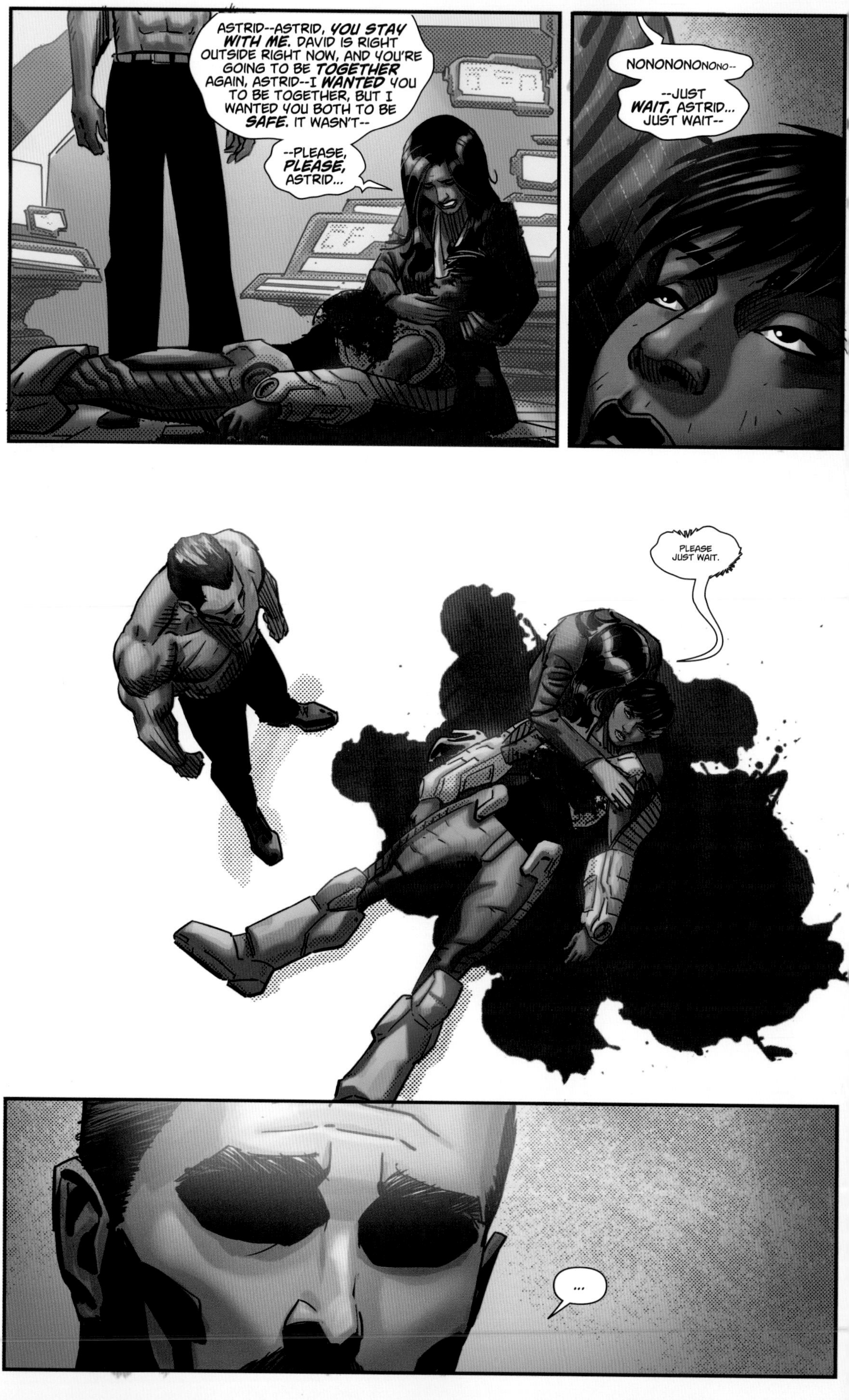
ASTRID--ASTRID, YOU STAY WITH ME. DAVID IS RIGHT OUTSIDE RIGHT NOW, AND YOU'RE GOING TO BE TOGETHER AGAIN, ASTRID--I WANTED YOU TO BE TOGETHER, BUT I WANTED YOU BOTH TO BE SAFE. IT WASN'T--
--PLEASE, PLEASE, ASTRID...
NONONONONONONO--
--JUST WAIT, ASTRID... JUST WAIT--
PLEASE JUST WAIT.
...

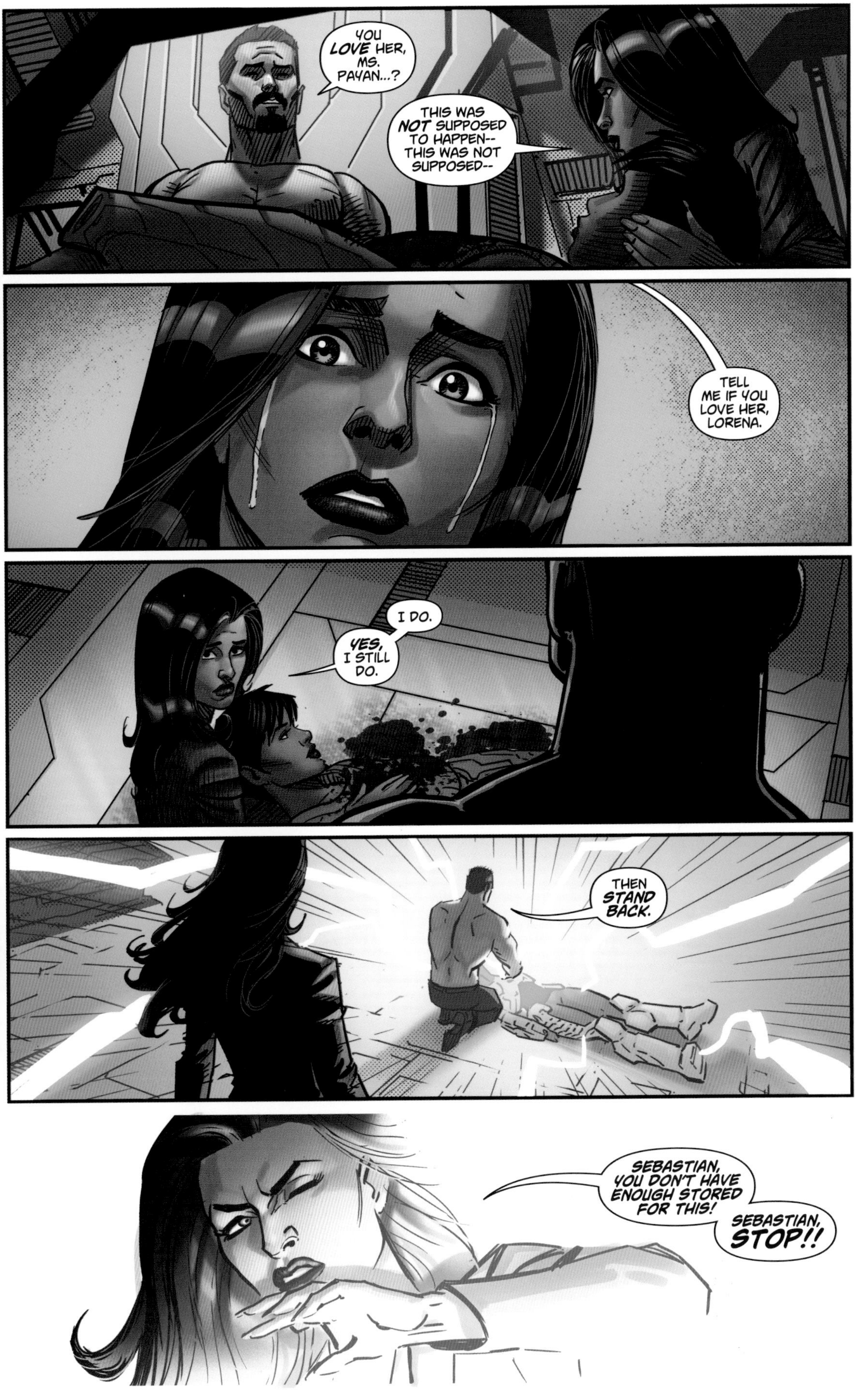
YOU LOVE HER, MS. PAYAN...?
THIS WAS NOT SUPPOSED TO HAPPEN-- THIS WAS NOT SUPPOSED--
TELL ME IF YOU LOVE HER, LORENA.
I DO.
YES, I STILL DO.
THEN STAND BACK.
SEBASTIAN, YOU DON'T HAVE ENOUGH STORED FOR THIS!
SEBASTIAN, STOP!!

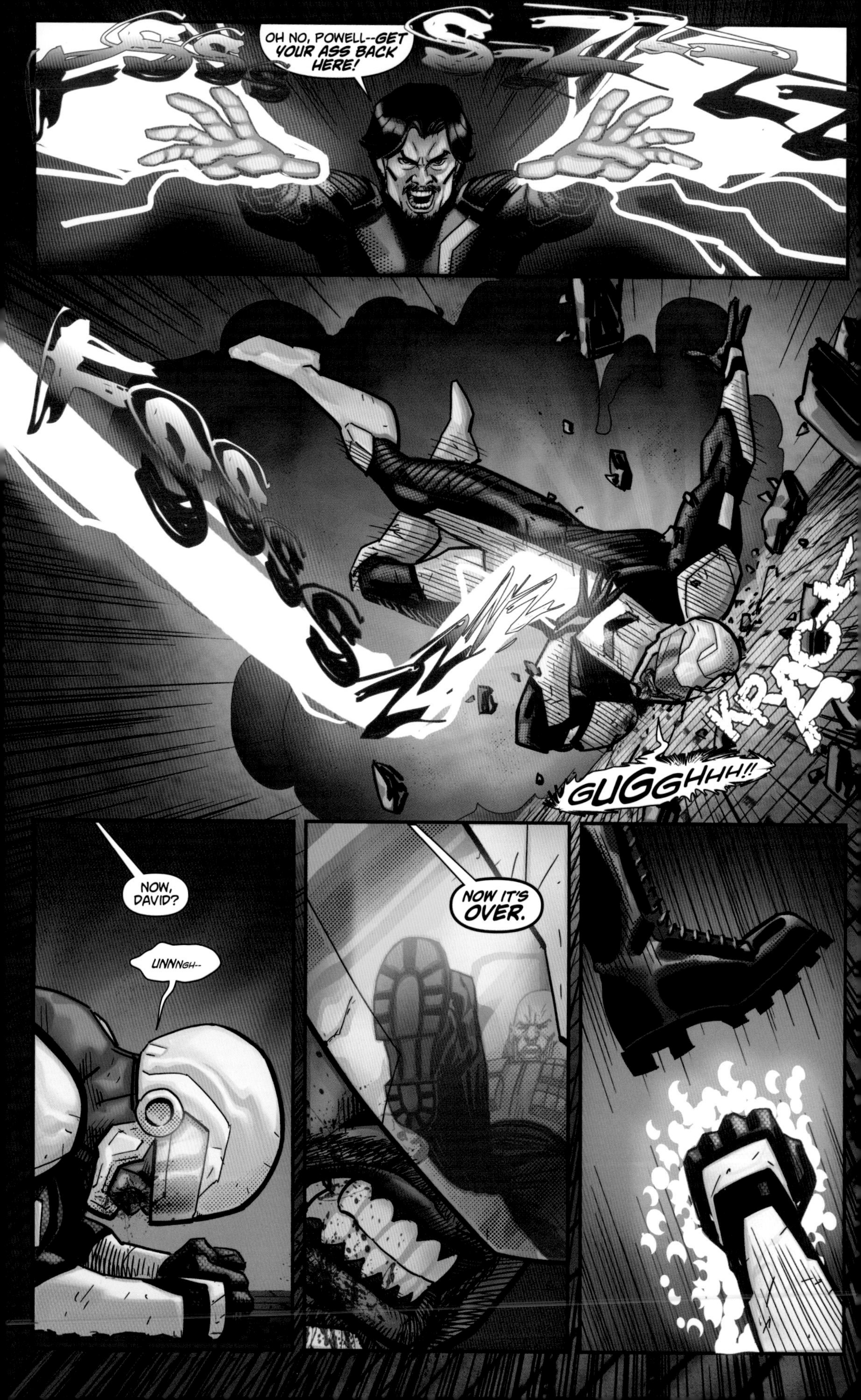

OH NO, POWELL--GET YOUR ASS BACK HERE!
KR-ACK
GUGGHHH!!
NOW, DAVID?
UNNNGH--
NOW IT'S OVER.

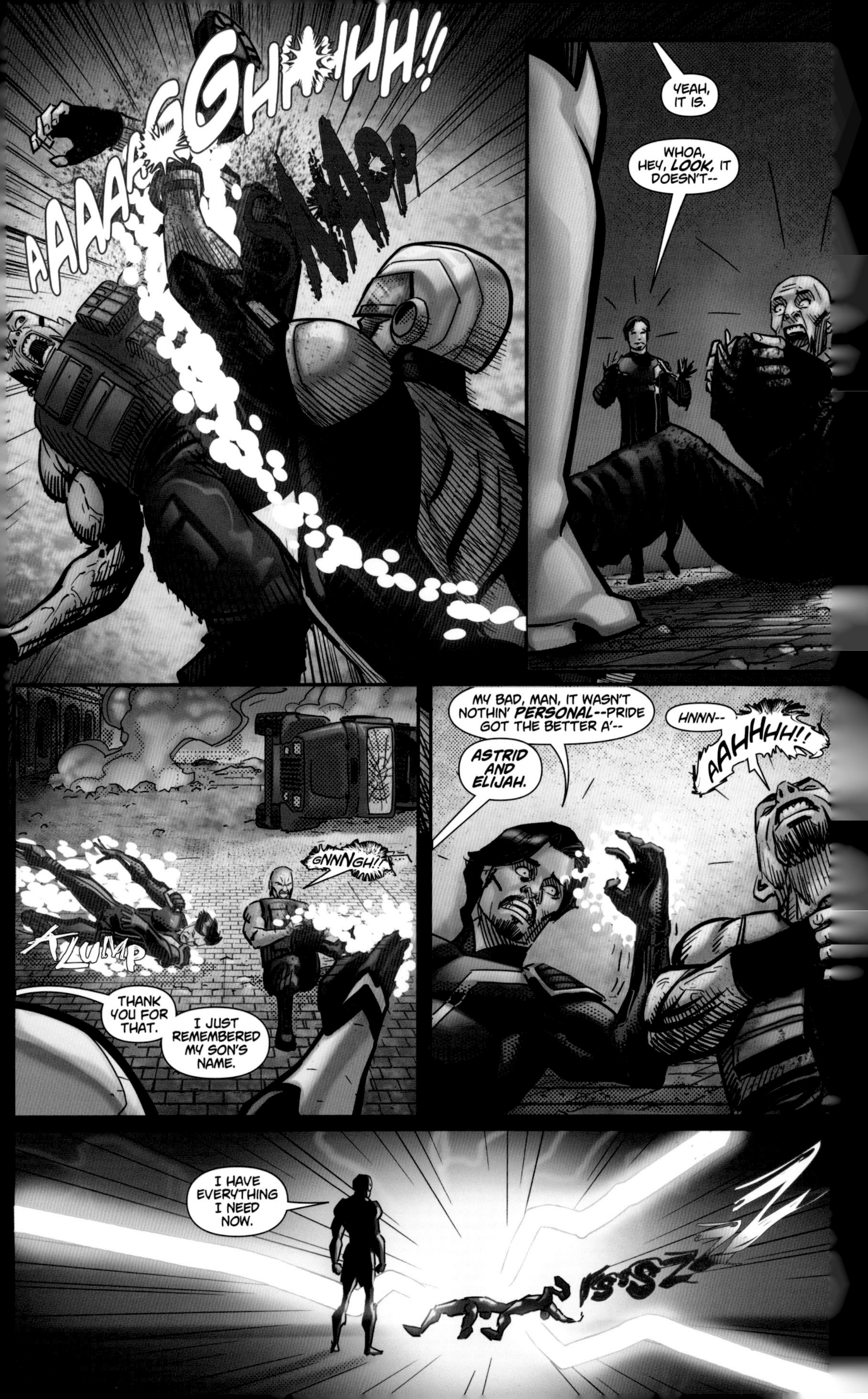
AAAAAGGHHHHH!!
SNAPP
YEAH, IT IS.
WHOA, HEY, LOOK, IT DOESN'T--
GNNNGH!!
KLUMP
THANK YOU FOR THAT.
I JUST REMEMBERED MY SON'S NAME.
MY BAD, MAN, IT WASN'T NOTHIN' PERSONAL--PRIDE GOT THE BETTER A'--
ASTRID AND ELIJAH.
HNNN--
AAHHHH!!
I HAVE EVERYTHING I NEED NOW.
ZZ
TSSSSZ

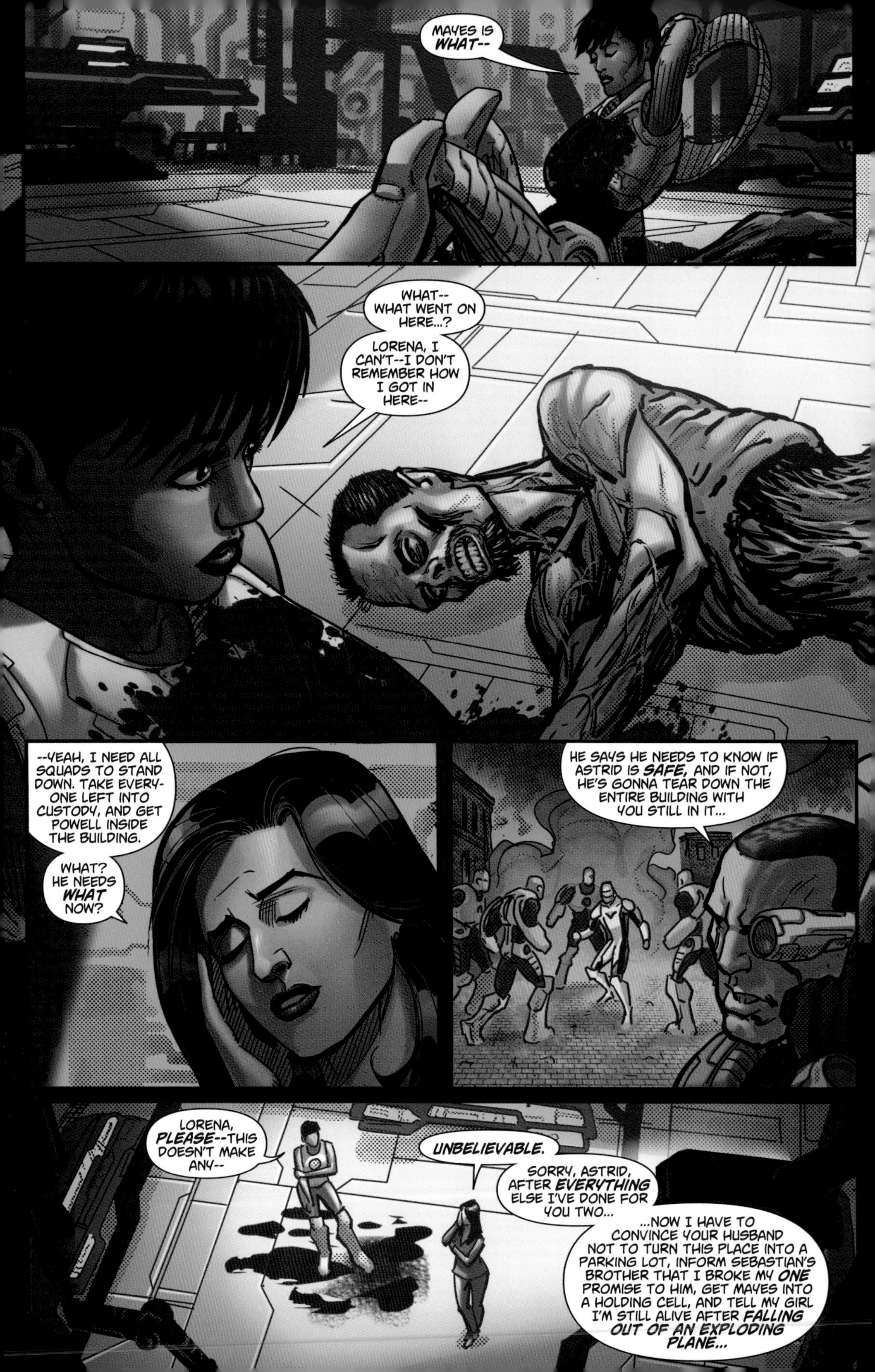
MAYES IS WHAT--
WHAT-- WHAT WENT ON HERE...?
LORENA, I CAN'T--I DON'T REMEMBER HOW I GOT IN HERE--
--YEAH, I NEED ALL SQUADS TO STAND DOWN. TAKE EVERY-ONE LEFT INTO CUSTODY, AND GET POWELL INSIDE THE BUILDING.
WHAT? HE NEEDS WHAT NOW?
HE SAYS HE NEEDS TO KNOW IF ASTRID IS SAFE, AND IF NOT, HE'S GONNA TEAR DOWN THE ENTIRE BUILDING WITH YOU STILL IN IT...
LORENA, PLEASE--THIS DOESN'T MAKE ANY--
UNBELIEVABLE.
SORRY, ASTRID, AFTER EVERYTHING ELSE I'VE DONE FOR YOU TWO...
...NOW I HAVE TO CONVINCE YOUR HUSBAND NOT TO TURN THIS PLACE INTO A PARKING LOT, INFORM SEBASTIAN'S BROTHER THAT I BROKE MY ONE PROMISE TO HIM, GET MAYES INTO A HOLDING CELL, AND TELL MY GIRL I'M STILL ALIVE AFTER FALLING OUT OF AN EXPLODING PLANE...

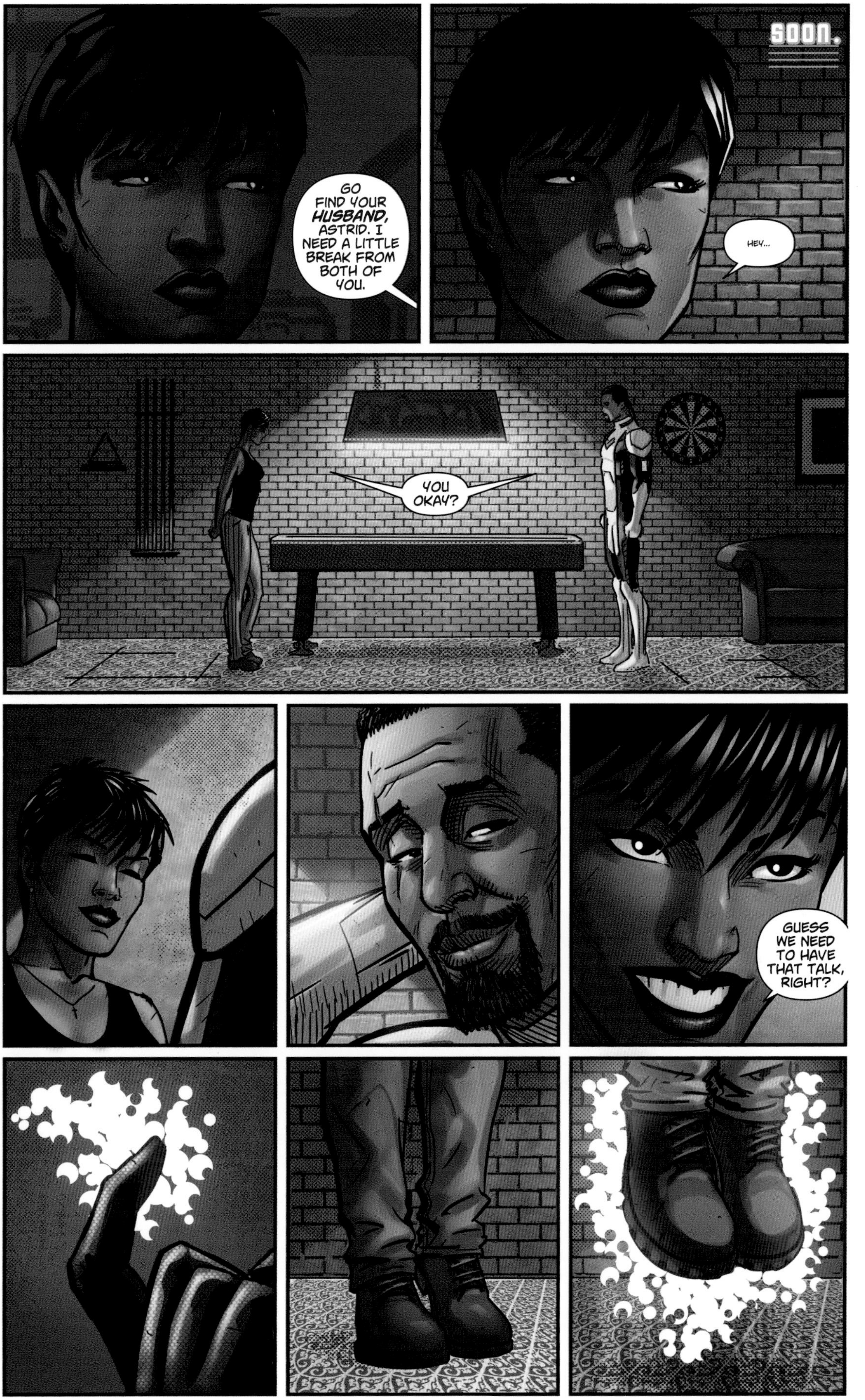
GO FIND YOUR HUSBAND, ASTRID. I NEED A LITTLE BREAK FROM BOTH OF YOU.
SOON.
HEY...
YOU OKAY?
GUESS WE NEED TO HAVE THAT TALK, RIGHT?

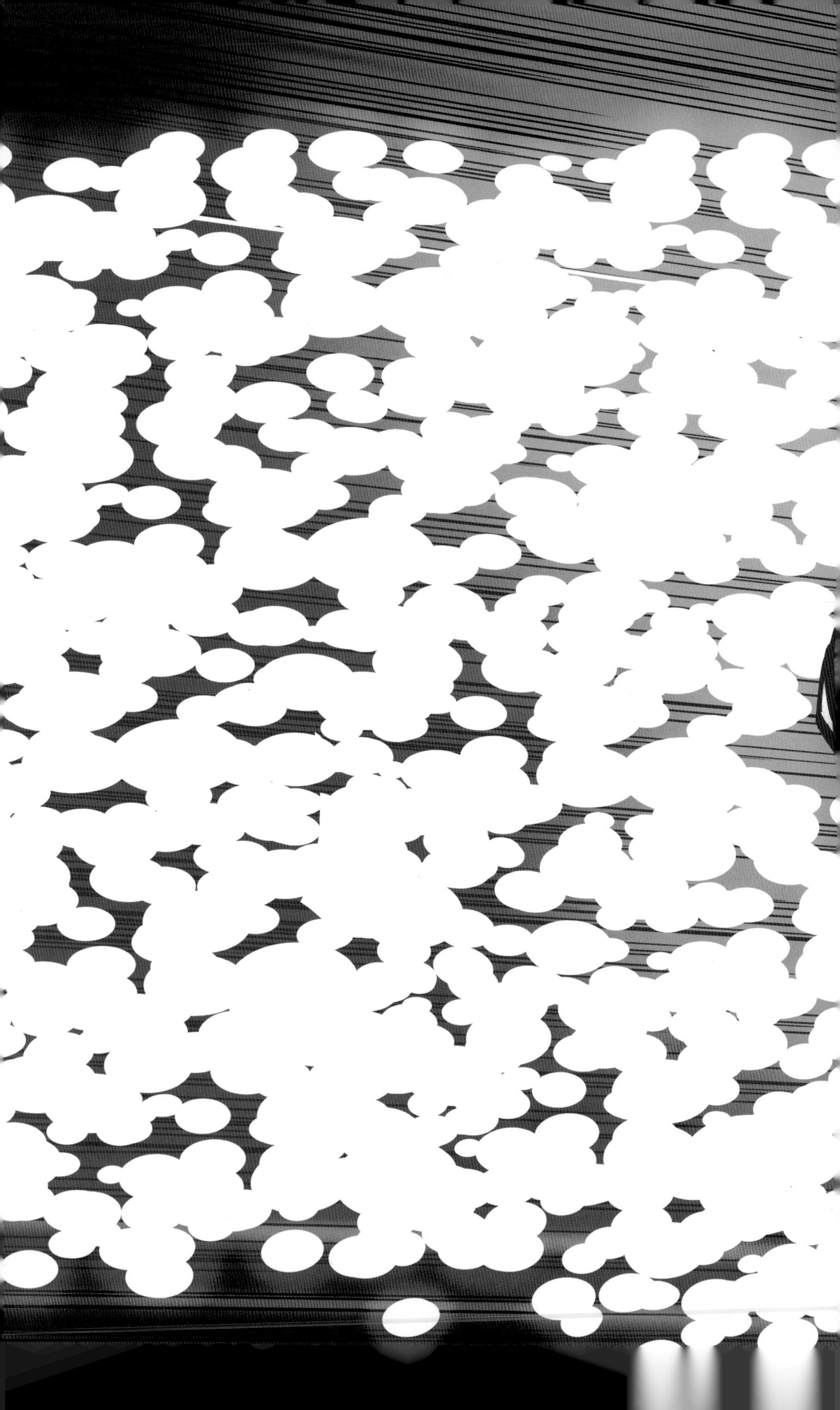

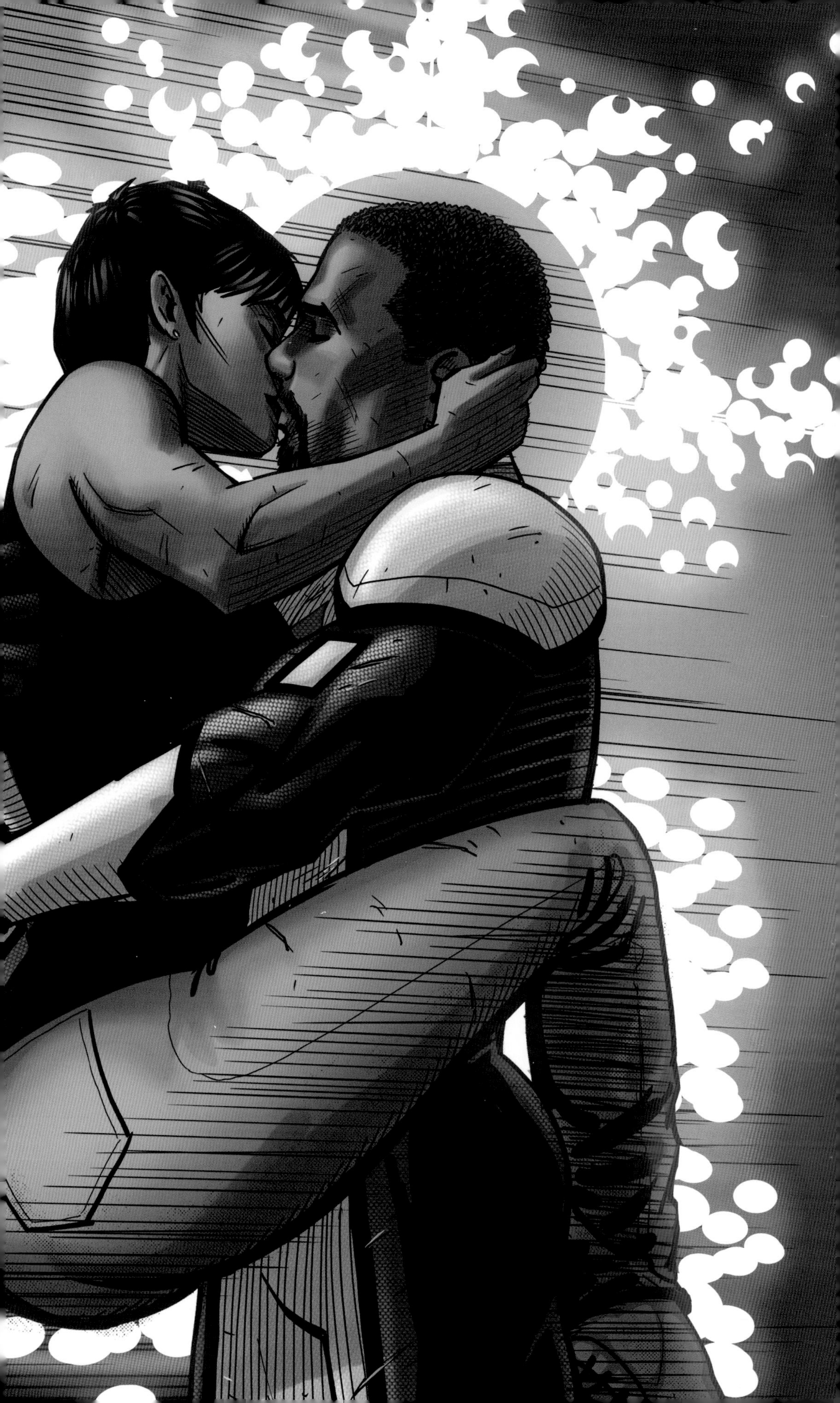

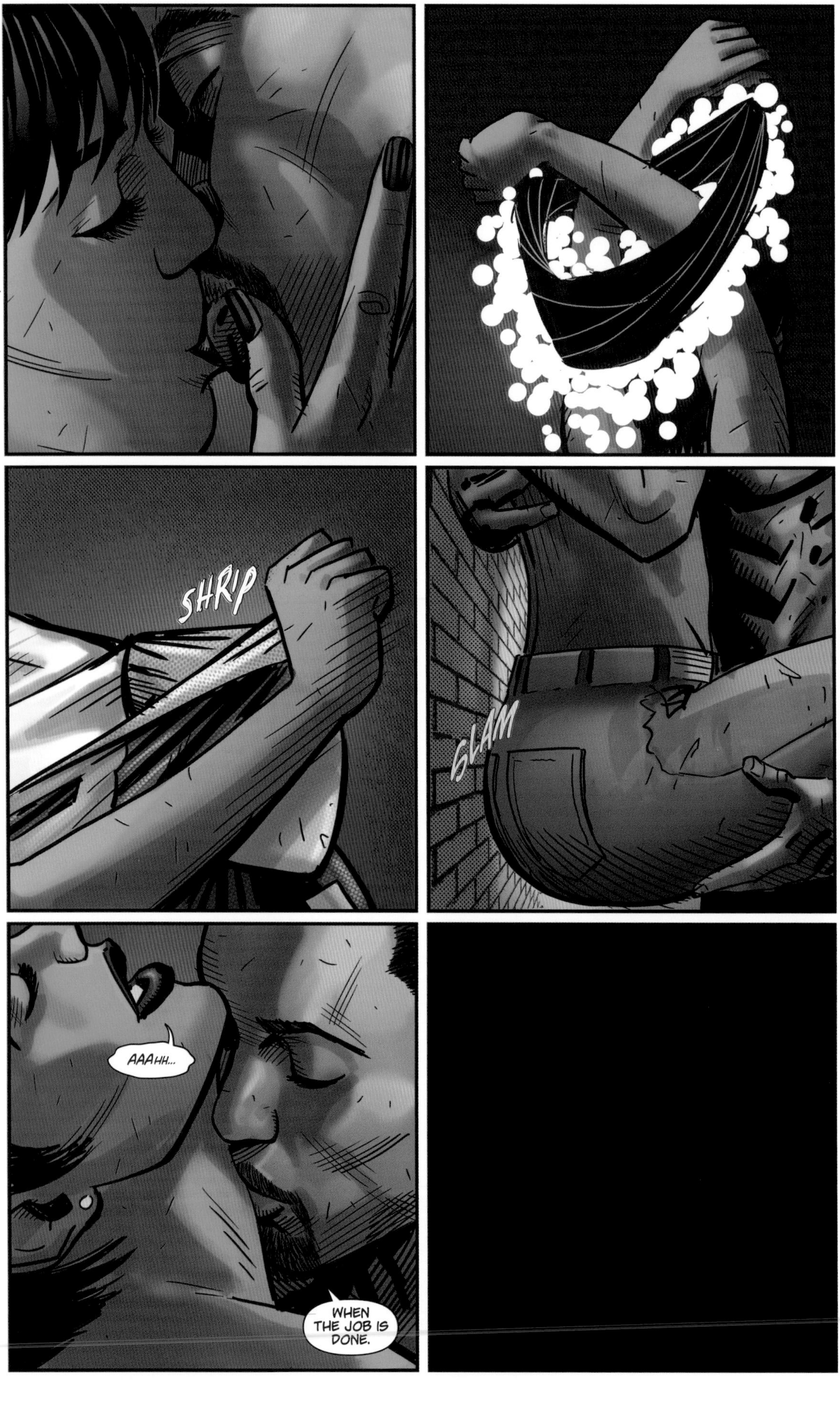

SHRIP
SLAM
AAAHH...
WHEN THE JOB IS DONE.

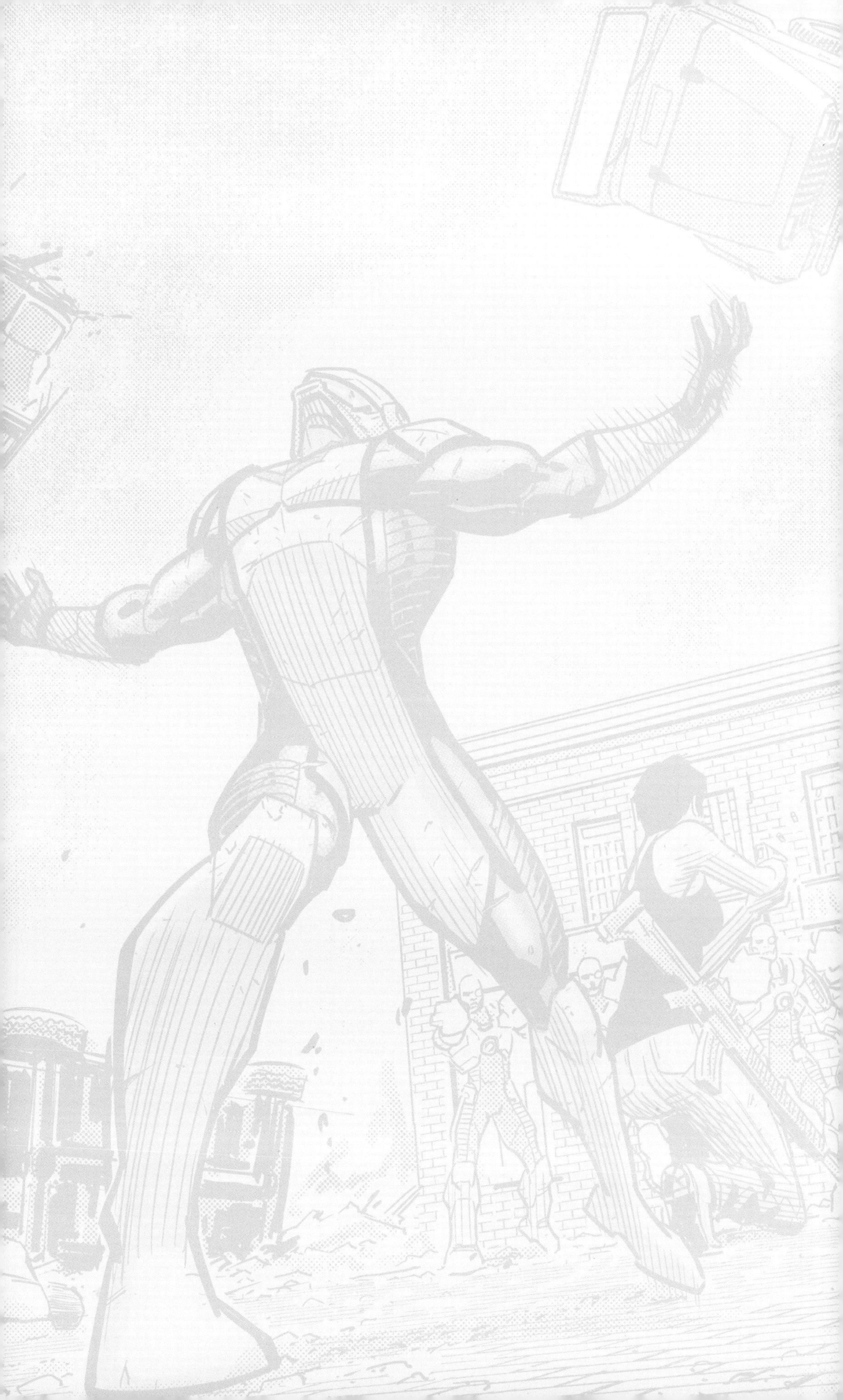

CHAPTER FIVE

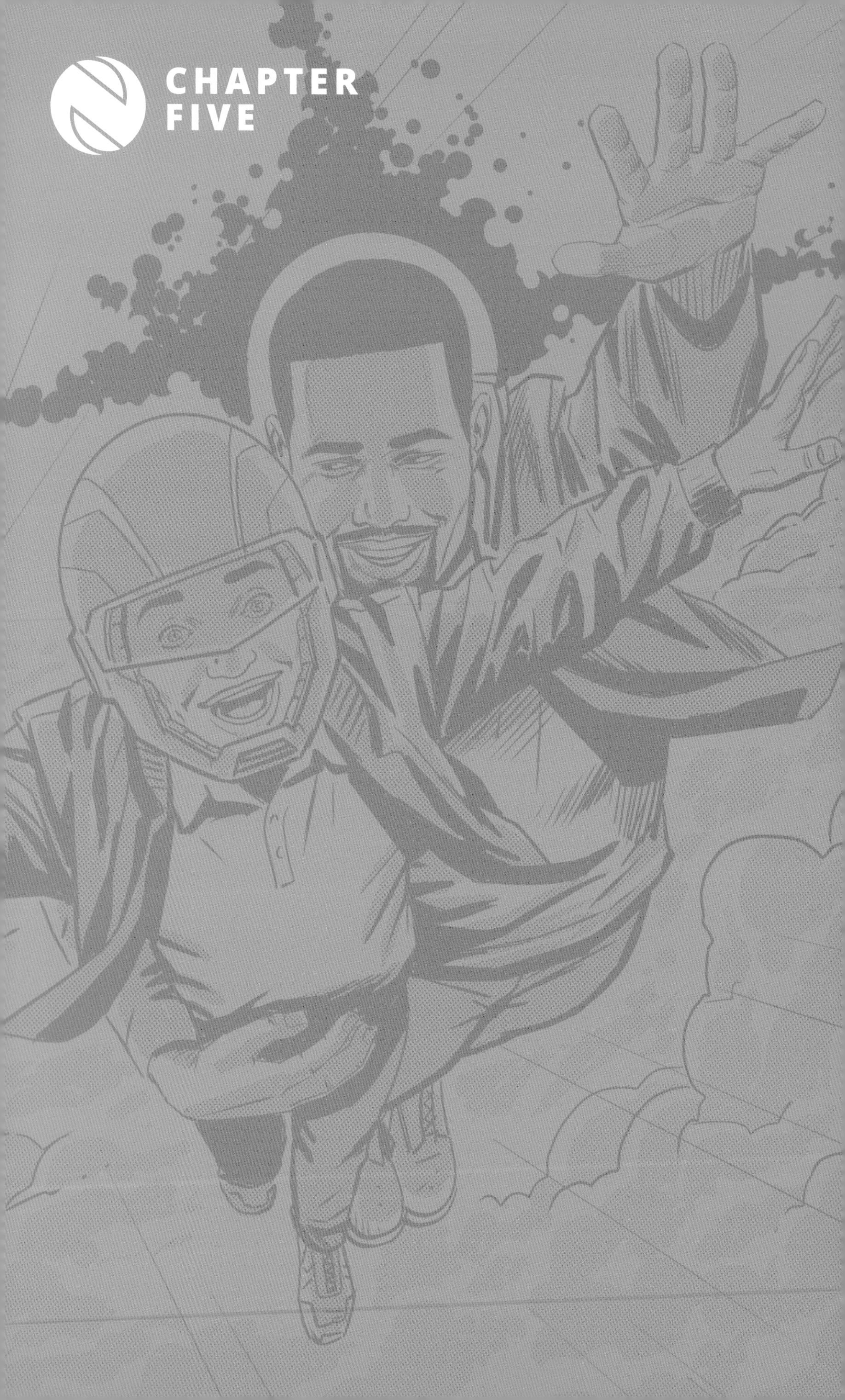

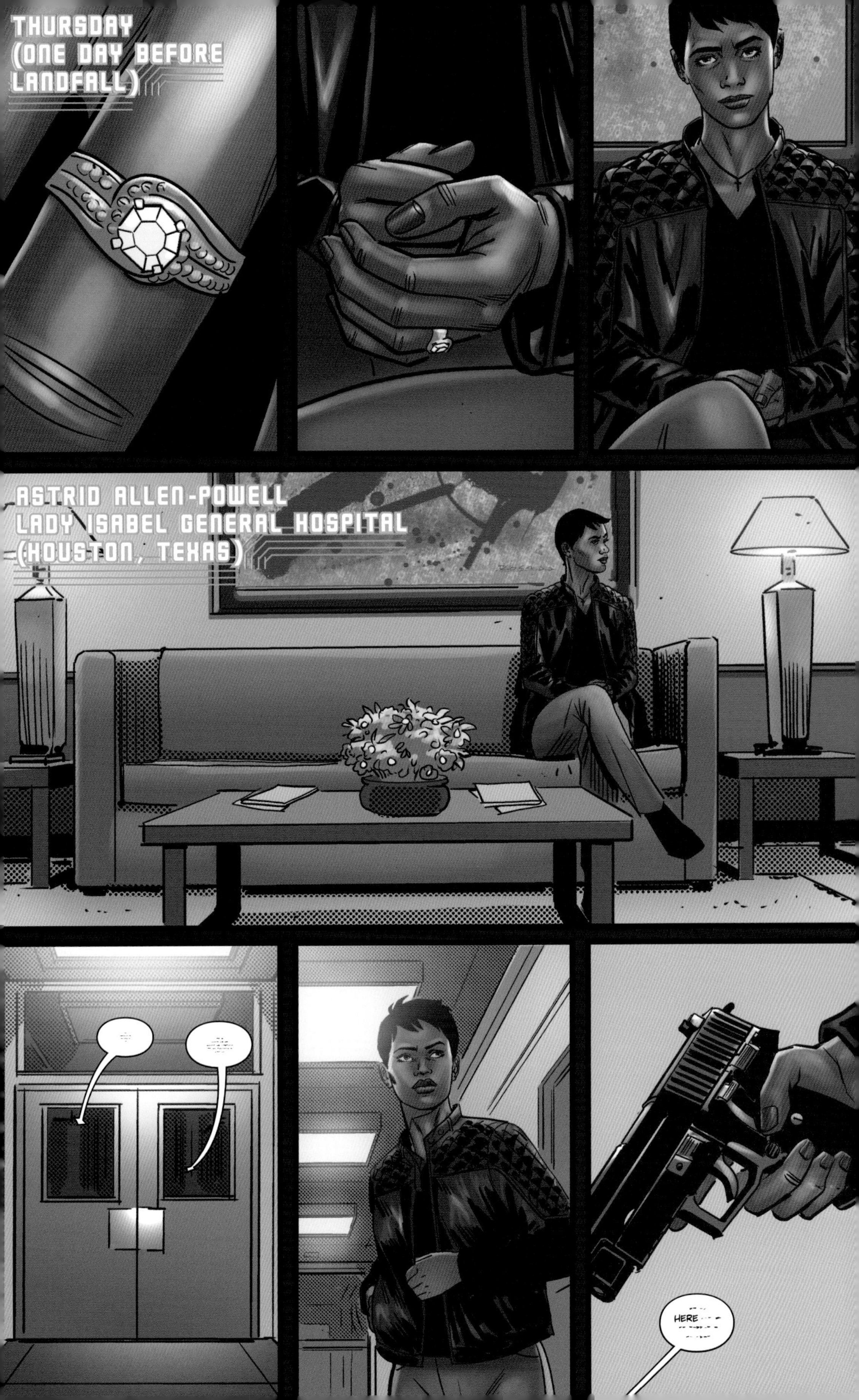
THURSDAY (ONE DAY BEFORE LANDFALL)
ASTRID ALLEN-POWELL
LADY ISABEL GENERAL HOSPITAL
(HOUSTON, TEXAS)
HERE

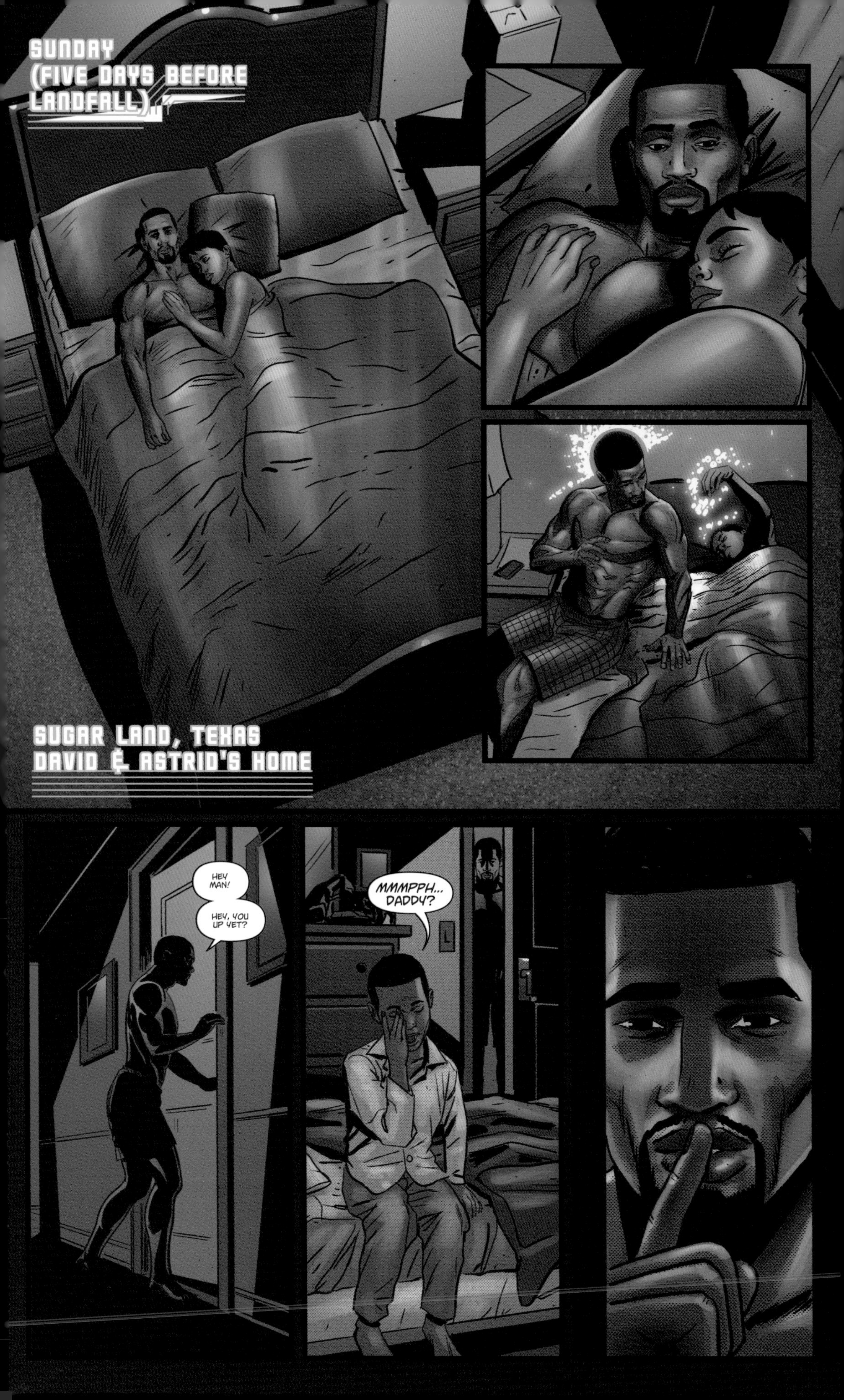
SUNDAY
(FIVE DAYS BEFORE LANDFALL)
SUGAR LAND, TEXAS
DAVID & ASTRID'S HOME
HEY MAN!
HEY, YOU UP YET?
MMMPPH... DADDY?

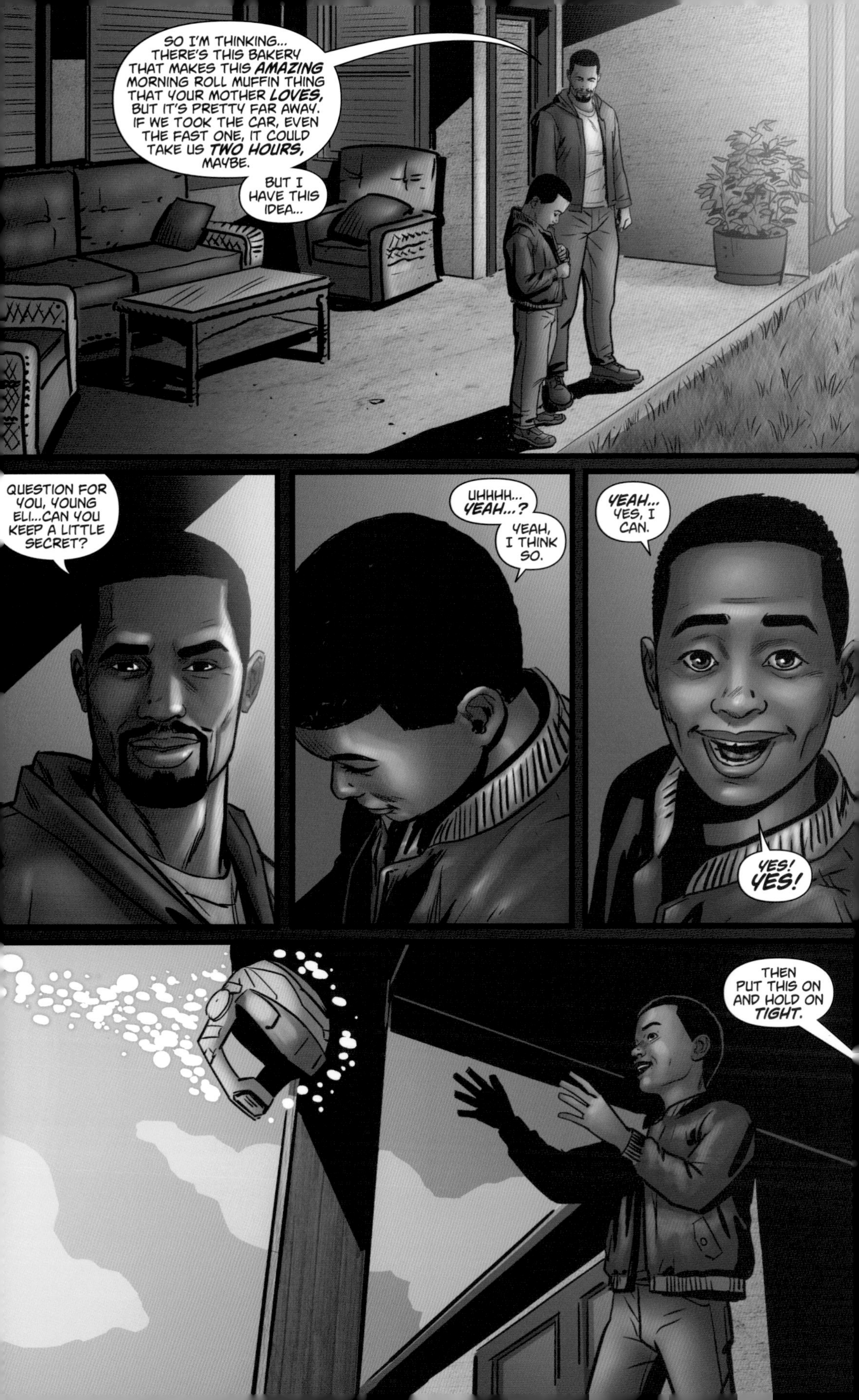
SO I'M THINKING... THERE'S THIS BAKERY THAT MAKES THIS *AMAZING* MORNING ROLL MUFFIN THING THAT YOUR MOTHER *LOVES,* BUT IT'S PRETTY FAR AWAY. IF WE TOOK THE CAR, EVEN THE FAST ONE, IT COULD TAKE US *TWO HOURS,* MAYBE.
BUT I HAVE THIS IDEA...
QUESTION FOR YOU, YOUNG ELI...CAN YOU KEEP A LITTLE SECRET?
UHHHH... *YEAH...?*
YEAH, I THINK SO.
YEAH... YES, I CAN.
YES! YES!
THEN PUT THIS ON AND HOLD ON *TIGHT.*

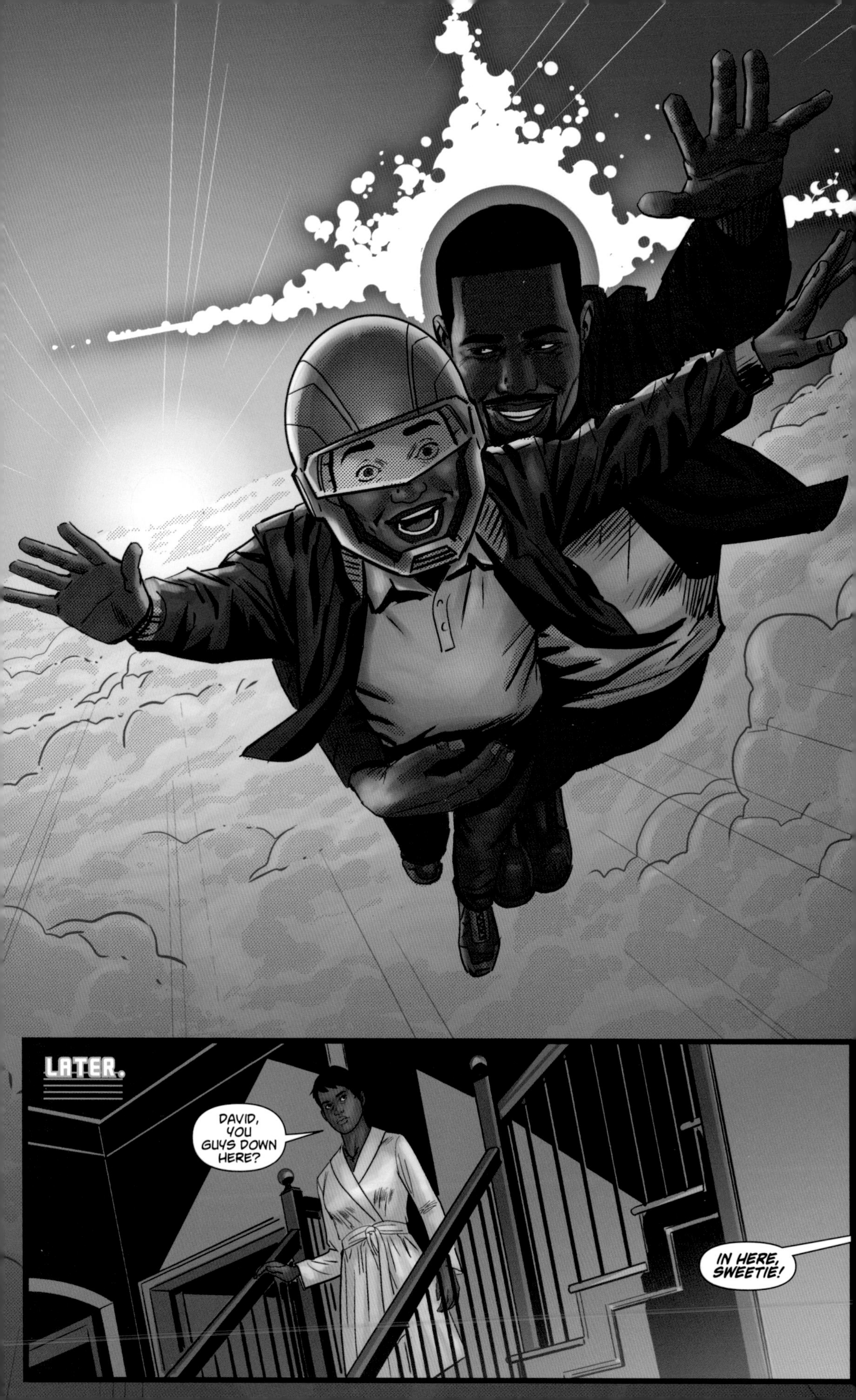
LATER.
DAVID, YOU GUYS DOWN HERE?
IN HERE, SWEETIE!

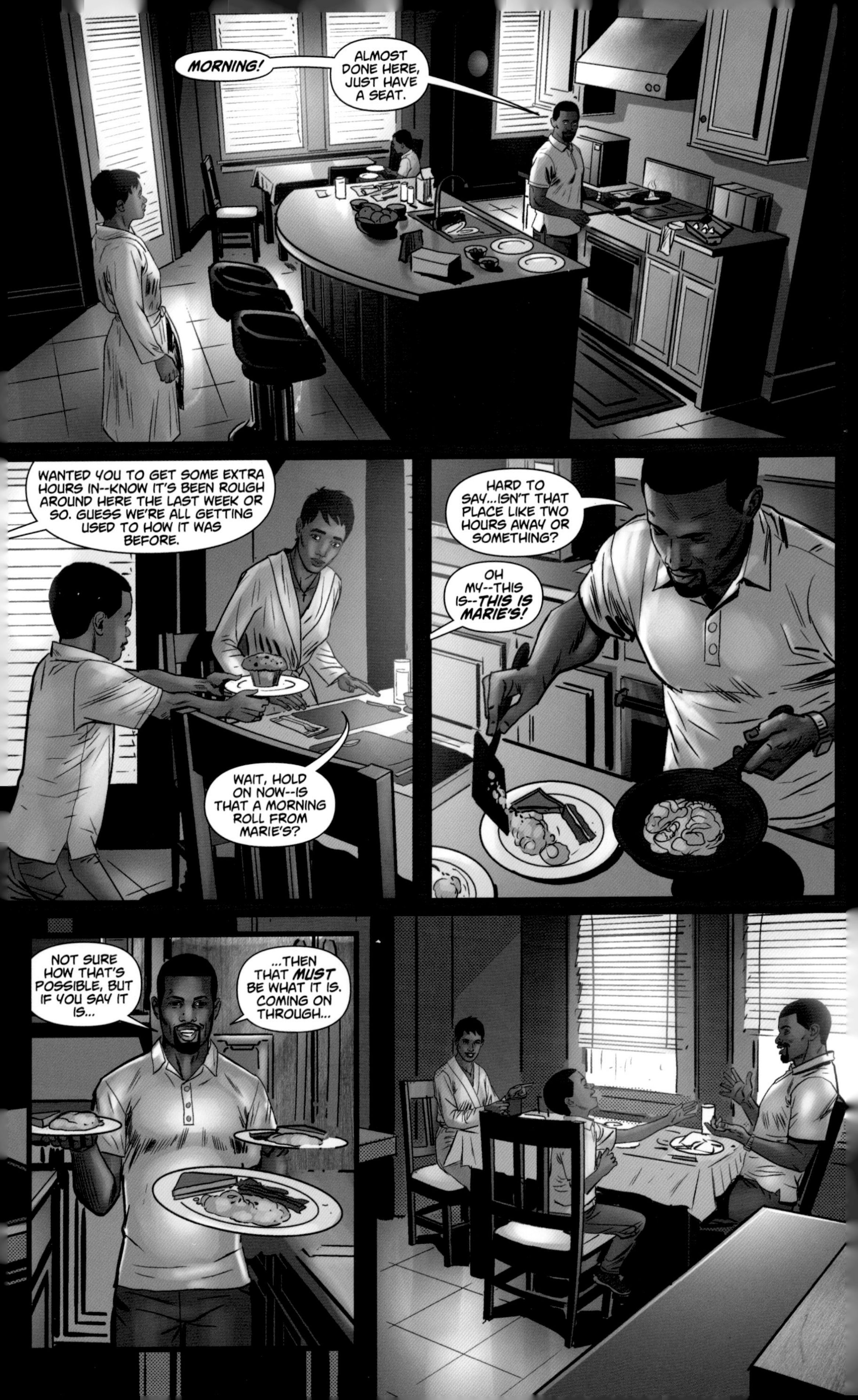
MORNING!
ALMOST DONE HERE, JUST HAVE A SEAT.
WANTED YOU TO GET SOME EXTRA HOURS IN--KNOW IT'S BEEN ROUGH AROUND HERE THE LAST WEEK OR SO. GUESS WE'RE ALL GETTING USED TO HOW IT WAS BEFORE.
WAIT, HOLD ON NOW--IS THAT A MORNING ROLL FROM MARIE'S?
HARD TO SAY...ISN'T THAT PLACE LIKE TWO HOURS AWAY OR SOMETHING?
OH MY--THIS IS--THIS IS MARIE'S!
NOT SURE HOW THAT'S POSSIBLE, BUT IF YOU SAY IT IS...
...THEN THAT MUST BE WHAT IT IS. COMING ON THROUGH...

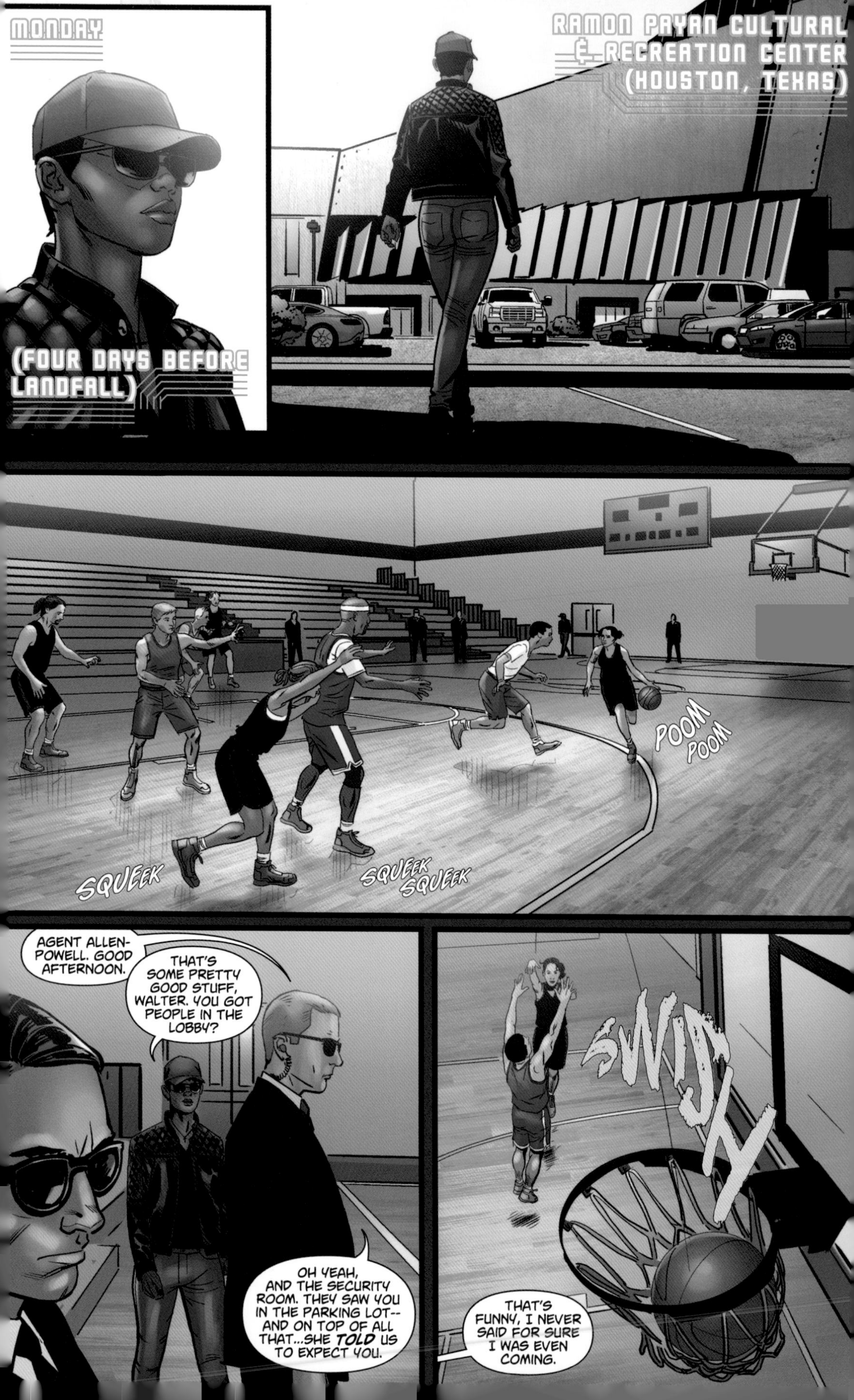
MONDAY
RAMON PAYAN CULTURAL & RECREATION CENTER (HOUSTON, TEXAS)
(FOUR DAYS BEFORE LANDFALL)
SQUEEK
SQUEEK SQUEEK
POOM POOM
AGENT ALLEN-POWELL. GOOD AFTERNOON.
THAT'S SOME PRETTY GOOD STUFF, WALTER. YOU GOT PEOPLE IN THE LOBBY?
OH YEAH, AND THE SECURITY ROOM. THEY SAW YOU IN THE PARKING LOT--AND ON TOP OF ALL THAT...SHE TOLD US TO EXPECT YOU.
SWISH
THAT'S FUNNY, I NEVER SAID FOR SURE I WAS EVEN COMING.

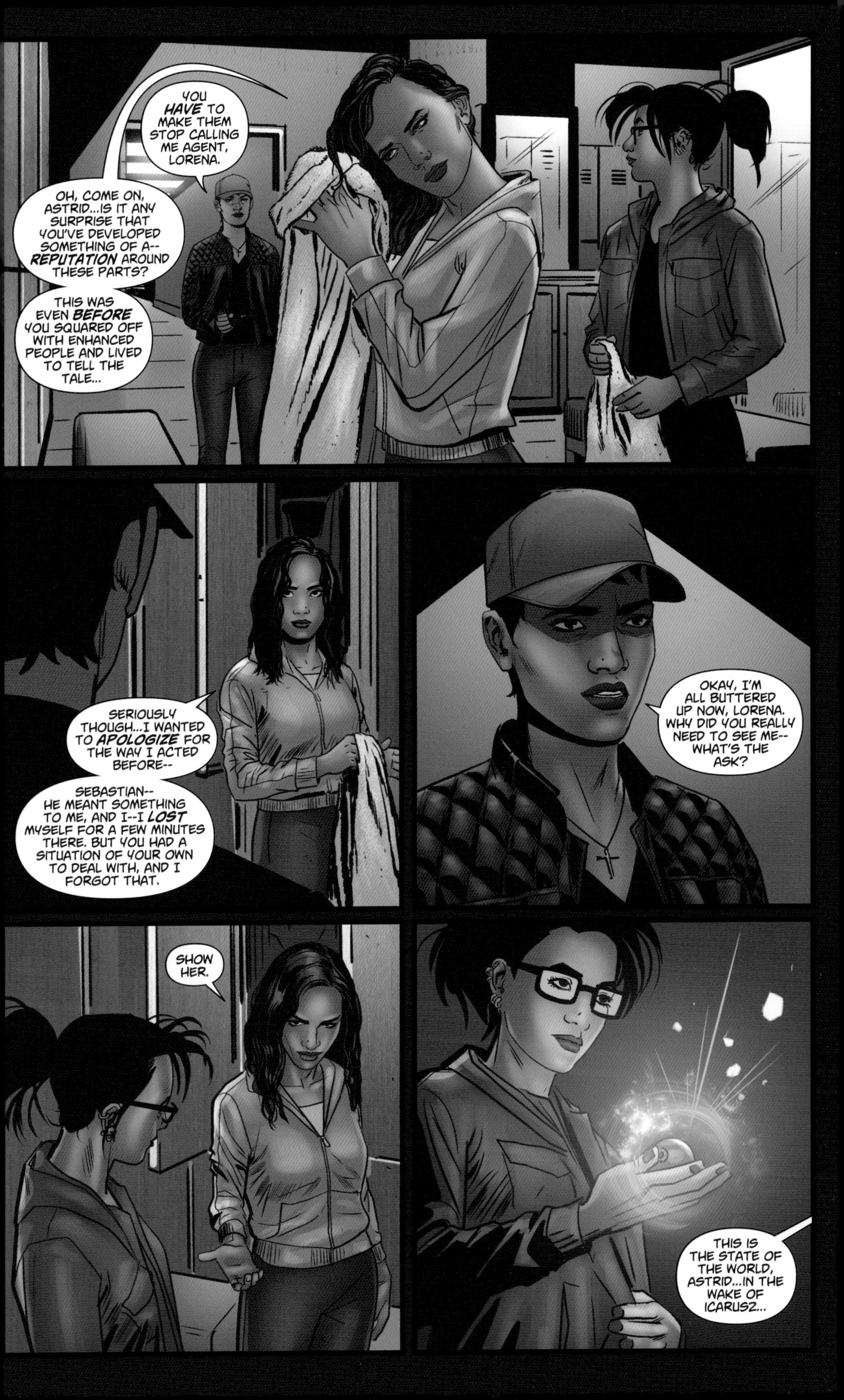

YOU *HAVE* TO MAKE THEM STOP CALLING ME AGENT, LORENA.
OH, COME ON, ASTRID...IS IT ANY SURPRISE THAT YOU'VE DEVELOPED SOMETHING OF A-- *REPUTATION* AROUND THESE PARTS?
THIS WAS EVEN *BEFORE* YOU SQUARED OFF WITH ENHANCED PEOPLE AND LIVED TO TELL THE TALE...
SERIOUSLY THOUGH...I WANTED TO *APOLOGIZE* FOR THE WAY I ACTED BEFORE--
SEBASTIAN-- HE MEANT SOMETHING TO ME, AND I--I *LOST* MYSELF FOR A FEW MINUTES THERE. BUT YOU HAD A SITUATION OF YOUR OWN TO DEAL WITH, AND I FORGOT THAT.
OKAY, I'M ALL BUTTERED UP NOW, LORENA. WHY DID YOU REALLY NEED TO SEE ME-- WHAT'S THE ASK?
SHOW HER.
THIS IS THE STATE OF THE WORLD, ASTRID...IN THE WAKE OF ICARUS2...

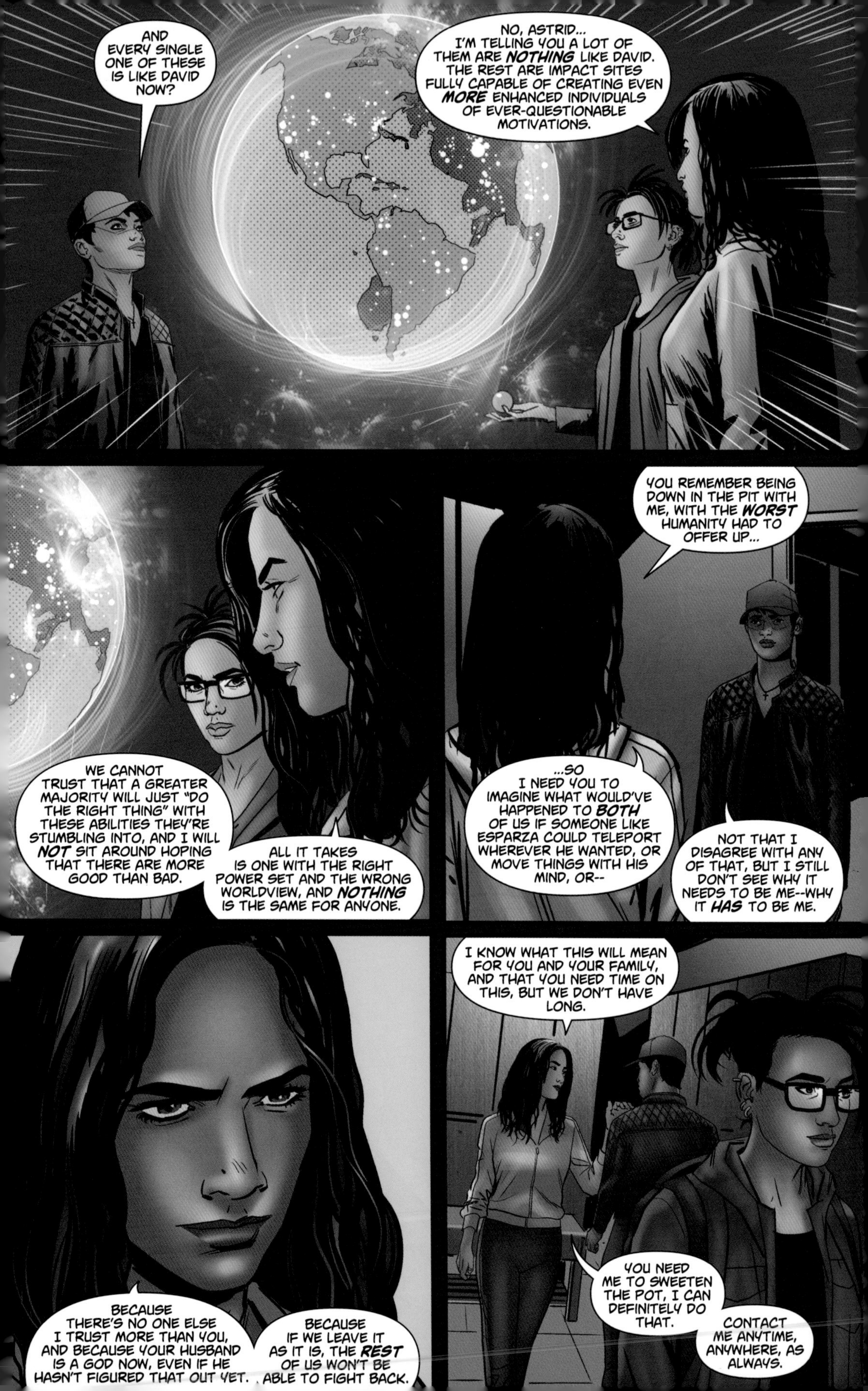
AND EVERY SINGLE ONE OF THESE IS LIKE DAVID NOW?
NO, ASTRID... I'M TELLING YOU A LOT OF THEM ARE NOTHING LIKE DAVID. THE REST ARE IMPACT SITES FULLY CAPABLE OF CREATING EVEN MORE ENHANCED INDIVIDUALS OF EVER-QUESTIONABLE MOTIVATIONS.
WE CANNOT TRUST THAT A GREATER MAJORITY WILL JUST "DO THE RIGHT THING" WITH THESE ABILITIES THEY'RE STUMBLING INTO, AND I WILL NOT SIT AROUND HOPING THAT THERE ARE MORE GOOD THAN BAD.
ALL IT TAKES IS ONE WITH THE RIGHT POWER SET AND THE WRONG WORLDVIEW, AND NOTHING IS THE SAME FOR ANYONE.
YOU REMEMBER BEING DOWN IN THE PIT WITH ME, WITH THE WORST HUMANITY HAD TO OFFER UP...
...SO I NEED YOU TO IMAGINE WHAT WOULD'VE HAPPENED TO BOTH OF US IF SOMEONE LIKE ESPARZA COULD TELEPORT WHEREVER HE WANTED, OR MOVE THINGS WITH HIS MIND, OR--
NOT THAT I DISAGREE WITH ANY OF THAT, BUT I STILL DON'T SEE WHY IT NEEDS TO BE ME--WHY IT HAS TO BE ME.
BECAUSE THERE'S NO ONE ELSE I TRUST MORE THAN YOU, AND BECAUSE YOUR HUSBAND IS A GOD NOW, EVEN IF HE HASN'T FIGURED THAT OUT YET.
BECAUSE IF WE LEAVE IT AS IT IS, THE REST OF US WON'T BE ABLE TO FIGHT BACK.
I KNOW WHAT THIS WILL MEAN FOR YOU AND YOUR FAMILY, AND THAT YOU NEED TIME ON THIS, BUT WE DON'T HAVE LONG.
YOU NEED ME TO SWEETEN THE POT, I CAN DEFINITELY DO THAT.
CONTACT ME ANYTIME, ANYWHERE, AS ALWAYS.

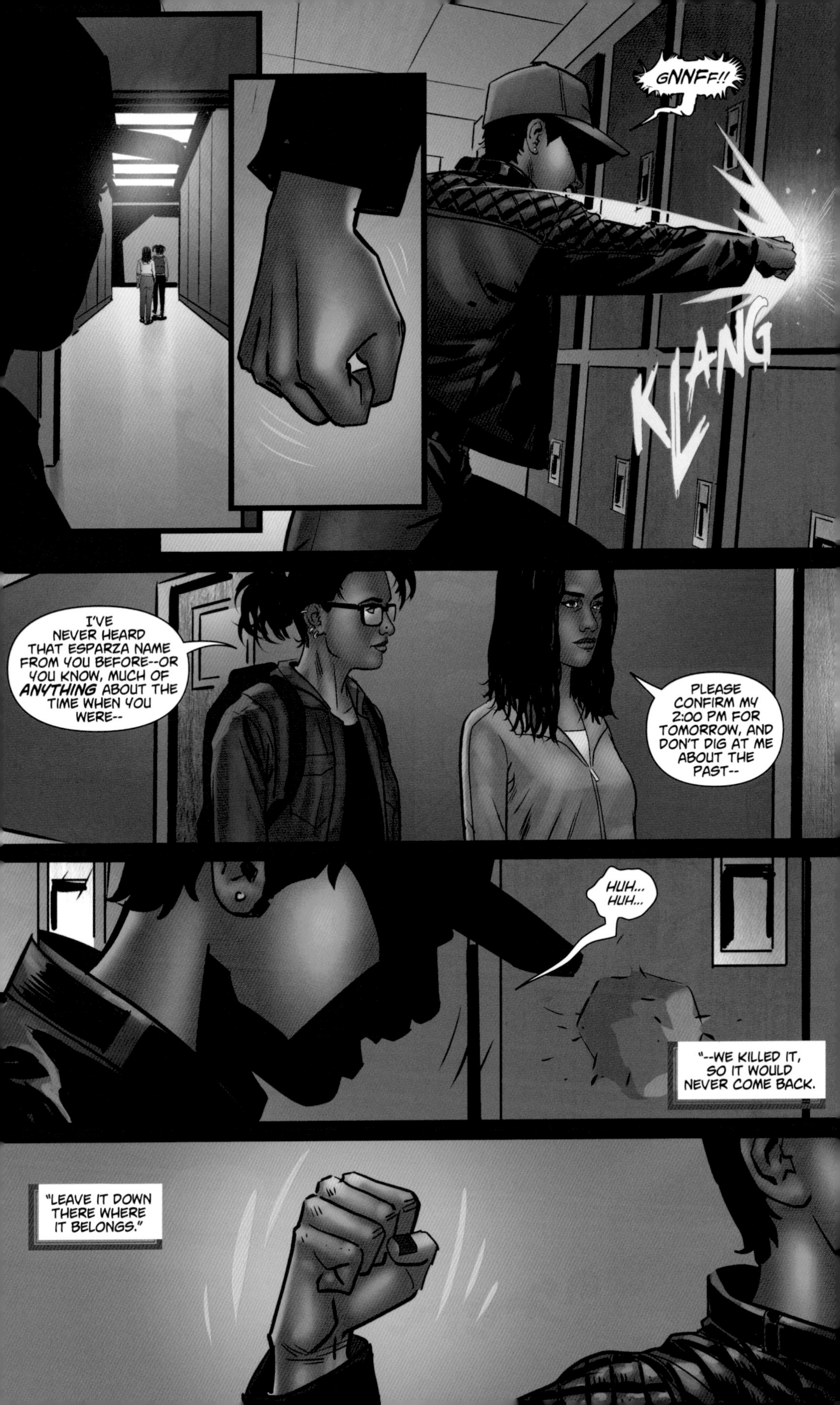
GNNFF!!
KLANG
I'VE NEVER HEARD THAT ESPARZA NAME FROM YOU BEFORE--OR YOU KNOW, MUCH OF *ANYTHING* ABOUT THE TIME WHEN YOU WERE--
PLEASE CONFIRM MY 2:00 PM FOR TOMORROW, AND DON'T DIG AT ME ABOUT THE PAST--
HUH... HUH...
"--WE KILLED IT, SO IT WOULD NEVER COME BACK.
"LEAVE IT DOWN THERE WHERE IT BELONGS."

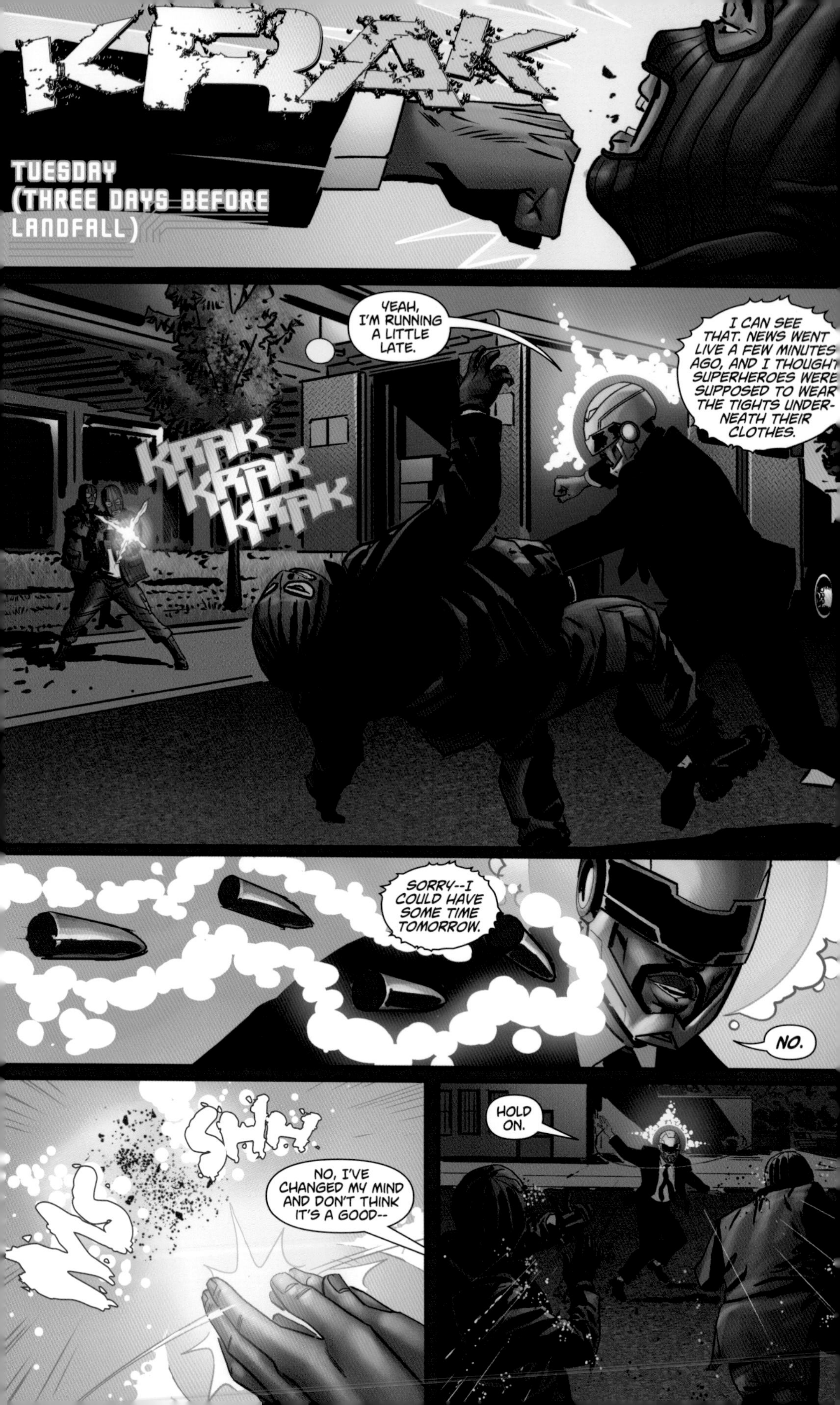
KRAK
TUESDAY (THREE DAYS BEFORE LANDFALL)
YEAH, I'M RUNNING A LITTLE LATE.
I CAN SEE THAT. NEWS WENT LIVE A FEW MINUTES AGO, AND I THOUGHT SUPERHEROES WERE SUPPOSED TO WEAR THE TIGHTS UNDERNEATH THEIR CLOTHES.
KRAK KRAK KRAK
SORRY--I COULD HAVE SOME TIME TOMORROW.
NO.
NO, I'VE CHANGED MY MIND AND DON'T THINK IT'S A GOOD--
HOLD ON.

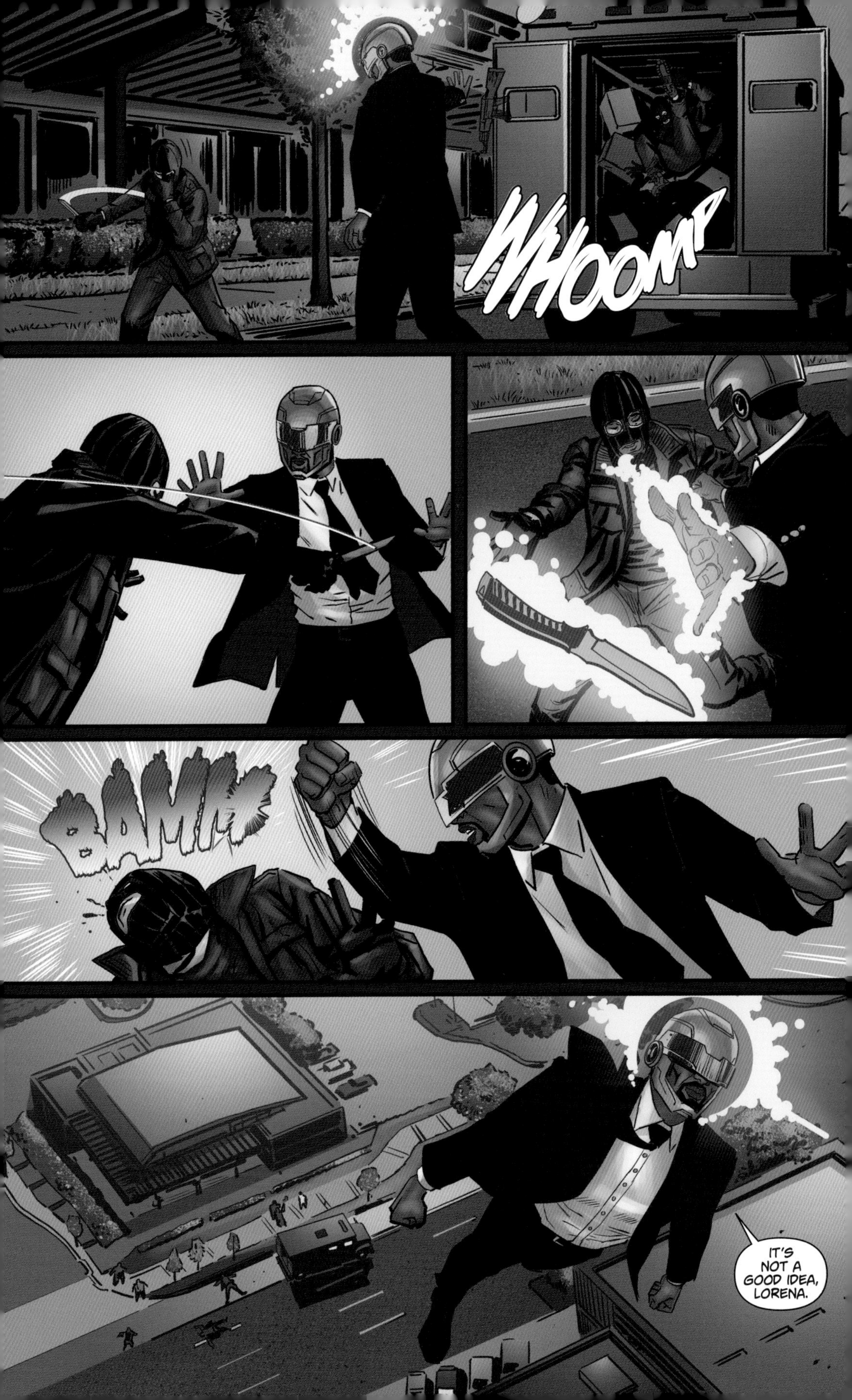
WHOOMP
BAMM
IT'S NOT A GOOD IDEA, LORENA.

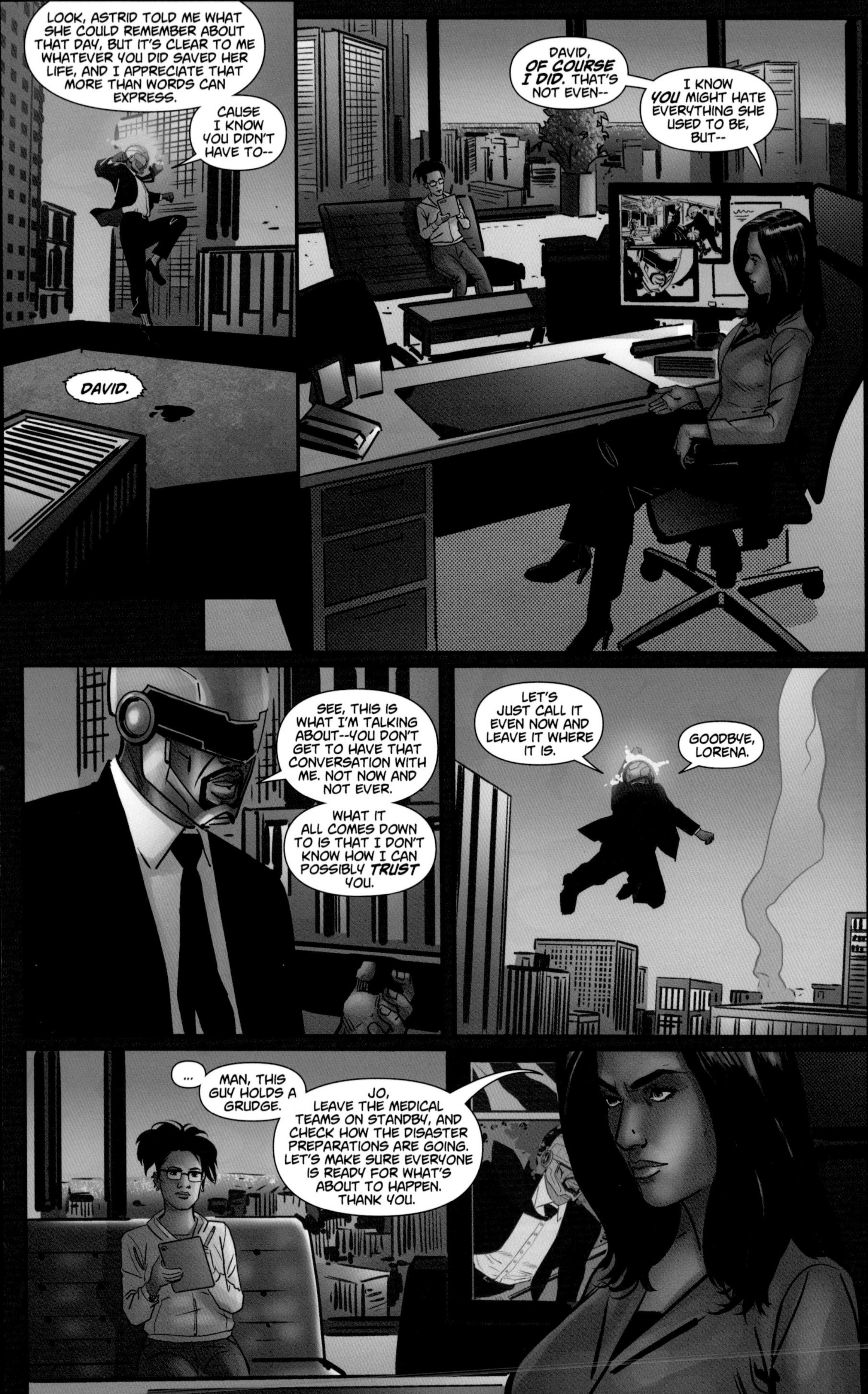

LOOK, ASTRID TOLD ME WHAT SHE COULD REMEMBER ABOUT THAT DAY, BUT IT'S CLEAR TO ME WHATEVER YOU DID SAVED HER LIFE, AND I APPRECIATE THAT MORE THAN WORDS CAN EXPRESS.
CAUSE I KNOW YOU DIDN'T HAVE TO--
DAVID, OF COURSE I DID. THAT'S NOT EVEN--
I KNOW YOU MIGHT HATE EVERYTHING SHE USED TO BE, BUT--
DAVID.
SEE, THIS IS WHAT I'M TALKING ABOUT--YOU DON'T GET TO HAVE THAT CONVERSATION WITH ME. NOT NOW AND NOT EVER.
WHAT IT ALL COMES DOWN TO IS THAT I DON'T KNOW HOW I CAN POSSIBLY TRUST YOU.
LET'S JUST CALL IT EVEN NOW AND LEAVE IT WHERE IT IS.
GOODBYE, LORENA.
...
MAN, THIS GUY HOLDS A GRUDGE.
JO, LEAVE THE MEDICAL TEAMS ON STANDBY, AND CHECK HOW THE DISASTER PREPARATIONS ARE GOING. LET'S MAKE SURE EVERYONE IS READY FOR WHAT'S ABOUT TO HAPPEN. THANK YOU.

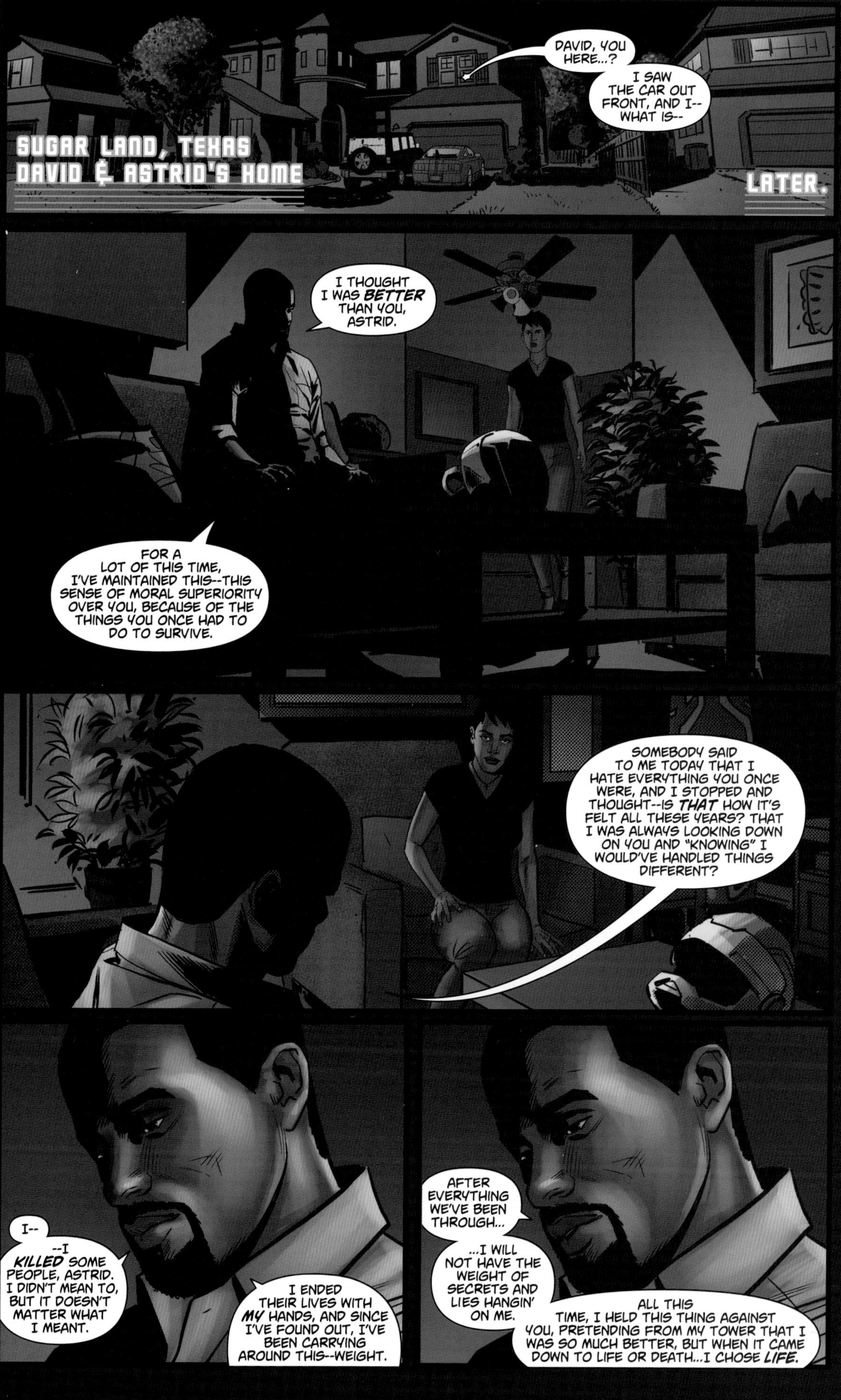
SUGAR LAND, TEXAS
DAVID & ASTRID'S HOME
LATER.
DAVID, YOU HERE...?
I SAW THE CAR OUT FRONT, AND I-- WHAT IS--
I THOUGHT I WAS BETTER THAN YOU, ASTRID.
FOR A LOT OF THIS TIME, I'VE MAINTAINED THIS--THIS SENSE OF MORAL SUPERIORITY OVER YOU, BECAUSE OF THE THINGS YOU ONCE HAD TO DO TO SURVIVE.
SOMEBODY SAID TO ME TODAY THAT I HATE EVERYTHING YOU ONCE WERE, AND I STOPPED AND THOUGHT--IS THAT HOW IT'S FELT ALL THESE YEARS? THAT I WAS ALWAYS LOOKING DOWN ON YOU AND "KNOWING" I WOULD'VE HANDLED THINGS DIFFERENT?
I--
--I KILLED SOME PEOPLE, ASTRID. I DIDN'T MEAN TO, BUT IT DOESN'T MATTER WHAT I MEANT.
I ENDED THEIR LIVES WITH MY HANDS, AND SINCE I'VE FOUND OUT, I'VE BEEN CARRYING AROUND THIS--WEIGHT.
AFTER EVERYTHING WE'VE BEEN THROUGH...
...I WILL NOT HAVE THE WEIGHT OF SECRETS AND LIES HANGIN' ON ME.
ALL THIS TIME, I HELD THIS THING AGAINST YOU, PRETENDING FROM MY TOWER THAT I WAS SO MUCH BETTER, BUT WHEN IT CAME DOWN TO LIFE OR DEATH...I CHOSE LIFE.

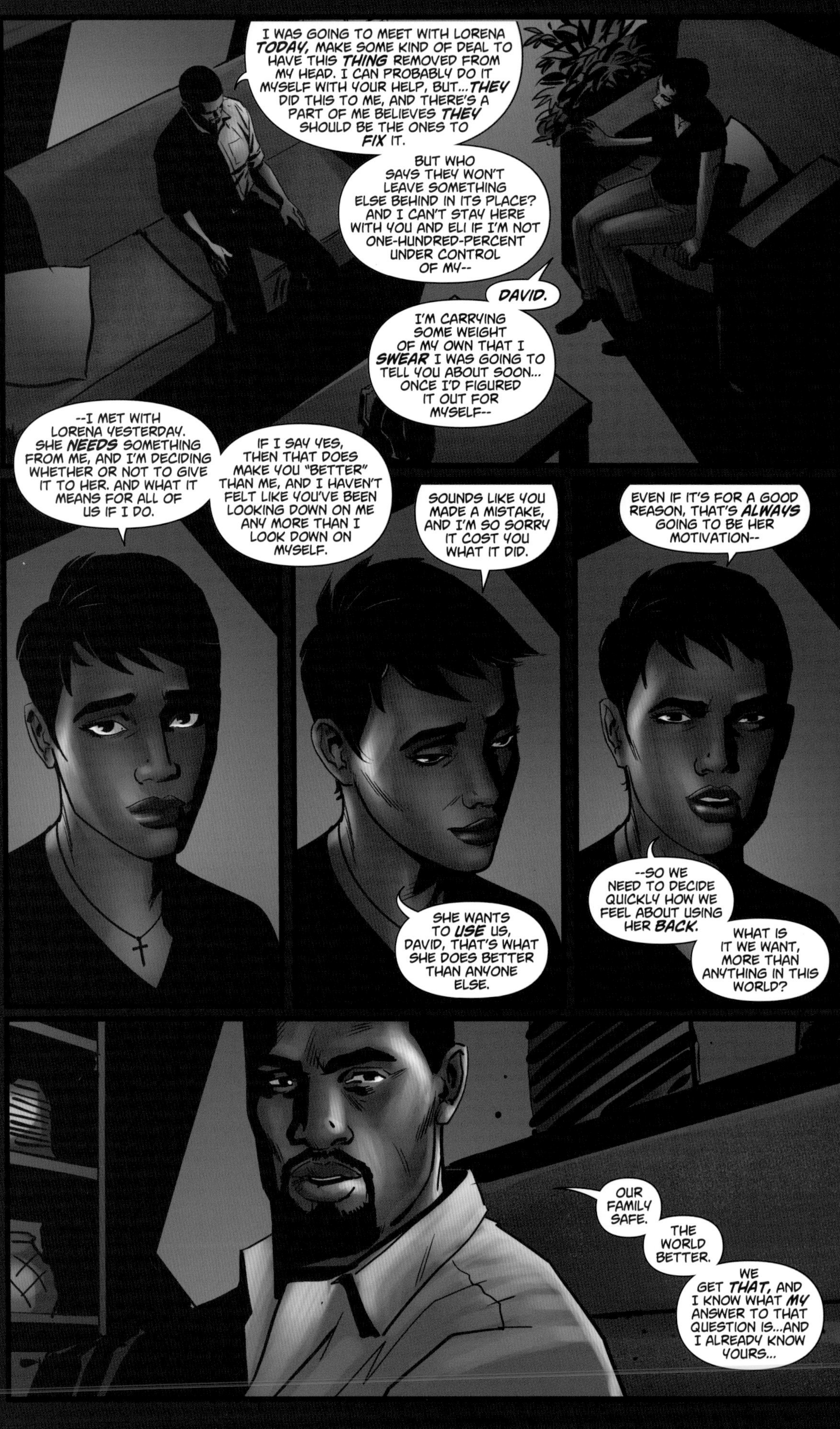

I WAS GOING TO MEET WITH LORENA TODAY, MAKE SOME KIND OF DEAL TO HAVE THIS THING REMOVED FROM MY HEAD. I CAN PROBABLY DO IT MYSELF WITH YOUR HELP, BUT...THEY DID THIS TO ME, AND THERE'S A PART OF ME BELIEVES THEY SHOULD BE THE ONES TO FIX IT.
BUT WHO SAYS THEY WON'T LEAVE SOMETHING ELSE BEHIND IN ITS PLACE? AND I CAN'T STAY HERE WITH YOU AND ELI IF I'M NOT ONE-HUNDRED-PERCENT UNDER CONTROL OF MY--
DAVID.
I'M CARRYING SOME WEIGHT OF MY OWN THAT I SWEAR I WAS GOING TO TELL YOU ABOUT SOON... ONCE I'D FIGURED IT OUT FOR MYSELF--
--I MET WITH LORENA YESTERDAY. SHE NEEDS SOMETHING FROM ME, AND I'M DECIDING WHETHER OR NOT TO GIVE IT TO HER. AND WHAT IT MEANS FOR ALL OF US IF I DO.
IF I SAY YES, THEN THAT DOES MAKE YOU "BETTER" THAN ME, AND I HAVEN'T FELT LIKE YOU'VE BEEN LOOKING DOWN ON ME ANY MORE THAN I LOOK DOWN ON MYSELF.
SOUNDS LIKE YOU MADE A MISTAKE, AND I'M SO SORRY IT COST YOU WHAT IT DID.
SHE WANTS TO USE US, DAVID, THAT'S WHAT SHE DOES BETTER THAN ANYONE ELSE.
EVEN IF IT'S FOR A GOOD REASON, THAT'S ALWAYS GOING TO BE HER MOTIVATION--
--SO WE NEED TO DECIDE QUICKLY HOW WE FEEL ABOUT USING HER BACK.
WHAT IS IT WE WANT, MORE THAN ANYTHING IN THIS WORLD?
OUR FAMILY SAFE.
THE WORLD BETTER.
WE GET THAT, AND I KNOW WHAT MY ANSWER TO THAT QUESTION IS...AND I ALREADY KNOW YOURS...

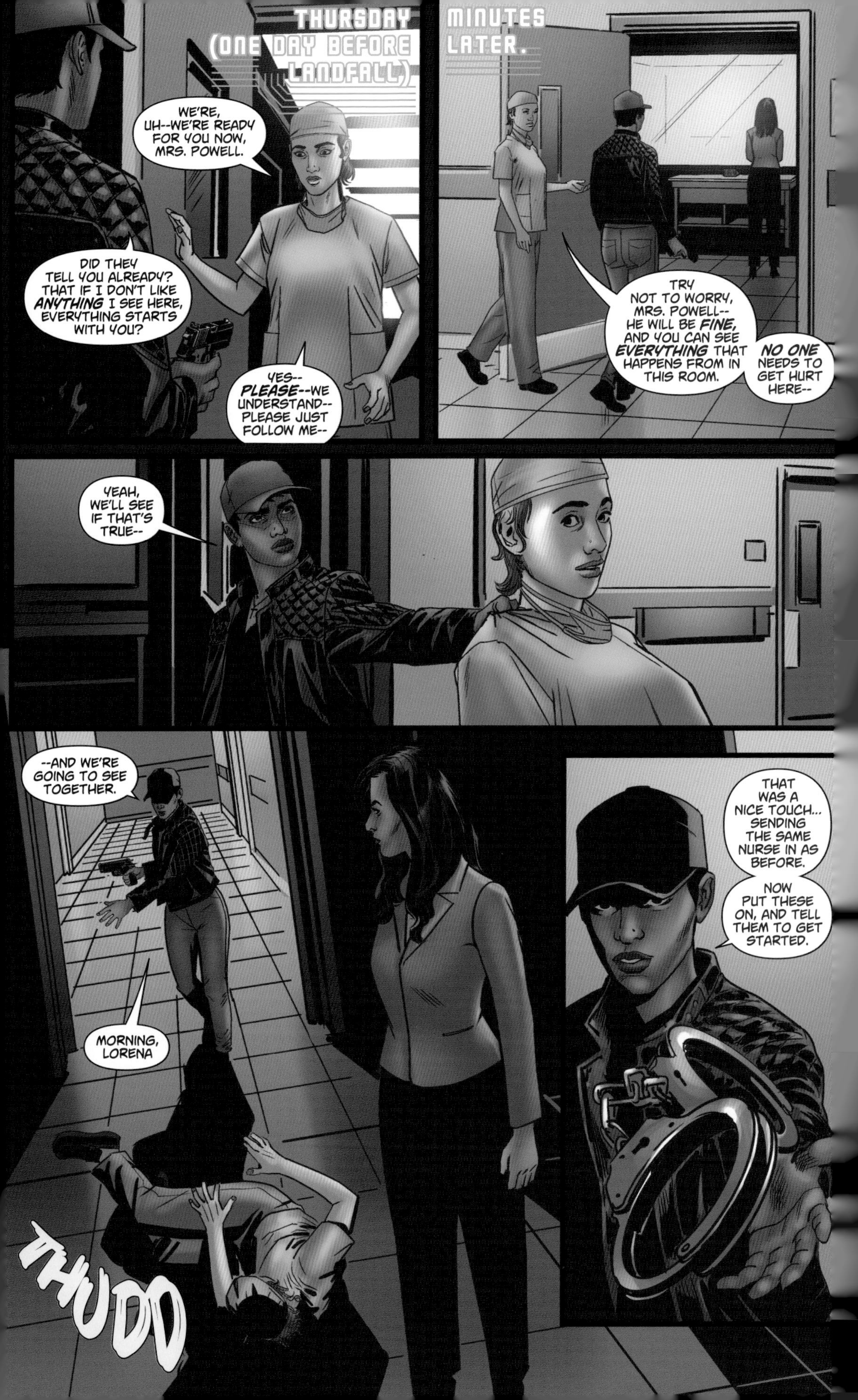

THURSDAY (ONE DAY BEFORE LANDFALL)
WE'RE, UH--WE'RE READY FOR YOU NOW, MRS. POWELL.
DID THEY TELL YOU ALREADY? THAT IF I DON'T LIKE ANYTHING I SEE HERE, EVERYTHING STARTS WITH YOU?
YES-- PLEASE--WE UNDERSTAND-- PLEASE JUST FOLLOW ME--
MINUTES LATER.
TRY NOT TO WORRY, MRS. POWELL-- HE WILL BE FINE, AND YOU CAN SEE EVERYTHING THAT HAPPENS FROM IN THIS ROOM.
NO ONE NEEDS TO GET HURT HERE--
YEAH, WE'LL SEE IF THAT'S TRUE--
--AND WE'RE GOING TO SEE TOGETHER.
MORNING, LORENA
THUDD
THAT WAS A NICE TOUCH... SENDING THE SAME NURSE IN AS BEFORE.
NOW PUT THESE ON, AND TELL THEM TO GET STARTED.

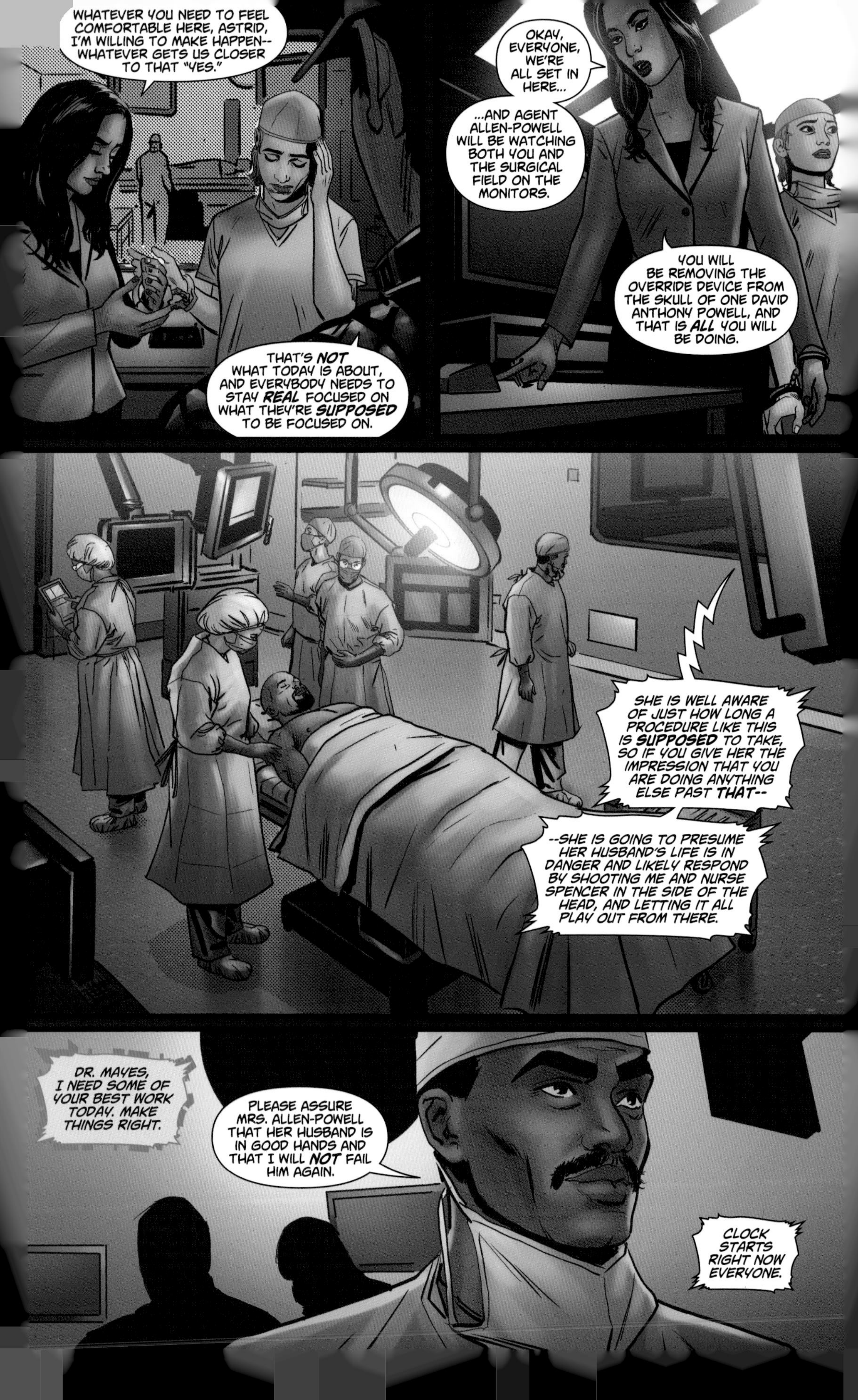
WHATEVER YOU NEED TO FEEL COMFORTABLE HERE, ASTRID, I'M WILLING TO MAKE HAPPEN-- WHATEVER GETS US CLOSER TO THAT "YES."
THAT'S NOT WHAT TODAY IS ABOUT, AND EVERYBODY NEEDS TO STAY REAL FOCUSED ON WHAT THEY'RE SUPPOSED TO BE FOCUSED ON.
OKAY, EVERYONE, WE'RE ALL SET IN HERE...
...AND AGENT ALLEN-POWELL WILL BE WATCHING BOTH YOU AND THE SURGICAL FIELD ON THE MONITORS.
YOU WILL BE REMOVING THE OVERRIDE DEVICE FROM THE SKULL OF ONE DAVID ANTHONY POWELL, AND THAT IS ALL YOU WILL BE DOING.
SHE IS WELL AWARE OF JUST HOW LONG A PROCEDURE LIKE THIS IS SUPPOSED TO TAKE, SO IF YOU GIVE HER THE IMPRESSION THAT YOU ARE DOING ANYTHING ELSE PAST THAT--
--SHE IS GOING TO PRESUME HER HUSBAND'S LIFE IS IN DANGER AND LIKELY RESPOND BY SHOOTING ME AND NURSE SPENCER IN THE SIDE OF THE HEAD, AND LETTING IT ALL PLAY OUT FROM THERE.
DR. MAYES, I NEED SOME OF YOUR BEST WORK TODAY. MAKE THINGS RIGHT.
PLEASE ASSURE MRS. ALLEN-POWELL THAT HER HUSBAND IS IN GOOD HANDS AND THAT I WILL NOT FAIL HIM AGAIN.
CLOCK STARTS RIGHT NOW EVERYONE.

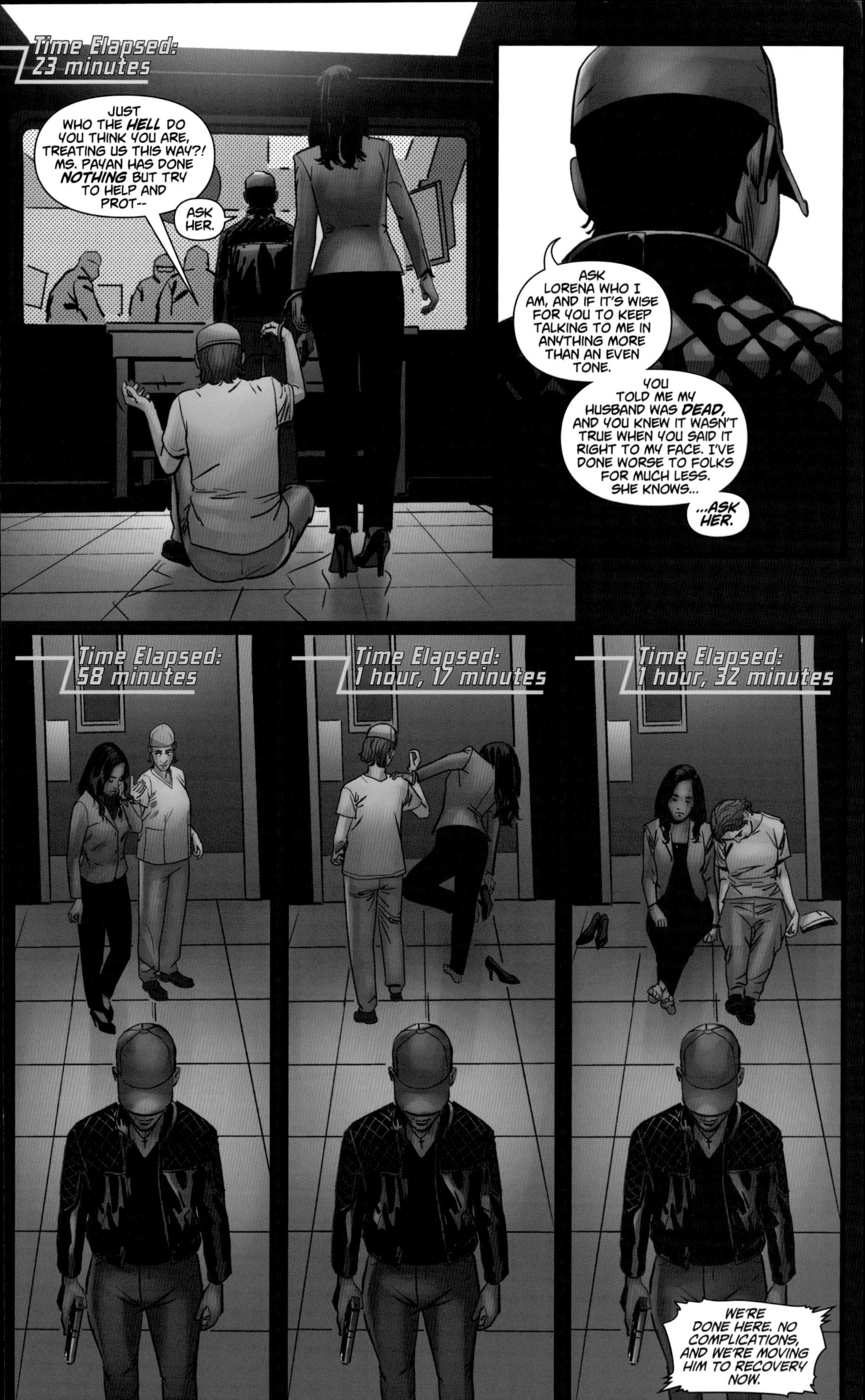
Time Elapsed: 23 minutes
JUST WHO THE HELL DO YOU THINK YOU ARE, TREATING US THIS WAY?! MS. PAYAN HAS DONE NOTHING BUT TRY TO HELP AND PROT--
ASK HER.
ASK LORENA WHO I AM, AND IF IT'S WISE FOR YOU TO KEEP TALKING TO ME IN ANYTHING MORE THAN AN EVEN TONE.
YOU TOLD ME MY HUSBAND WAS DEAD, AND YOU KNEW IT WASN'T TRUE WHEN YOU SAID IT RIGHT TO MY FACE. I'VE DONE WORSE TO FOLKS FOR MUCH LESS. SHE KNOWS...
...ASK HER.
Time Elapsed: 58 minutes
Time Elapsed: 1 hour, 17 minutes
Time Elapsed: 1 hour, 32 minutes
WE'RE DONE HERE. NO COMPLICATIONS, AND WE'RE MOVING HIM TO RECOVERY NOW.

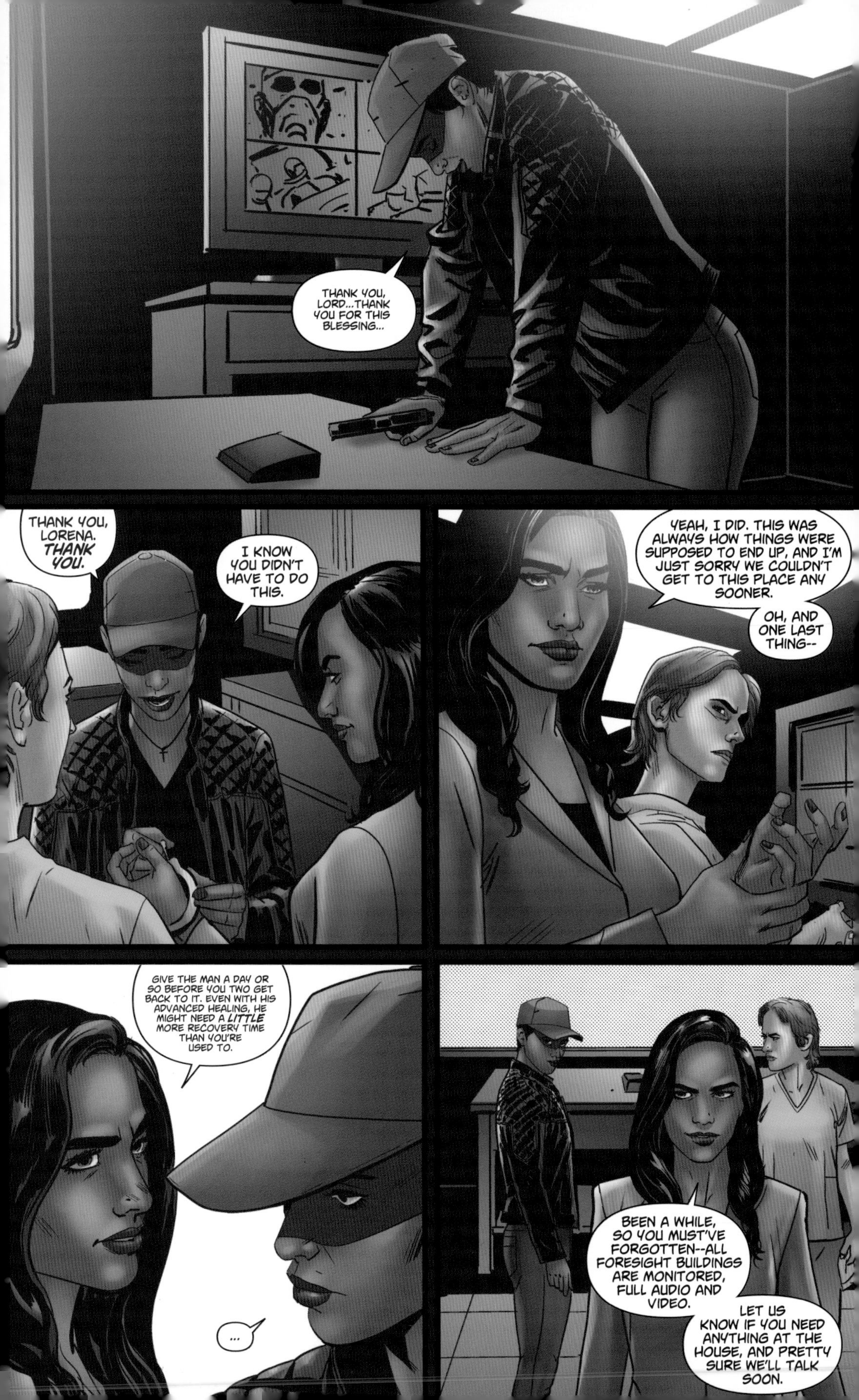
THANK YOU, LORD...THANK YOU FOR THIS BLESSING...
THANK YOU, LORENA. *THANK YOU.*
I KNOW YOU DIDN'T HAVE TO DO THIS.
YEAH, I DID. THIS WAS ALWAYS HOW THINGS WERE SUPPOSED TO END UP, AND I'M JUST SORRY WE COULDN'T GET TO THIS PLACE ANY SOONER.
OH, AND ONE LAST THING--
GIVE THE MAN A DAY OR SO BEFORE YOU TWO GET BACK TO IT. EVEN WITH HIS ADVANCED HEALING, HE MIGHT NEED A *LITTLE* MORE RECOVERY TIME THAN YOU'RE USED TO.
...
BEEN A WHILE, SO YOU MUST'VE FORGOTTEN--ALL FORESIGHT BUILDINGS ARE MONITORED, FULL AUDIO AND VIDEO.
LET US KNOW IF YOU NEED ANYTHING AT THE HOUSE, AND PRETTY SURE WE'LL TALK SOON.

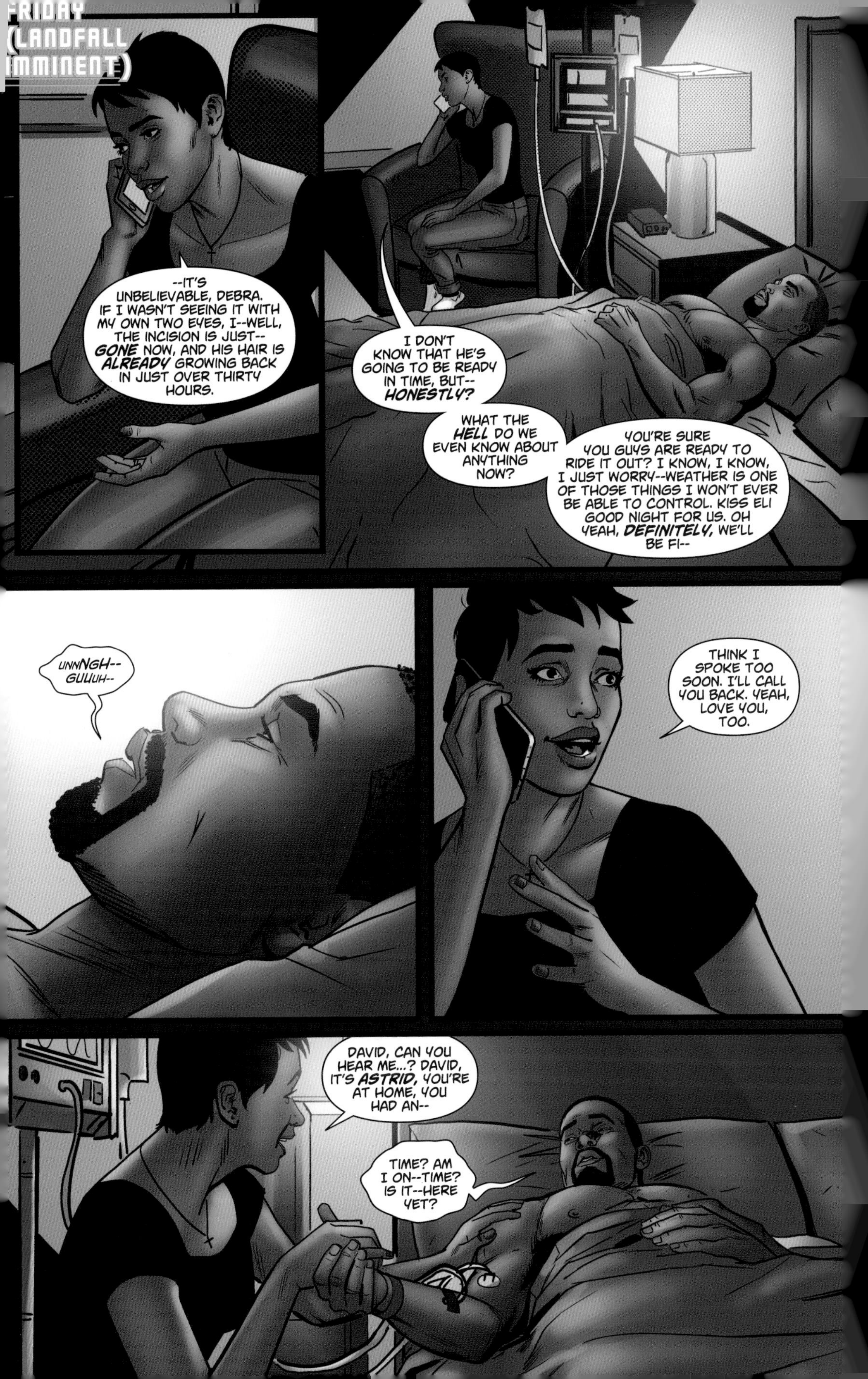
FRIDAY (LANDFALL IMMINENT)
--IT'S UNBELIEVABLE, DEBRA. IF I WASN'T SEEING IT WITH MY OWN TWO EYES, I--WELL, THE INCISION IS JUST-- GONE NOW, AND HIS HAIR IS ALREADY GROWING BACK IN JUST OVER THIRTY HOURS.
I DON'T KNOW THAT HE'S GOING TO BE READY IN TIME, BUT-- HONESTLY?
WHAT THE HELL DO WE EVEN KNOW ABOUT ANYTHING NOW?
YOU'RE SURE YOU GUYS ARE READY TO RIDE IT OUT? I KNOW, I KNOW, I JUST WORRY--WEATHER IS ONE OF THOSE THINGS I WON'T EVER BE ABLE TO CONTROL. KISS ELI GOOD NIGHT FOR US. OH YEAH, DEFINITELY, WE'LL BE FI--
UNNNGH-- GUUUH--
THINK I SPOKE TOO SOON. I'LL CALL YOU BACK. YEAH, LOVE YOU, TOO.
DAVID, CAN YOU HEAR ME...? DAVID, IT'S ASTRID, YOU'RE AT HOME, YOU HAD AN--
TIME? AM I ON--TIME? IS IT--HERE YET?

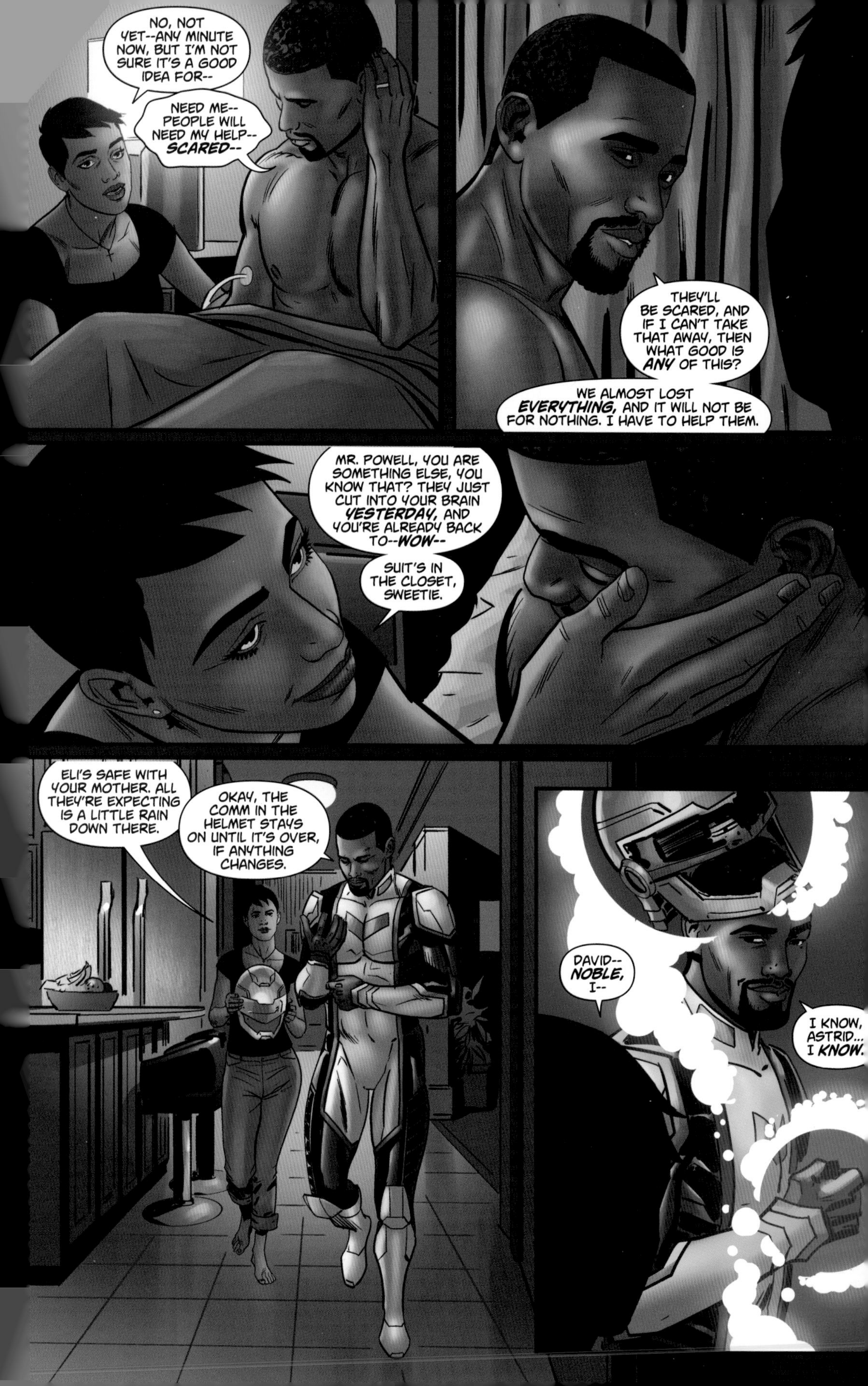
NO, NOT YET--ANY MINUTE NOW, BUT I'M NOT SURE IT'S A GOOD IDEA FOR--
NEED ME--PEOPLE WILL NEED MY HELP--SCARED--
THEY'LL BE SCARED, AND IF I CAN'T TAKE THAT AWAY, THEN WHAT GOOD IS ANY OF THIS?
WE ALMOST LOST EVERYTHING, AND IT WILL NOT BE FOR NOTHING. I HAVE TO HELP THEM.
MR. POWELL, YOU ARE SOMETHING ELSE, YOU KNOW THAT? THEY JUST CUT INTO YOUR BRAIN YESTERDAY, AND YOU'RE ALREADY BACK TO--WOW--
SUIT'S IN THE CLOSET, SWEETIE.
ELI'S SAFE WITH YOUR MOTHER. ALL THEY'RE EXPECTING IS A LITTLE RAIN DOWN THERE.
OKAY, THE COMM IN THE HELMET STAYS ON UNTIL IT'S OVER, IF ANYTHING CHANGES.
DAVID--NOBLE, I--
I KNOW, ASTRID... I KNOW.

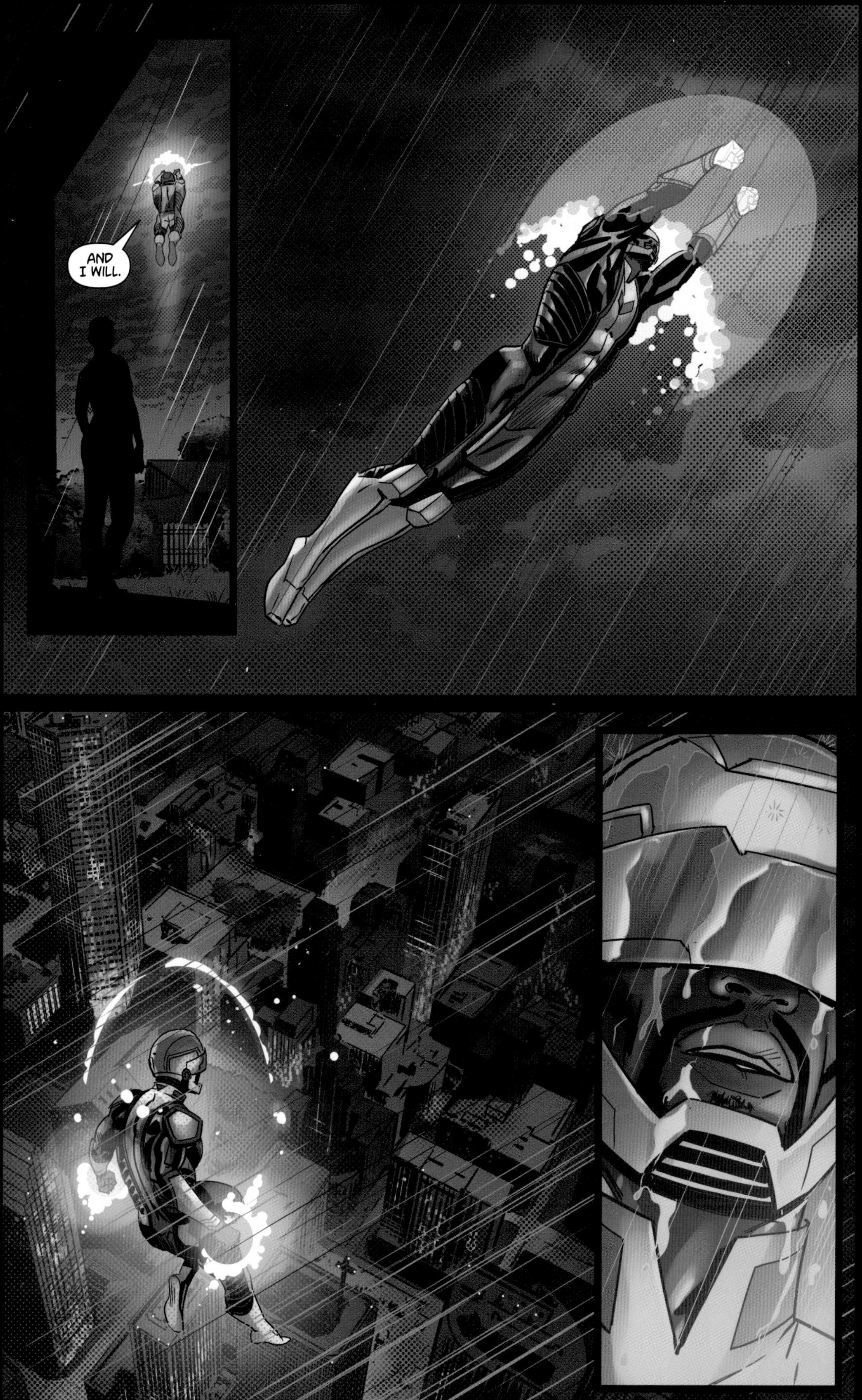
AND I WILL.

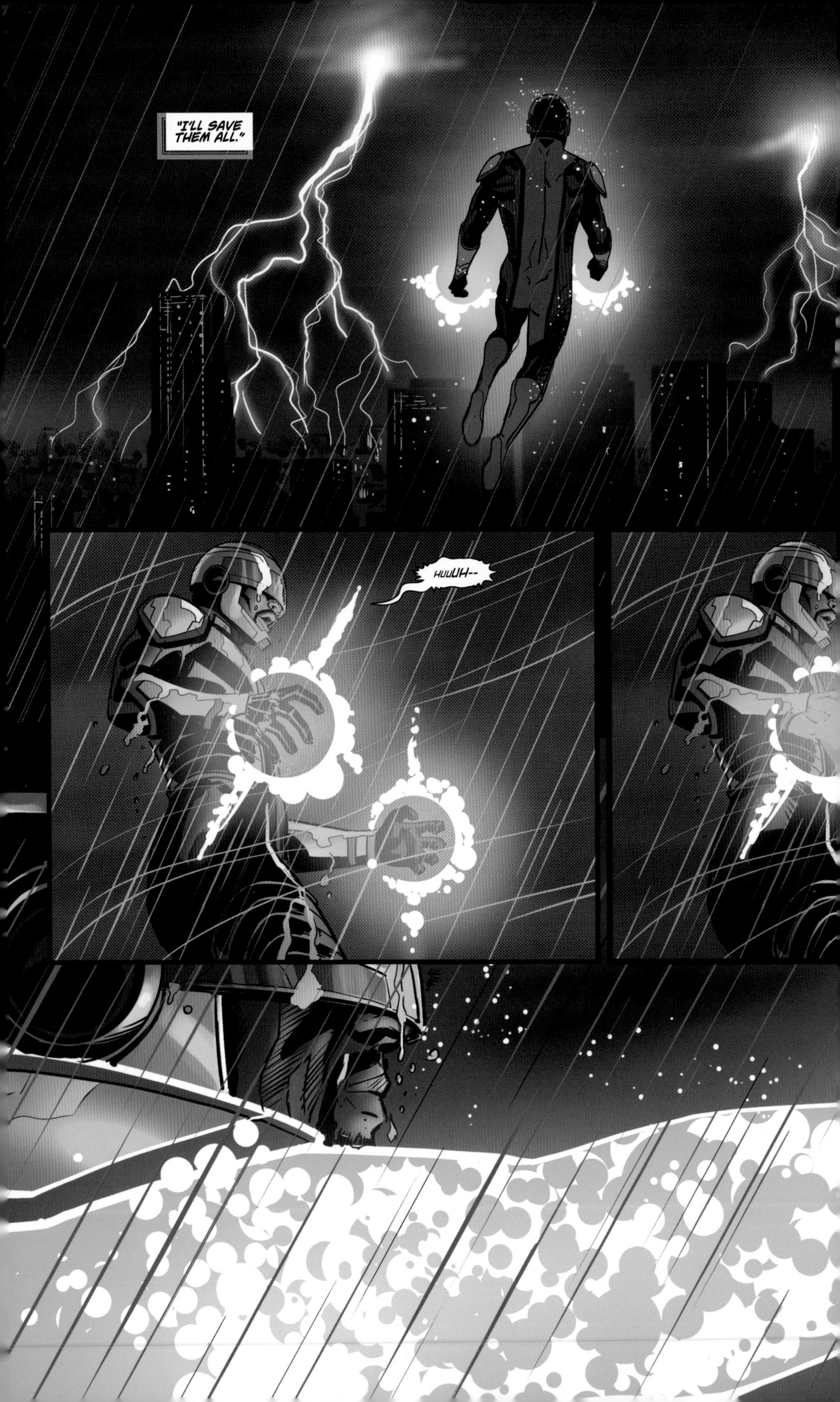
"I'LL SAVE THEM ALL."
HUUUH--

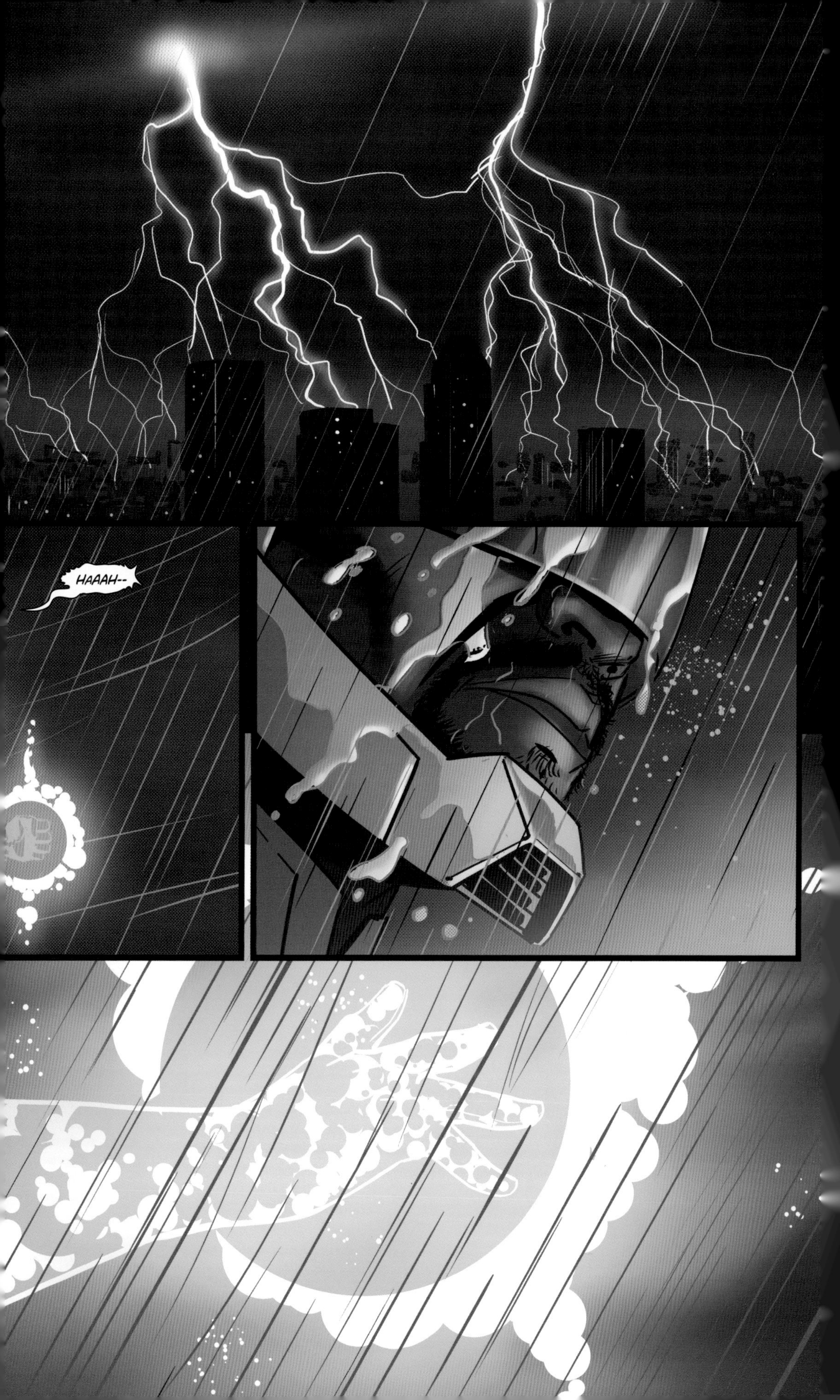
HAAAH--

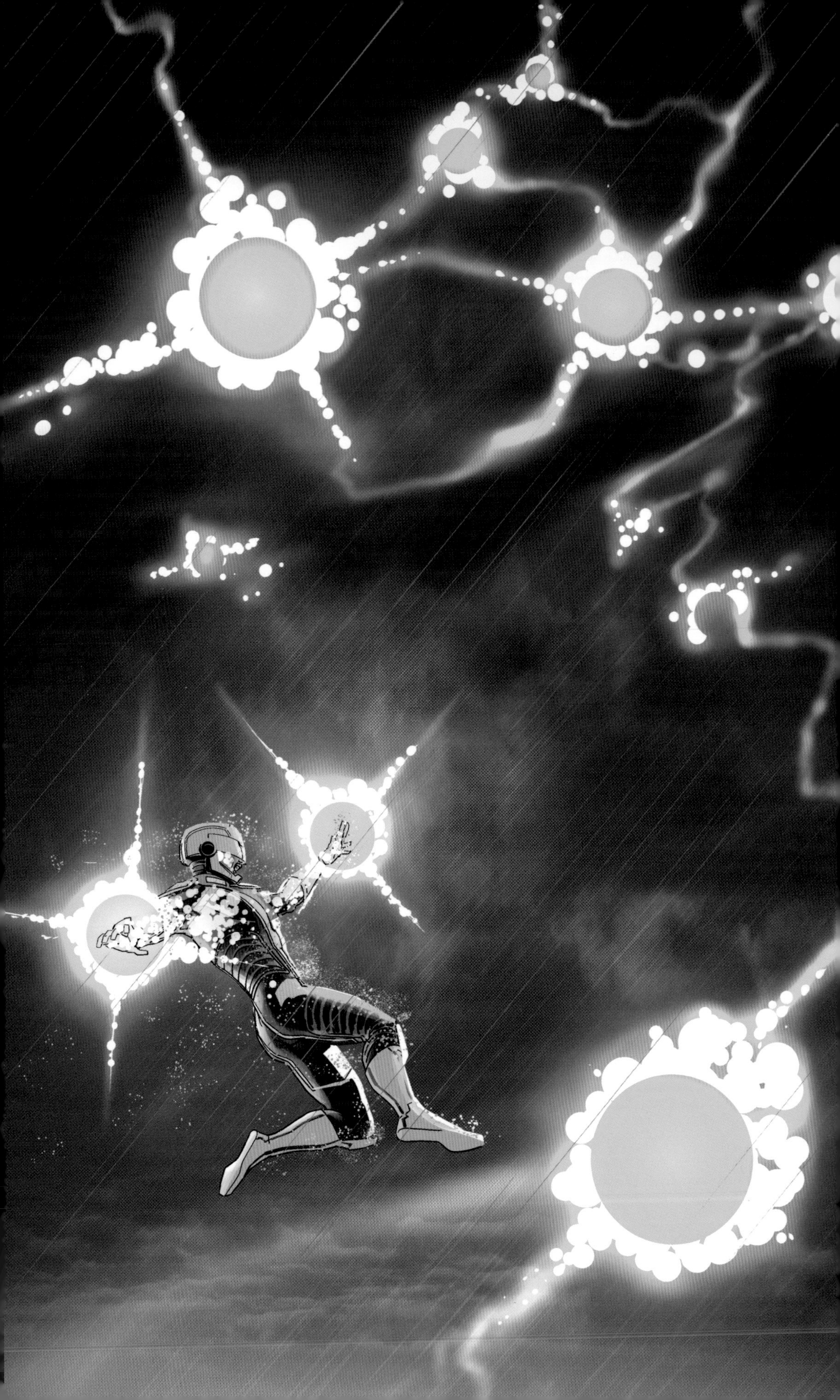

COVER GALLERY

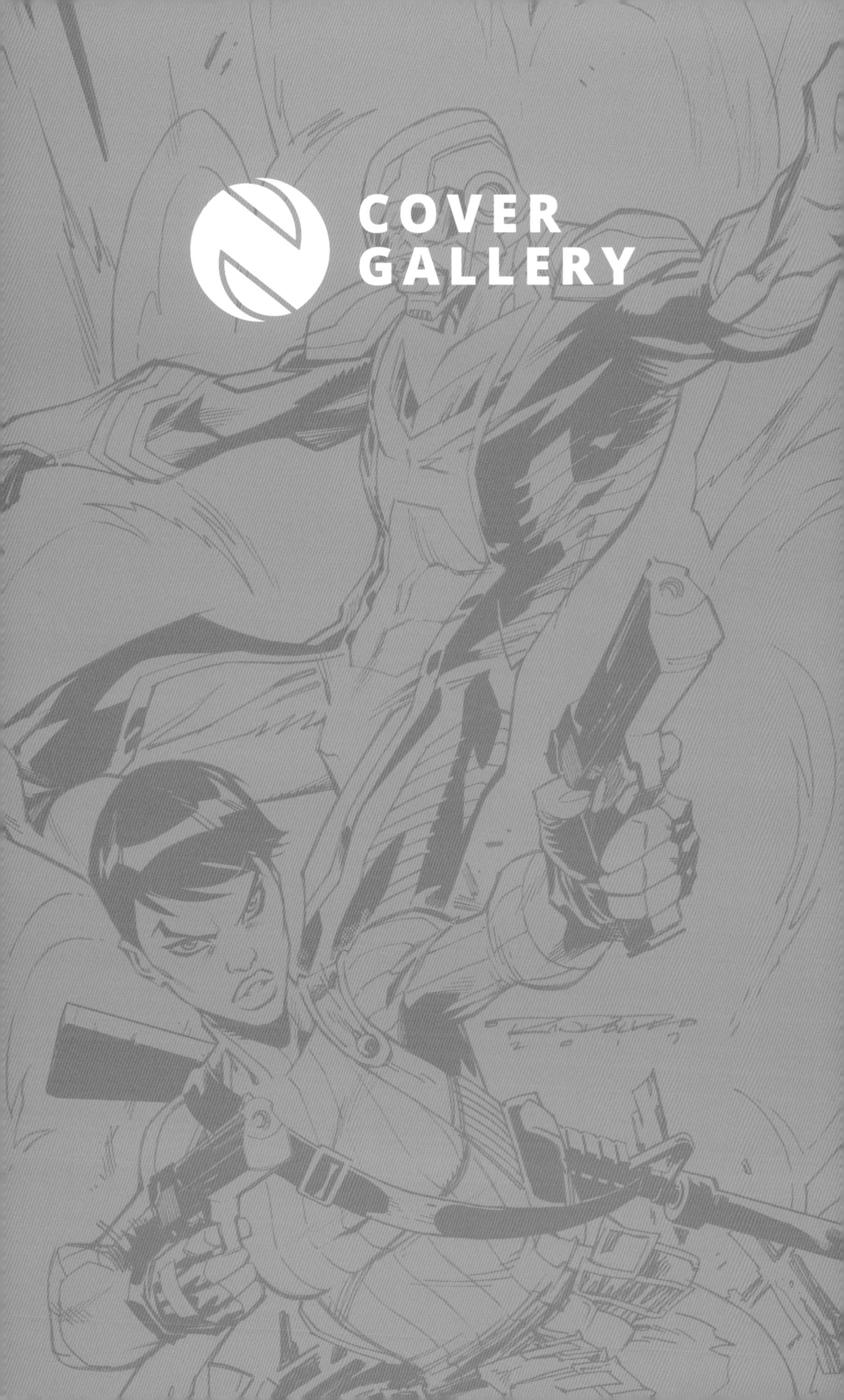

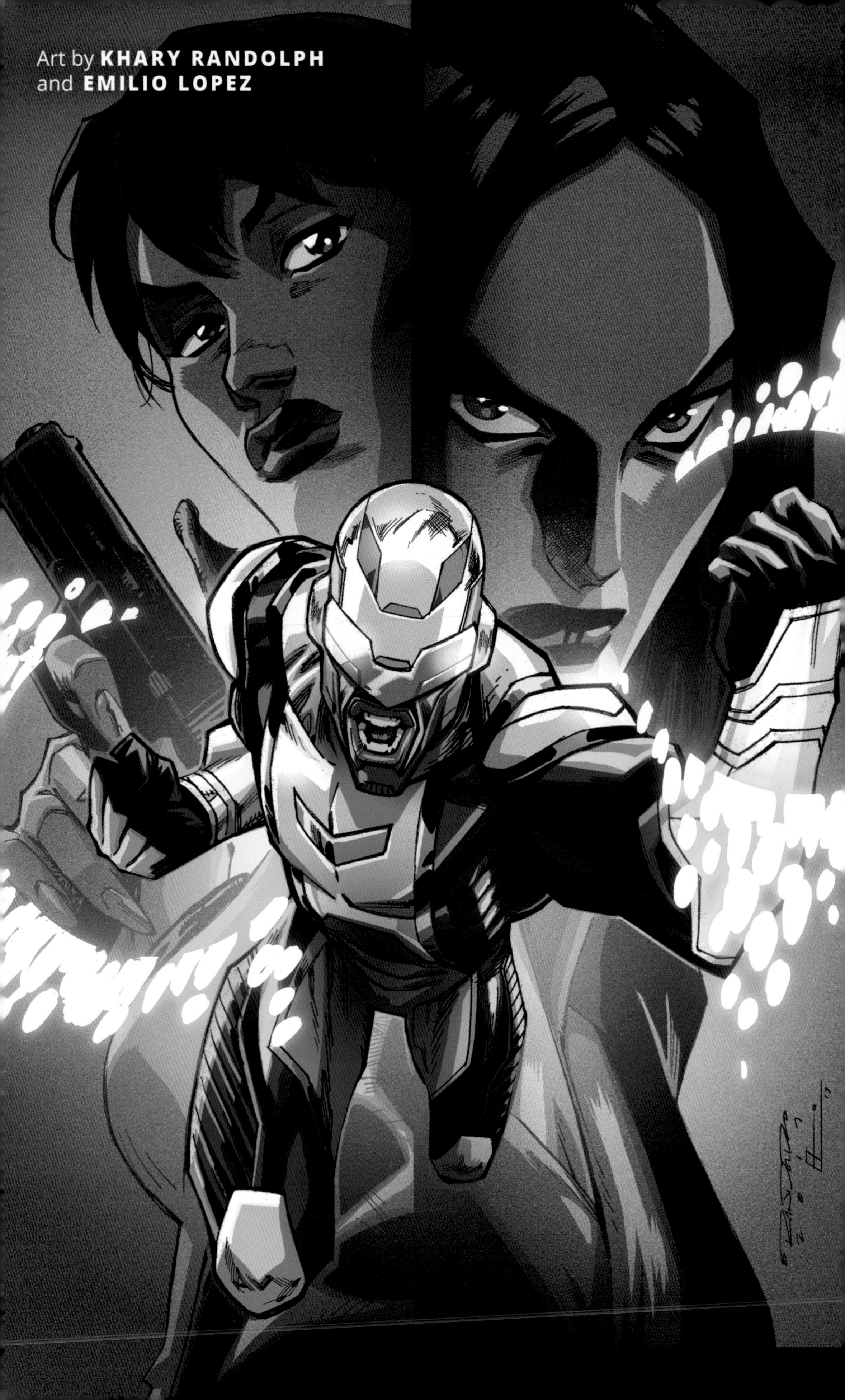

Art by **KHARY RANDOLPH**
and **EMILIO LOPEZ**

Art by **KHARY RANDOLPH**
and **EMILIO LOPEZ**

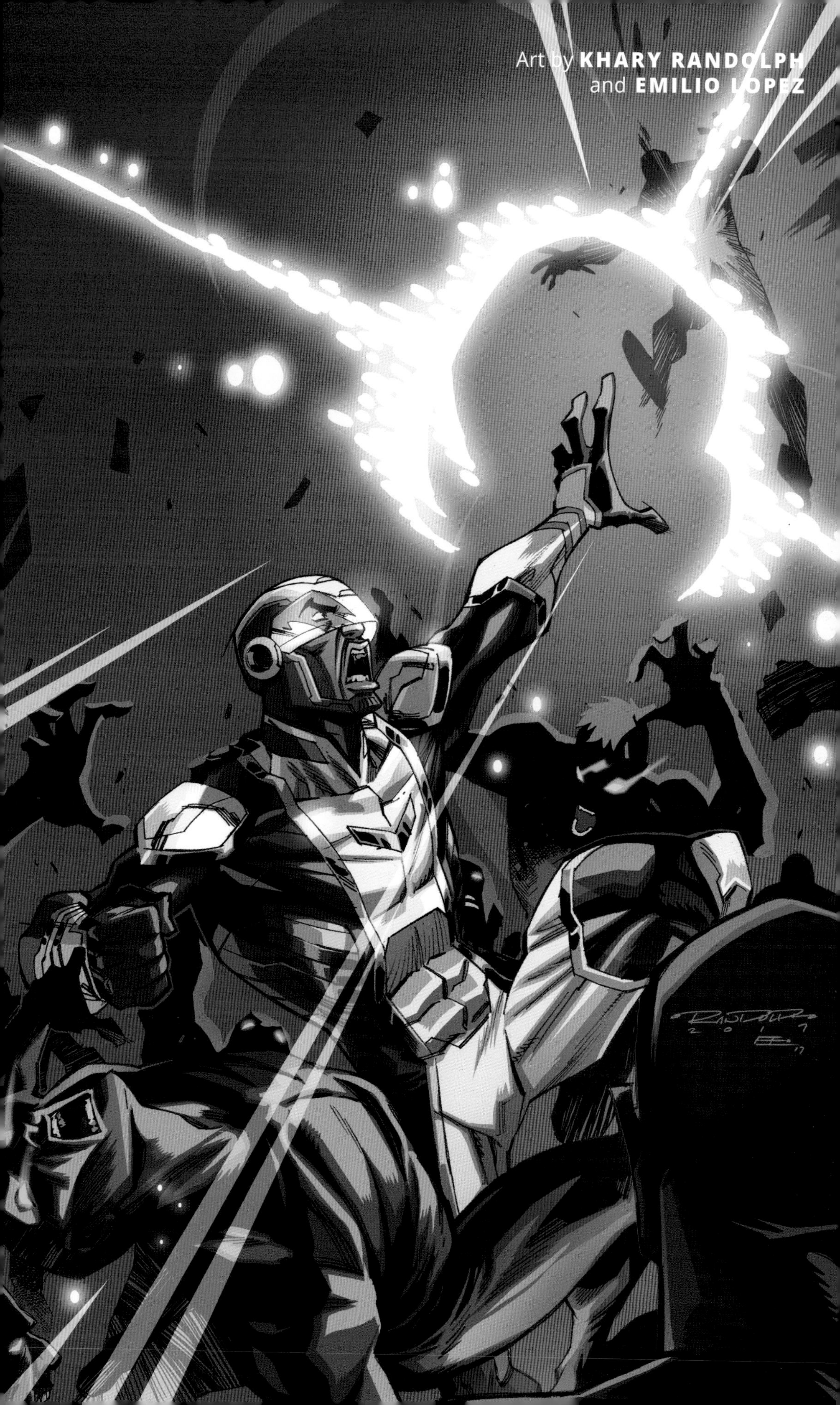

Art by **KHARY RANDOLPH**
and **EMILIO LOPEZ**

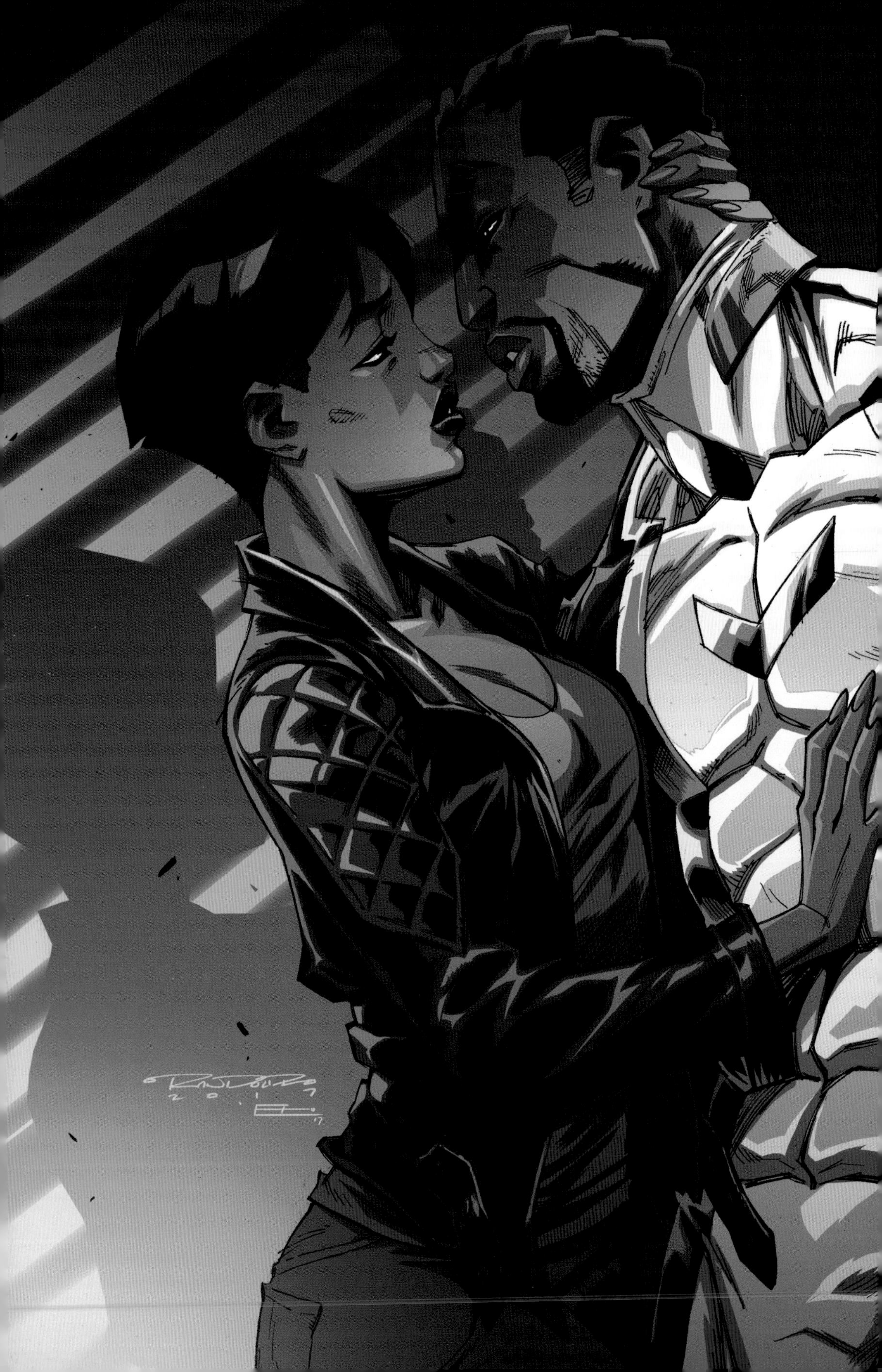

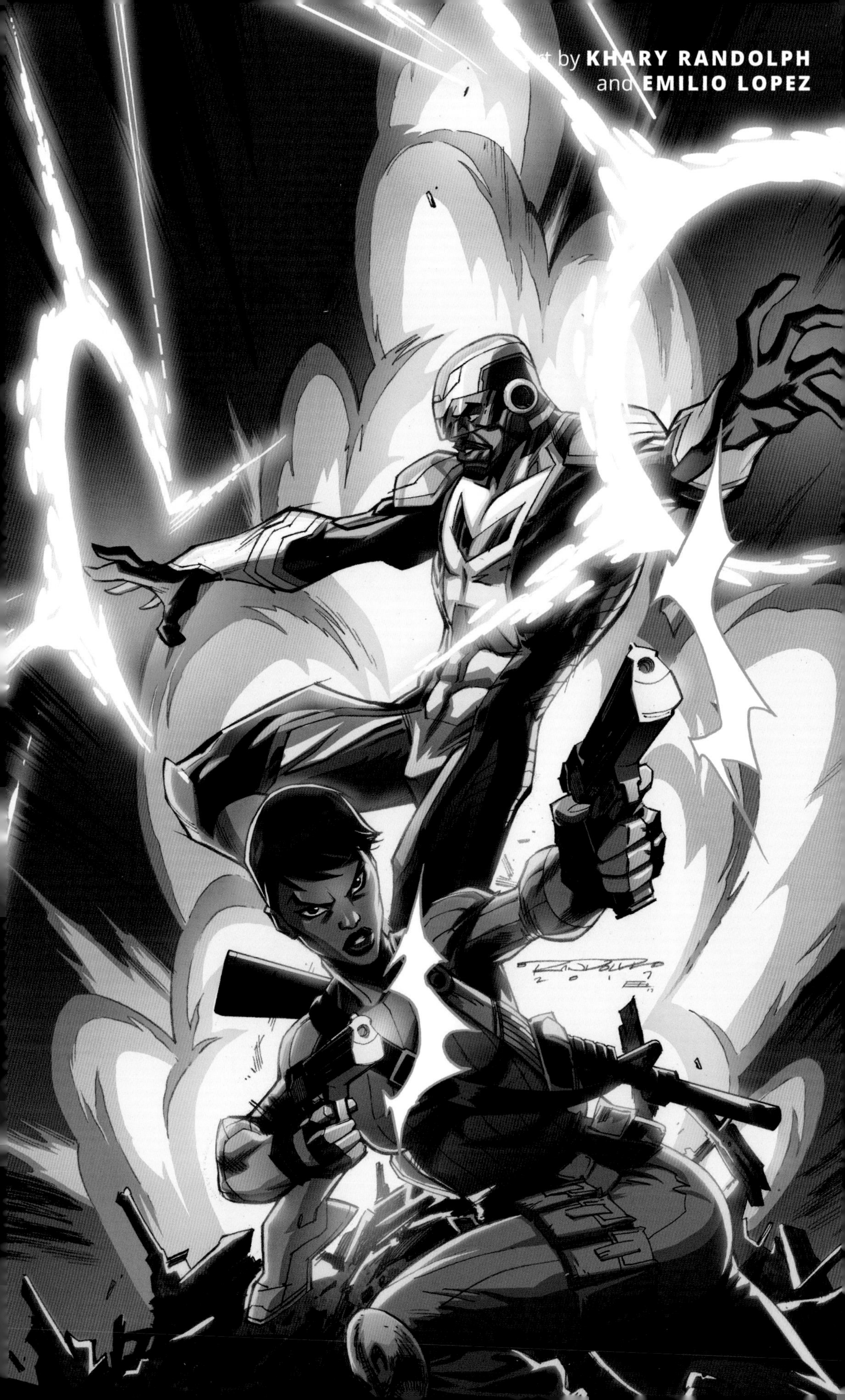

Art by **KHARY RANDOLPH** and **EMILIO LOPEZ**

Art by **KHARY RANDOLPH**
and **EMILIO LOPEZ**

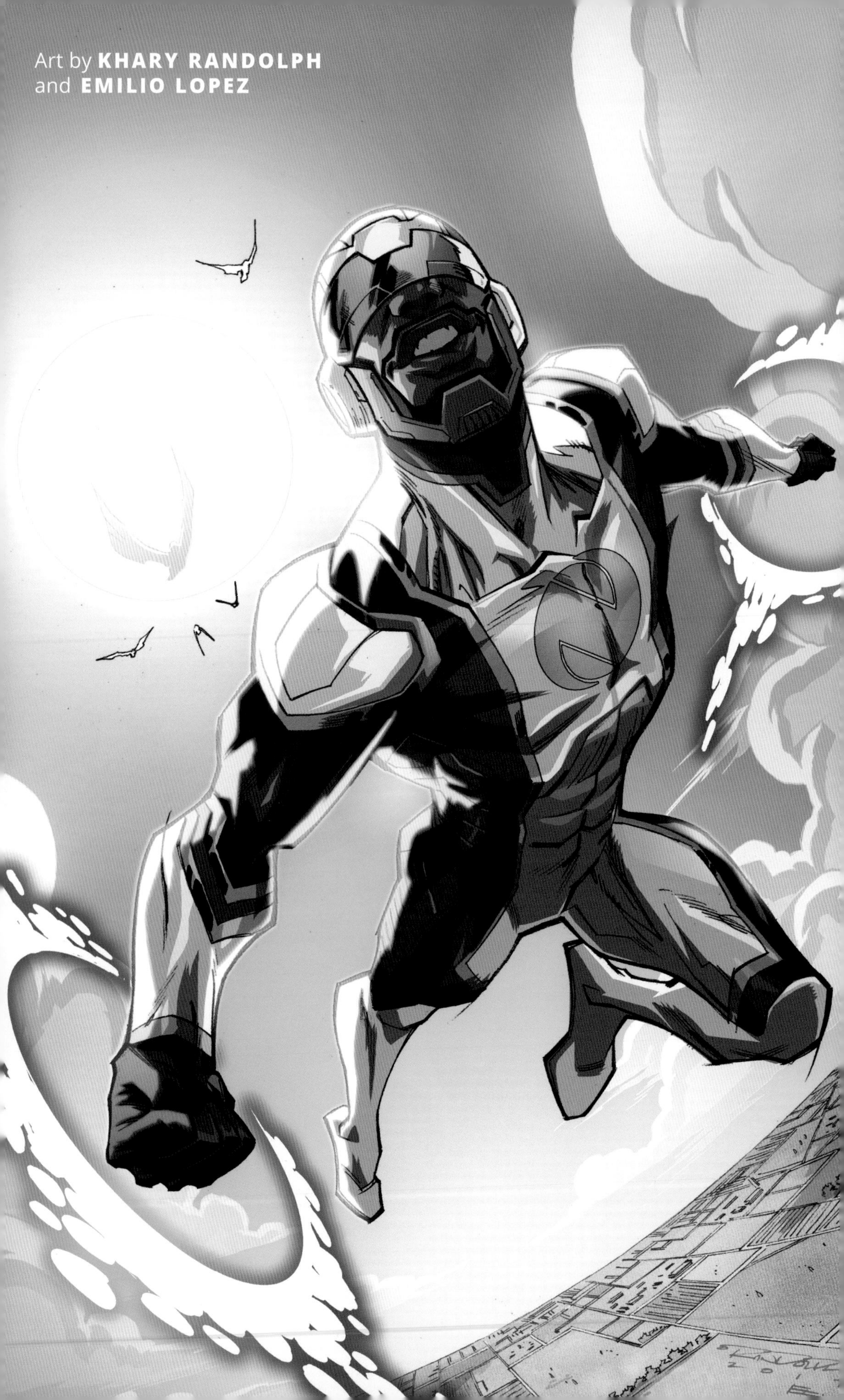

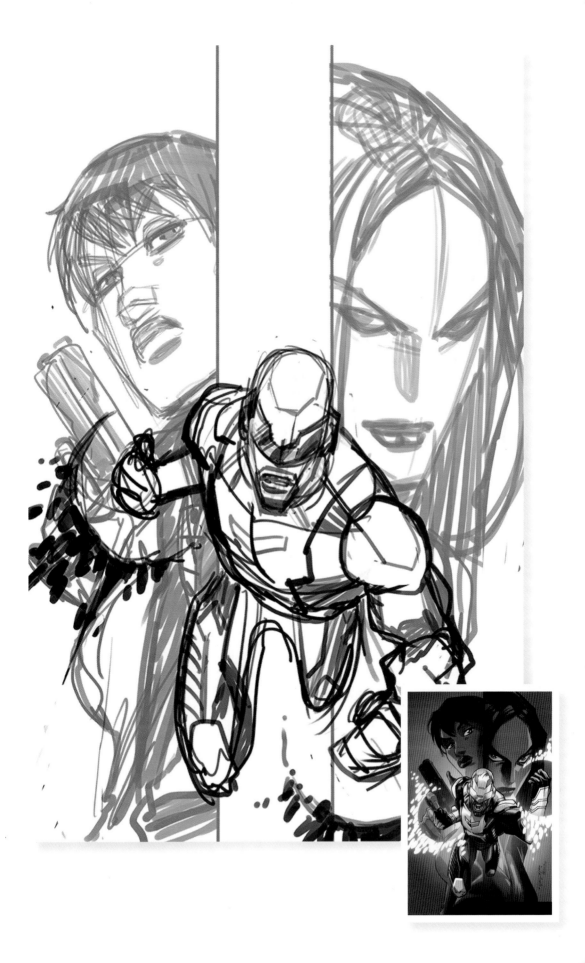

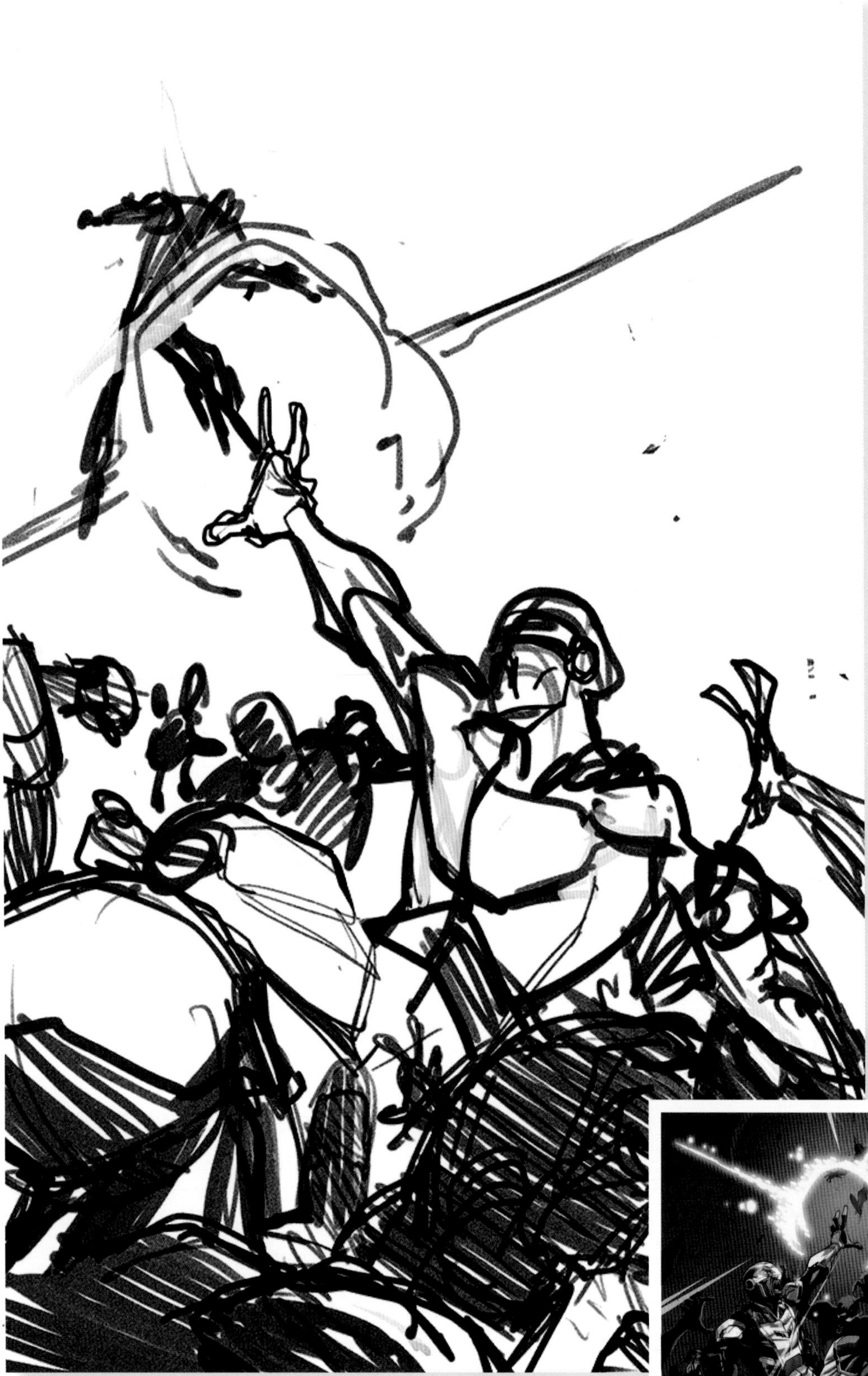
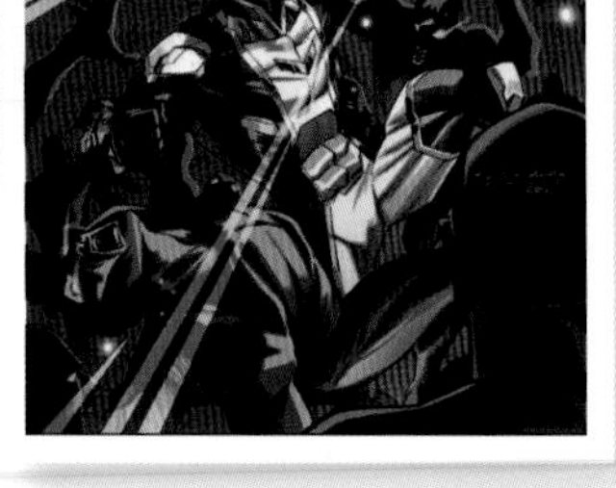

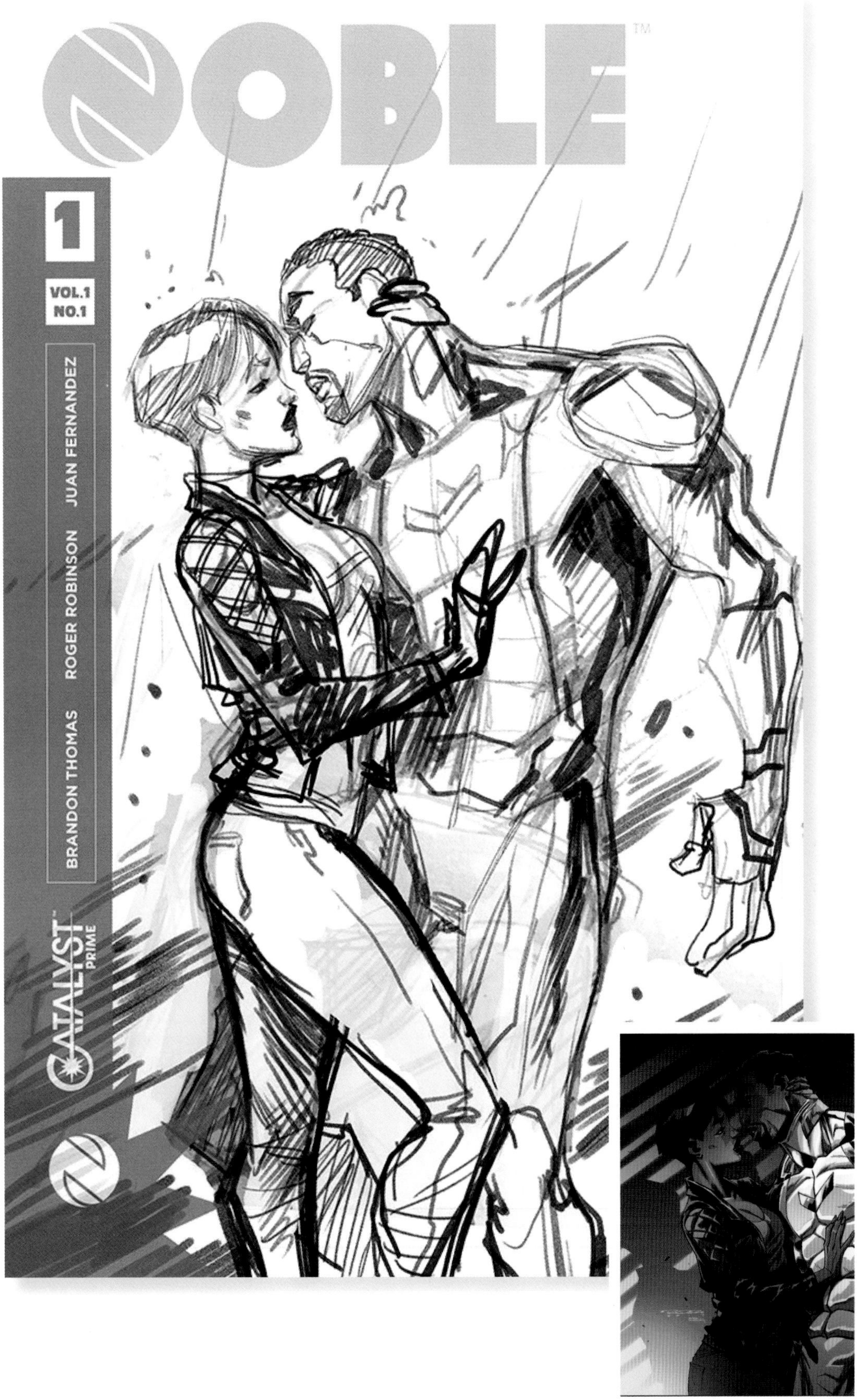
NOBLE™
1
VOL.1
NO.1
BRANDON THOMAS
ROGER ROBINSON
JUAN FERNANDEZ
CATALYST PRIME

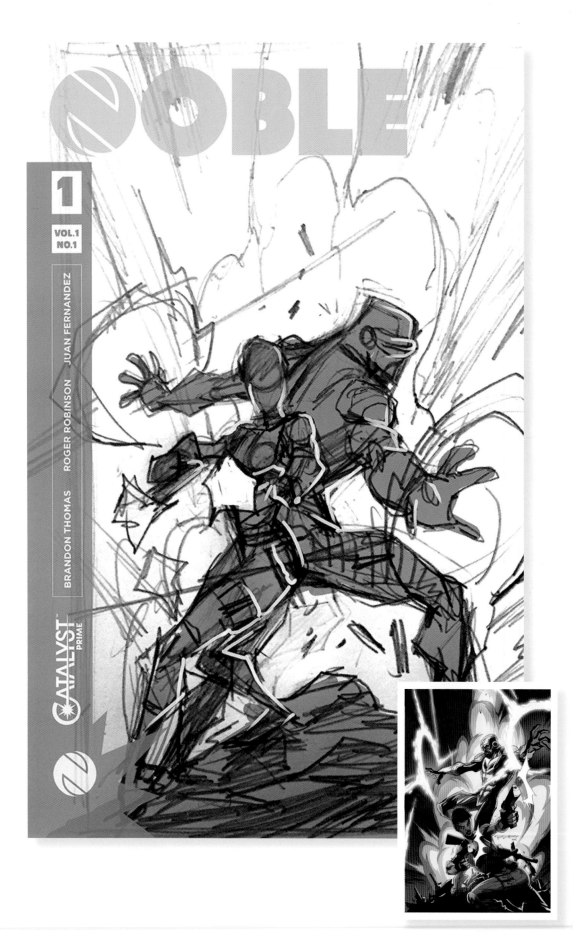

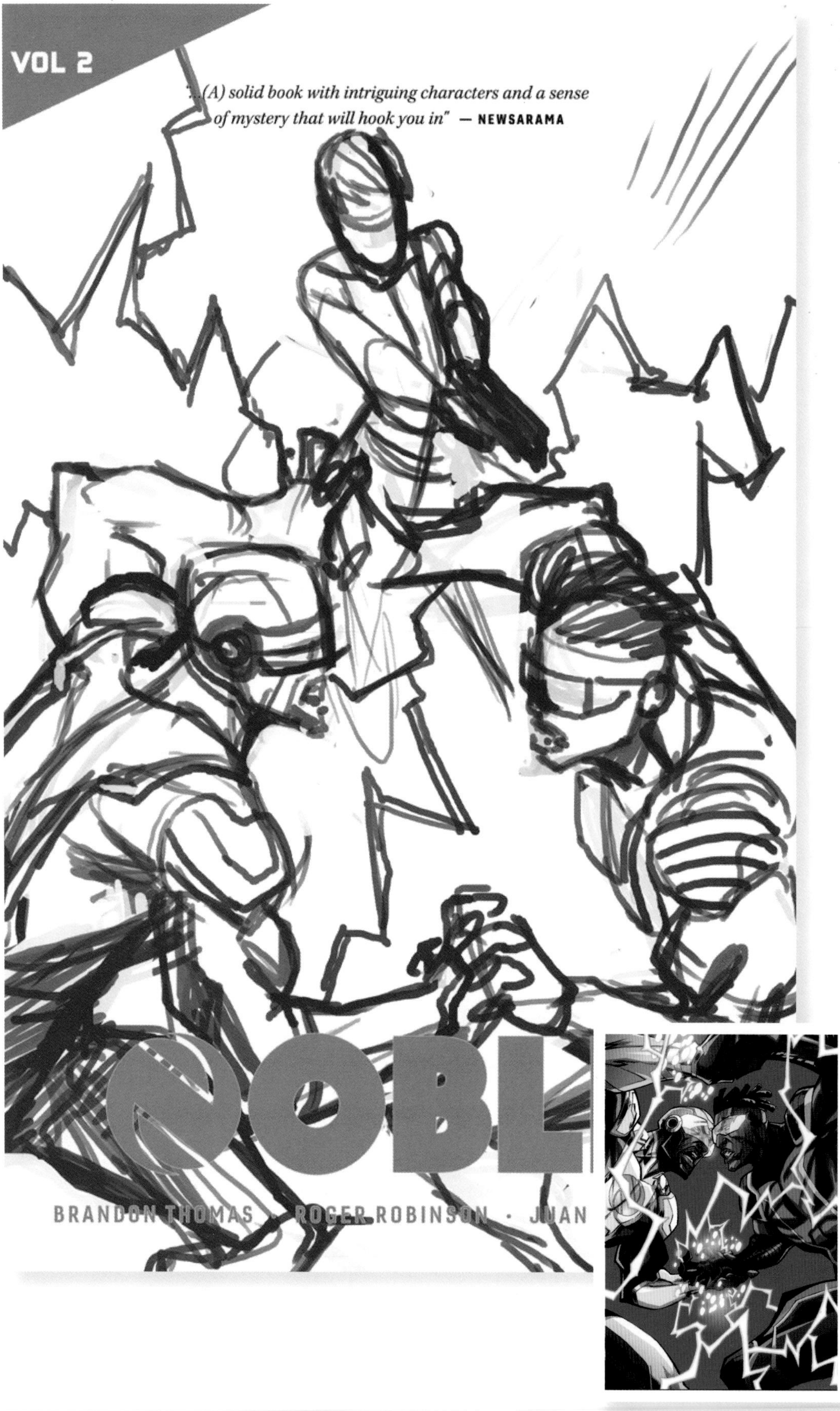
VOL 2
"...(A) solid book with intriguing characters and a sense of mystery that will hook you in" — NEWSARAMA
NOBL
BRANDON THOMAS · ROGER ROBINSON · JUAN